THE KUZARI

JUDAH HALEVI

THE KUZARI

(KITAB AL KHAZARI)

An Argument for
the Faith of Israel

Introduction by Henry Slonimsky

Schocken Books • New York

Translated from the Arabic by Hartwig Hirschfeld.
First published 1905 by George Routledge and Sons, Ltd.

© 1964 by Schocken Books Inc.
First SCHOCKEN PAPERBACK edition 1964

Third Printing, 1971

Library of Congress Catalog Card No. 64–15222
Manufactured in the United States of America

TABLE OF CONTENTS

82453

Contents

INTRODUCTION

The publisher gratefully acknowledges permission of *The Jewish Frontier* for use of material in the introduction by Henry Slonimsky, first published therein.

JUDAH HALEVI: AN INTRODUCTION

by Henry Slonimsky

I. THE MAN AND HIS POETRY

Judah Halevi (b. ca. 1080) is the greatest poet and one of the profoundest thinkers Judaism has had since the closing of the canon. He plumbed depths in religion and reflection on history, and he made claims for Israel so strange and inordinate, that he would be merely an anomaly unless profoundly related to his time and viewed centrally from that history and destiny in which he was rooted and of which he is clearly the deepest expression and interpretation. The overshadowing event of his time was the struggle of Christian and Moslem for Spain; and, farther afield, for the mastery of the Holy Land. In Spain, the community of Israel was ground between upper and nether millstones; and in Palestine, the last spark of hope seemed finally extinguished with the advent of the Crusaders. Israel appeared to be doomed. Judah Halevi's poetry and prose are the response evoked by that world situation.

The general setting was the *reconquista*, the gradual reconquest of Spain by the Christians from the north, where they had been pushed in the first great Moslem irruption into Europe four centuries earlier. And, though Judah Halevi's life span was marked at its beginning and end by two fierce counterattacks from the south—the Almoravides in the 1080's and the Almohades in the 1140's—the victorious advance from the north remained unchecked.

The *reconquista* was a curious fusion of crusading religious fanaticism with astute political realism. While the Arab ruling classes were ruthlessly eliminated and the peasantry allowed to remain, the Jews, as politically innocuous and economically valuable, were treated with indulgence at the instance and special pleading of the Jewish court grandees and permitted to take refuge in the north. But their condition remained forever precarious, and that is the crux of the matter. The court Jews who dominated Jewish policy, the *gevirim* and *nesiim* to whom Judah Halevi as Moses ibn Ezra and others before him tirelessly addressed poems and hymns of praise, and who were hailed each in turn by the trusting masses as the final savior of Israel, were capable of nothing better than parleying and manoeuvering for position with the powers that be.

Judah Halevi belonged by birth and tradition to this upper stratum of court Jewry, and his material existence may have been linked up with this group. Its attitude toward life—its views on love, religion, philosophy, politics, and the future of Israel—Judah Halevi undoubtedly shared for the first half of his life. And the radical break with this outlook on life constitutes the secret of his power, clears the way for that efflorescence in poetry and thinking which makes of him the unique figure he is.

The shock which brought about this complete inner change in him, this reversal of all the values he and his class had lived by, led, among the masses, to the revival of a Messianic mood and apocalyptic hopes. As an aftermath of the great struggle of which the Jewish masses were witnesses and victims caught between two fires, minor Messiahs began to appear among them, old apocalypses dealing with the "end" once again emerged, and calculations as to the exact date of that "end"—as the coming of the Messiah is usually designated among Jews—were made by consulting signs and stars. And, while Judah Halevi shared to the full these moods and hopes, he knew better than any of them, better than the practical politicians whose principle was opportunism, better than the eschatological astrologers who calculated ends, better than the vague votaries of Messianic enthusiasm, how truly to interpret the great events of the times.

Born in Toledo while it was still Mohammedan, he went south for his education to the old seats of learning. Those were his happy *Wanderjahre,* and they were spent, according to the fine civilization of the age, not merely in absorbing Jewish learning in the regular Talmudical schools, but in assimilating everything he could of the science and philosophy which Arabic culture had to offer; cultivating the poetic arts in both Arabic and Hebrew; fraternizing with young men of like gifts and inclinations; and frankly enjoying life. The love poems of his youth, it may be said in passing, are certainly not academic exercises in imagined passion. Love was in the mores of his time for the members of his class, and, while native fastidiousness may have led him to avoid the profligacy characteristic of the rich of his class, the tenderness and sensuousness of his love poems are too authentic to allow any doubt of the realness of the experience.

He returned to Toledo, then in Christian hands, to practice medicine, but he speaks ironically of his patients and his profession. "Thus we heal Babylon, but it cannot be healed." His work as a physician did not fill his life. His contacts with the south continued unabated, despite the fluctuation of arms, and his literary activity increased. Besides his love songs, this period of poetic production was marked by poems addressed to friends and court functionaries, poems of praise and homage to court Jews in either Christian or Mohammedan service, possibly patrons of the poet, certainly men whom he regarded as the leaders of his class and of Jewry.

As the years went by, however, and he witnessed one Jewish community after another going down in destruction as it was caught between two fires in the advance of the Christian armies, a new light dawned on him to which he gave expression in a new type of poetry—an insight which found mature and conscious formulation in his later and most powerful poems and the great prose work of his closing years. This insight —that whoever won in the struggles of the *reconquista*, Israel was bound to lose, that, although some powerful court Jew might find protection for his people in the north as they fled their burning homes in the south, such asylum would be merely a refuge built on quicksand—slowly ripened into conviction.

There came a point where Judah Halevi's poems of homage to Jewish grandees ceased, and another type of writing, another way of thinking, came into predominance. In a poem which still trembles with the concrete detail of death and murder recently witnessed, our poet sums up its final meaning for him. "Between the armies of Seir and Kedar (i.e., Christian and Moslem), my army is lost. Whenever they fight their fight, it is *we* who fall, and thus it has been in former times in Israel." And so again in another poem of this period: "The enemies battle like wild beasts, the princes of Eliphas with the rams of Nevayot (i.e., Christians with Moslems), but between the two the young sheep (of Israel) are undone."

The new poems dealing with the destiny of Israel begin to follow a definite pattern: they are marked by grief over the loss of God's proximity which was Israel's distinction of old; they depict conditions in Spain; they lament the loss of Jerusalem to the Crusaders; they raise questions as to the future. And, while the older poets dealing with the same themes had followed a similar pattern, namely, the triadic scheme of the lost ideal of the past, the hopeless present, and the prospect of salvation in some future, Judah Halevi differs from them in his definiteness and concreteness, in his realistic treatment of the present, and in his interpretation of the struggles of the time as the actual birth-pangs of the imminent Messiah. His poems do not end on a vague note of hope, but are charged with new resolution and conviction. His espousal of the Messianic hopes current in his day assumes an almost political character, and the belief itself is merely the index of an entire change of viewpoint.

What is this change of heart? It is the rejection of the entire basis on which the existence of Spanish Jewry rested: culture of the senses and the mind, love-making and philosophy, economic dependence on the princely courts and political security that hinged upon the favor of the princes, the building up of this life in the north as rapidly as it was being destroyed in the south. Judah Halevi saw that it could not go on.

It was not merely the eternal political opportunism which he rejected as inadequate and which he realized must be replaced by a far more radical cure, but all the things that went with it and were part and parcel of the same scheme, above all, the evaporation of religion in the intelligentsia. The enlightenment which came in the train of philosophical studies had led not to a higher and freer faith on the basis of pure reason, but merely to a decay of the inner sanctions of the old religion, and even to a readiness on occasion to forsake Judaism—as if Christianity were any the less subject to the same rationalistic critique.

Judah Halevi saw that, if the return to Zion must be the political remedy at a time when all seemed lost, the return to God must go along with it, the return to traditional Judaism with all its transcendent claims, as a means of renewing power; the return, therefore, to Revelation and Election. He realized that the Jewish religion shares the fate of the Jewish people, that when both seem doomed, the moment has come for supreme re-assertion, that the political and the religious go hand in hand for the Jews.

However, such changes of heart are never easy, and again and again he falters. In poems of intense personal pathos he records these trepidations and fluctuations of his heart. The process means uprooting, from country, language, home—therefore, a kind of death; and in his case it did lead to death, but to death and transfiguration. For, in the drama of his personal life, he enacted, on a kind of ideal stage, the deepest drama of Israel.

II. THE MAN AND HIS THOUGHT

The Kuzari, Judah Halevi's philosophical master-piece, written between 1130–1140, is a book of defense, as the full Arabic title expressly states, and as that title goes on to say, a defense of a despised religion; despised, we may add, not merely by the world, by the two great religious powers who between them divide the inhabited globe, but secretly also by the educated and powerful among its own adherents. So that with hardly a place to stand, pushed so to speak to the edge of things by enemies from without and by doubt within, Judah Halevi still opposes to that world a philosophy of history (as we should say today) or more strictly a theology of history, whereby a supreme place is vindicated for his people and for its religion in the economy of world events. Everything of "pure" philosophy which the book contains is entirely sub-servient to this main purpose and is invented ad hoc. That purpose is the eminently practical and life-giving one of asserting a primary place in history for his people chronically threatened with external annihila-tion and internal disruption. The time and the scene could hardly have appeared more fraught with doom and disaster: Judah Halevi picked that moment as precisely the time for grandiose self-assertion.

The anti-rationalist tone of the book which makes it unique among all the products of Jewish mediaeval thinking is not just a new fashion in philosophy but is to be understood from an entirely different motiva-

tion. It is directed against the enemy within the gates.
All the Jewish magnates and intellectuals of the day
had gone through the school of Arabic philosophy.
The educated, enlightened and superior people of that
generation had insensibly substituted a set of metaphysical propositions for the ancestral religion. In
any case its old vigor had slackened and relaxed; its
great texts and images allegorized and symbolized.
Judah Halevi's idea of defending the Jewish religion
was not by showing its identity with rational truth,
as all his predecessors and his successors after him
tried to do. He did not have that ambition. He sees
that the Jewish religion is not reducible to a sum of
abstract propositions. Propositions in philosophy can
always be debated both ways; and even at their best
they never pierce deeper than the plane of argument.
He tries to vindicate for it a securer place, a place
beyond all reason. As against the influences of Arabic
philosophy he re-asserts the original historical character of the Jewish religion, constituted by historic
fate and historic election. The great scene at Sinai
puts it in possession of the truth. And as the doctrine
there imparted is the sole source of religious truth, so
the people chosen to be its bearer is alone capable of
realizing the religious life, and is therefore the core
and heart of mankind. Sinai being the one authentic
event in religious history, Christianity and Islam are
inevitably derivative and imitative. But with all that
they are assigned a high place. Israel has indeed a
central position in history, but Judah Halevi robs the
idea of chosenness of all hate and intolerance, and in
the broad humanism of his Messianic conception he
leaves far behind him the limitations of Mediaeval

feeling. The two world-religions perform a function in their place and time, and in the end will be converted to the truth. The seed in the ground, Israel among the nations, though apparently disrupted and dying, transmutes the surrounding earth and loam by a magic alchemy into its own higher life. And towards his own people there is a polarity of attitude manifest throughout—the polarity furnished by its high promise and its miserable present. His book is an elaborate theory of an innate superhuman distinctiveness inhering in the Jewish people and amounting to a special soul-form; but the actual fact which confronts him, and which his poet's eye made him perceive all the more unflinchingly, was a condition of shabby dilapidation, an outer and inner disarray. What helps him to overcome the discrepancy is unbounded love and faith. Judah Halevi's steadfast belief in the meaning of Jewish history enables him to overarch the present by spanning Sinai with Messiah.

Two great themes dominate the book, the one culminating in the other; the first deals with the difference between an historical religion and a religion of reason, and the second gives a theory of the Jewish people. As for the first, he is not opposed to philosophy as such; he merely contests its claim to supplant religion, to be a religion in its own right. And he makes his point by an amazingly modern and valid analysis of the God-idea offered by each. But the climax towards which everything converges is the notion of Election, and of the unique and supernatural character of the Jewish people and its history. There is of course a touch of irony, deliberate or implicit, in every elaborately maintained extreme, in every soberly defended audacity of thought. But Judah Halevi is dealing with extremes; he is dealing with a people living in a chronically desperate situation, a people every element of whose life and history is so extreme that living for it becomes plausible and tolerable only on the basis of transcendental assumptions. In any case this is Judah Halevi's thesis and he adheres to it throughout.

Judah Halevi's apology for Judaism arises out of a polemic with the prevailing power of the day; that power was philosophy—the educated beliefs of his contemporaries. He insists that metaphysics does not yield truth in the higher reaches. There may be a preliminary area in which the light of reason gives us sure guidance both in questions of God and in the field of ethics, but for ultimates the real source of religious truth is Revelation.

Philosophy indeed appears as a Promethean undertaking. It is an attempt to reach God through man's unaided efforts, through his will to know. Man's intellect, by appropriating the great truths of metaphysics, fuses (so we are told) with the "Active Intellect" which presides over this earth from its seat in the lunar sphere and, through the Active Intellect, with God. The human mind becomes as eternal as the truths which it assimilates, as the objects which it comprehends, chief among them being God. And there is a point where knowledge and understanding become contemplation and emotion, and philosophy takes on the character of religion for the higher man, and the philosopher at the peak of vision is the true prophet, the seer of God.

Judah Halevi denies this power of the intellect to

establish communion with God. For one thing the actual historic fact refutes the claim made for philosophers: they do not figure in any special way among great religious leaders or prophets. On the contrary, and unreasonable as it may appear, prophets and men of religious power seem to be chosen from ranks outside the class of philosophers.

Moreover communion with God seems to be a gift of God, not a product of the efforts of men. And here precisely is the difference between real and apparent religion. Attainment of God, living contact with him, cannot be achieved by man's reason out of its own resources. The point of departure is always with God; the genuine religious experience or event is always due to the spontaneity, the free grace, the self-revelation of God. It is he who reaches out and seeks man. Revelation alone then establishes the true, the real religion. This real or historical religion is basically different from the intellectual religion of the philosophers and God is a radically different being in both. The God of philosophy remains the far-off unmoved goal towards which man aspires and towards which he raises himself by his own cognitive efforts. The God of religion does not remain at rest in self-sufficiency but reaches out actively and with solicitude to call and raise man to himself.

The opposition between the two may be expressed in a somewhat different way. For philosophy God is an object of knowledge, standing in exactly the same relation to the theoretic faculty as any other object we set out to know. God is indeed a supreme object in the sense of being the first cause, but that is merely a logical pre-eminence, not a supremacy of concern or value. And this is reflected in the contemplative character of the Aristotelian religiosity, in the note of theoretic peace and imperturbability which pervades it. But while philosophy is primarily the knowing of God, religion is living with God. The religious man is impelled to God not by a desire to know but by a yearning to be with him, by love; bliss and misery coincide, in the Psalmist's phrase, with being near to God or cast from him. The whole relation is a dynamic of longing, entirely different from the serenity of the theoretic attitude. The God of Abraham and the God of Aristotle are two different gods.

This superiority of the religious experience over the theoretic understanding finds psychological expression in the assumption by Judah Halevi of a separate religious faculty, higher than the understanding, whereby union with God is achieved. The Hebrew term employed is the strange *ha-inyan ha-elohi;* it is used indifferently to indicate the double direction which obtains here, objectively the revelation coming from God, subjectively the power to apperceive it. It thus replaces intellect or rational soul which had till now served the philosopher to establish the relation with the unseen world. And one might suppose that in all this Judah Halevi is being motivated by a disinterested desire to distinguish the religious experience for its own sake, as something superior to the study and meditation of the philosopher. But his real intention is to provide a rationale for Israel's supernatural place and function.

For the religious faculty has been granted only to Israel. Israel has it by direct inheritance from the first man. Adam coming from the hand of God himself had it in full measure, and it was bequeathed in each generation to one or a few who were the "heart" or "treasure" of mankind in that generation—by a divine insistence on a hierarchy of being, which subordinates plant to animal and animal to man and among men the "husk" to the "treasure." When it finally passed on to Jacob it became the peculiar heritage and the common possession (though in endless degrees of variation) of the whole household of Israel, which by virtue of this is the "heart" or "treasure" of mankind. In all other respects, in understanding and moral qualities, there is no distinction between Israel and the nations, but this faculty constitutes the specific difference between them. In itself a mere disposition or potentiality, the religious faculty is brought to full fruition through the efficacy of the ritual and ceremonial law. The ceremonial law is thus not the opaque and irrational appendage which it seemed to the Jewish rationalists, but rather the agency prescribed by God to serve the superrational purpose of achieving living contact with Him. And along with the superrational efficacy of the ritual a similar religious pre-eminence inheres in the Holy Land, and a similar virtue resides in the Hebrew language. This is to be understood in a precise manner. As certain precious vines can grow only in a definite place and only through specific cultivation, so religion, the highest life of man, the constant communion with God, can come to full fruit and flower only through the union of all the requisite elements—the chosen people residing in the Holy Land, speaking the first and noblest tongue of men and performing the prescribed ordinances of ritual. The magic of exact co-ordination of elements is as necessary on the highest plane of creation as on the lower plane of nature in the production of orchid or peacock.

Particularism could seem to go no further with this concentration of religion on one people and the exclusion of the rest of the world. But the bare fact that the theme of the book is the conversion of a heathen king to the Jewish faith should be enough to indicate the true intention of the author. Mankind is not to be excluded from the life with God; nothing could be further from the spirit and intention of the book. But it is primarily a theory of first and last things and of the place of Judaism in this scheme; and it was written to remind the Jewish people of that supreme fact in the moment of deepest danger and decline. Jews and Judaism may be the least of these now; they were and shall be first—but this in a world-embracing scheme involving all men. Meanwhile those among the nations who observe the moral law given by God to all men shall have their reward from God, and if they join the Jewish faith they shall be accounted equals in all respects except the highest one of eligibility for prophecy. And even that invidious distinction shall disappear in the coming of the Messiah, when all peoples will have attained *ha-inyan ha-elohi,* and the seed in the ground will have assimilated all the earth to its own higher substance. Judah Halevi makes express use in this highest connection of the most tragic and beautiful of all symbols—the death and resurrection of the seed in the dark earth.

But that is the end, the final light. For the present the immediate concern is with the long hard road, and for that the Jews must have their courage renewed.

Judah Halevi is impressed and overwhelmed with the one idea that the Jews are in a pre-eminent and unique sense the God-bearing people of history. He devotes his life to recalling them to that one thought. His poetry, his philosophy, his journey to the Holy Land, his whole personality in which the very soul of the race seems embodied, all serve to inculcate and impress the one idea.

To us as well as to his contemporaries, he gives two answers, a lived life and a book. He provides the exemplar or archetype of the tragic-heroic life of high resolve, return to faith and active endeavor. And he writes an apology for Judaism designed, first, to prove its world historic mission as against the two world powers who between them seem to fill the entire stage; and, second, to restore and reopen the sources of religious power in a people despised, discouraged, and depressed.

As for the man himself, he seems to be Israel's own answer to its problem. Only one profoundly rooted in his people and its substance could produce such an answer. In Judah Halevi the genius of Judaism comes to consciousness.

THE BOOK AL KHAZARI

THE BOOK AL KHAZARI

PART ONE

I WAS asked to state what arguments and replies I
could bring to bear against the attacks of philosophers
and followers of other religions, and also against [Jewish]
sectarians who attacked the rest of Israel. This reminded me of something I had once heard concerning
the arguments of a Rabbi who sojourned with the
King of the Khazars. The latter, as we know from
historical records, became a convert to Judaism about
four hundred years ago. To him came a dream, and it appeared as if an angel addressed him, saying : ' Thy way
of thinking is indeed pleasing to the Creator, but not thy
way of acting.' Yet he was so zealous in the performance of the Khazar religion, that he devoted himself
with a perfect heart to the service of the temple and
sacrifices. Notwithstanding this devotion, the angel
came again at night and repeated : ' Thy way of thinking is pleasing to God, but not thy way of acting.' This
caused him to ponder over the different beliefs and
religions, and finally become a convert to Judaism
together with many other Khazars. As I found among
the arguments of the Rabbi, many which appealed to
me, and were in harmony with my own opinions, I
resolved to write them down exactly as they had been
spoken.[1]

When the King of Khazar (as is related) dreamt that

his way of thinking was agreeable to God, but not his
way of acting, and was commanded in the same dream
to seek the God-pleasing work, he inquired of a philosopher concerning his religious persuasion. The philosopher replied : There is no favour or dislike in [the
nature of] God, because He is above desire and intention. A desire intimates a want in the person who feels
it, and not till it is satisfied does he become (so to speak)
complete. If it remains unfulfilled, he lacks completion.
In a similar way He is, in the opinion of philosophers,
above the knowledge of individuals, because the latter
change with the times, whilst there is no change in God's
knowledge. He, therefore, does not know thee, much
less thy thoughts and actions, nor does He listen to thy
prayers, or see thy movements. If philosophers say
that He created thee, they only use a metaphor, because
He is the Cause of causes in the creation of all creatures,
but not because this was His intention from the beginning. He never created man. For the world is without
beginning, and there never arose a man otherwise than
through one who came into existence before him, in
whom were united forms, gifts, and characteristics inherited from father, mother, and other relations, besides
the influences of climate, countries, foods and water,
spheres, stars and constellations. Everything is reduced to a Prime Cause ; not to a Will proceeding from
this, but an Emanation from which emanated a second,
a third, and fourth cause.

The Cause and the caused are, as thou seest, intimately connected with one another, their coherence
being as eternal as the Prime Cause and having no
beginning. Every individual on earth has his com-
pleting causes ; consequently an individual with perfect

causes becomes perfect, and another with imperfect causes remains imperfect, as the negro who is able to receive nothing more than the human shape and speech in its least developed form. The philosopher, however, who is equipped with the highest capacity, receives through it the advantages of disposition, intelligence and active power, so that he wants nothing to make him perfect. Now these perfections exist but *in abstracto*, and require instruction and training to become practical, and in order that this capacity, with all its completeness or deficiencies and endless grades, may become visible. In the perfect person a light of divine nature, called Active Intellect, is with him, and its Passive Intellect is so closely connected therewith that both are but one. The person [of such perfection] thus observes that he is The Active Intellect himself, and that there is no difference between them. His organs—I mean the limbs of such a person—only serve for the most perfect purposes, in the most appropriate time, and in the best condition, as if they were the organs of the Active Intellect, but not of the material and passive Intellect, which used them at an earlier period, sometimes well, but more often improperly. The Active Intellect, however, is always successful. This degree is the last and most longed-for goal for the perfect man whose soul, after having been purified, has grasped the inward truths of all branches of science, has thus become equal to an angel, and has found a place on the nethermost step of seraphic beings. This is the degree of the Active Intellect, viz. that angel whose degree is below the angel who is connected with the sphere of the moon. There are spiritual forces, detached from matter, but eternal like

the Prime Cause and never threatened by decay.
Thus the soul of the perfect man and that Intellect
become One, without concern for the decay of his body
or his organs, because he becomes united to the other.
His soul is cheerful while he is alive, because it enjoys
the company of Hermes, Asclepios, Socrates, Plato
and Aristotle ; nay, he and they, as well as every one
who shares their degree, and the Active Intellect, are
one thing. This is what is called allusively and approximately *Pleasure of God.* Endeavour to reach it, and
the true knowledge of things, in order that thy intellect
may become active, but not passive. Keep just ways
as regards character and actions, because this will help
thee to effect truth, to gain instruction, and to become
similar to this Active Intellect. The consequence of
this will be contentment, humility, meekness, and
every other praiseworthy inclination, accompanied by
the veneration of the Prime Cause, not in order to
receive favour from it, or to divert its wrath, but solely
to become like the Active Intellect in finding the truth,
in describing everything in a fitting manner, and in
rightly recognizing its basis. These are the characteristics of the [Active] Intellect. If thou hast reached
such disposition of belief, be not concerned about the
forms of thy humility or religion or worship, or the
word or language or actions thou employest. Thou
mayest even choose a religion in the way of humility,
worship, and benediction, for the management of thy
temperament, thy house and [the people of thy]
country, if they agree to it. Or fashion thy religion
according to the laws of reason set up by philosophers,
and strive after purity of soul. In fine, seek purity of
heart in which way thou art able, provided thou hast

acquired the sum total of knowledge in its real essence ; then thou wilt reach thy goal, viz. the union with this Spiritual, or rather Active Intellect. Maybe he will communicate with thee or teach thee the knowledge of what is hidden through true dreams and positive visions.

2. Said to him the Khazari : Thy words are convincing, yet they do not correspond to what I wish to find. I know already that my soul is pure and that my actions are calculated to gain the favour of God. To all this I received the answer that this way of action does *not* find favour, though the intention does. There must no doubt be a way of acting, pleasing by its very nature, but not through the medium of intentions. If this be not so, why, then, do Christian and Moslim, who divide the inhabited world between them, fight with one another, each of them serving his God with pure intention, living either as monks or hermits, fasting and praying ? For all that they vie with each other in committing murders, believing that this is a most pious work and brings them nearer to God. They fight in the belief that paradise and eternal bliss will be their reward. It is, however, impossible to agree with both.

3. The Philosopher replied : The philosophers' creed knows no manslaughter, as they only cultivate the intellect.

4. Al Khazari : What could be more erroneous, in the opinion of the philosophers, than the belief that the world was created in six days, or that the Prime Cause spoke with mortals, not to mention the philosophic doctrine, which declares the former to be above knowing details. In addition to this one might expect the gift of prophecy quite common among philosophers,

considering their deeds, their knowledge, their researches after truth, their exertions, and their close
connexion with all things spiritual, also that wonders,
miracles, and extraordinary things would be reported
of them. Yet we find that true visions are granted to
persons who do not devote themselves to study or to
the purification of their souls, whereas the opposite is
the case with those who strive after these things. This
proves that the divine influence as well as the souls
have a secret which is not identical with what thou
sayest, O Philosopher.

After this the Khazari said to himself : I will ask
the Christians and Moslims, since one of these per-
suasions is, no doubt, the God-pleasing one. As regards
the Jews, I am satisfied that they are of low station,
few in number, and generally despised.

He then invited a Christian scholastic, and put
questions to him concerning the theory and practice
of his faith.

The Scholastic replied : I believe that all things
are created, whilst the Creator is eternal ; that He
created the whole world in six days ; that all mankind
sprang from Adam, and after him from Noah, to whom
they trace themselves back ; that God takes care of
the created beings, and keeps in touch with man ; that
He shows wrath, pleasure, and compassion ; that He
speaks, appears, and reveals Himself to His prophets
and favoured ones ; that He dwells among those who
please him   In short [I believe] in all that is written
in the Tōrāh and the records of the Children of Israel,
which are undisputed, because they are generally
known as lasting, and have been revealed before a
vast multitude. Subsequently the divine essence

became embodied in an embryo in the womb of a
virgin taken from the noblest ranks of Israelitish women.
She bore Him with the semblance of a human being,
but covering a divinity, seemingly a prophet, but in
reality a God sent forth.   He is the Messiah, whom
we call the Son of God, and He is the Father, and the
Son and the Holy Spirit.   We condense His nature into
one thing, although the Trinity appears on our
tongues.   We believe in Him and in His abode among
the Children of Israel, granted to them as a distinction,
because the divine influence never ceased to be attached
to them, until the masses rebelled against this Messiah,
and they crucified Him.   Then divine wrath burdened
them everlastingly, whilst the favour was confined to
a few who followed the Messiah, and to those nations
which followed these few.   We belong to their number.
Although we are not of Israelitish descent, we are well
deserving of being called Children of Israel, because
we follow the Messiah and His twelve Israelitish
companions who took the place of the tribes.   Many
Israelites followed these twelve [apostles], and became
the leaven, as it were, for the Christians.   We are
worthy of the degree of the Children of Israel.   To us
was also granted victory, and expansion over the
countries.   All nations are invited to this religion, and
charged to practise it, to adore the Messiah and the
cross on which He was put, and the like.   Our laws and
regulations are derived from the Apostle Simon, and
from ordinations taken from the Tōrā, which we study.
Its truth is indisputable, as is also the fact that it came
from God.   It is also stated in the New Testament:
I came not to destroy one of the laws of Moses, but I
came to confirm and enlarge it.[1a]

5. Then said the Khazari : I see here no logical
conclusion ; nay, logic rejects most of what thou sayest.
If both appearance and experience are so palpable
that they take hold of the whole heart, compelling belief
in a thing of which one is not convinced they render
the matter more feasible by a semblance of logic.
This is how natural philosophers deal with strange
phenomena which come upon them unawares,
and which they would not believe if they only heard
of them without seeing them. When they have examined them, they discuss them, and ascribe them to
the influence of stars or spirits without disproving
ocular evidence. As for me, I cannot accept these
things, because they come upon me suddenly, not
having grown up in them. My duty is to investigate
further.

He then invited one of the Doctors of Islām, and
questioned him regarding his doctrine and observance.

The Doctor said : We acknowledge the unity and
eternity of God, and that all men are derived from
Adam-Noah. We absolutely reject embodiment,[2]
and if any element of this appears in the Writ, we
explain it as a metaphor and allegory. At the same
time we maintain that our Book is the Speech of God,
being a miracle [3] which we are bound to accept for its
own sake, since no one is able to bring anything similar
to it, or to one of its verses.[4] Our prophet is the Seal
of the prophets,[5] who abrogated every previous law,[6]
and invited all nations to embrace Islām. The reward
of the pious consists in the return of his spirit to his
body in paradise and bliss, where he never ceases to
enjoy eating, drinking, woman's love, and anything
he may desire. The requital of the disobedient con-

sists in being condemned to the fire of hell, and his
punishment knows no end.

6. Said to him the Khazari : If any one is to be
guided in matters divine, and to be convinced that
God speaks to man, whilst he considers it improbable, he must be convinced of it by means of generally
known facts, which allow no refutation, and particularly imbue him with the belief that God has spoken
to man. Although your book may be a miracle, as
long as it is written in Arabic,[7] a non-Arab, as I am,
cannot perceive its miraculous character ; and even if
it were read to me, I could not distinguish between it
and any other book written in the Arabic language.

7. The Doctor replied : Yet miracles were performed by him, but they were not used as evidence for
the acceptance of his law.

8. Al Khazari : Exactly so ; but the human mind
cannot believe that God has intercourse with man,
except by a miracle which changes the nature of things.
He then recognizes that to do so He alone is capable
who created them from nought. It must also have
taken place in the presence of great multitudes, who
saw it distinctly, and did not learn it from reports and
traditions. Even then they must examine the matter
carefully and repeatedly, so that no suspicion of
imagination or magic can enter their minds. Then
it is possible that the mind may grasp this extraordinary matter, viz. that the Creator of this world
and the next, of the heavens and lights, should hold
intercourse with this contemptible piece of clay, I
mean man, speak to him, and fulfil his wishes and
desires.

9. The Doctor : Is not our Book full of the stories

of Moses and the Children of Israel ? No one can
deny what He did to Pharaoh, how He divided the
sea, saved those who enjoyed His favour, but drowned
those who had aroused His wrath. Then came the
manna and the quails during forty years, His speaking
to Moses on the mount, making the sun stand still for
Joshua, and assisting him against the mighty. [Add
to this] what happened previously, viz. the Flood, the
destruction of the people of Lot ; is this not so well
known that no suspicion of deceit and imagination
is possible ?

10. Al Khazari : Indeed, I see myself compélled to
ask the Jews, because they are the relic of the Children
of Israel. For I see that they constitute in themselves
the evidence for the divine law on earth.

He then invited a Jewish Rabbi, and asked him
about his belief.

11. The Rabbi replied : I believe in the God of
Abraham, Isaac and Israel, who led the children of
Israel out of Egypt with signs and miracles ; who fed
them in the desert and gave them the land, after having
made them traverse the sea and the Jordan in a miraculous way ; who sent Moses with His law, and subsequently thousands of prophets, who confirmed His law
by promises to the observant, and threats to the disobedient. Our belief is comprised in the Tōrāh—a
very large domain.

12. I had not intended to ask any Jew, because I
am aware of their reduced condition and narrow-
minded views, as their misery left them nothing com-
mendable. Now shouldst thou, O Jew, not have said
that thou believest in the Creator of the world, its
Governor and Guide, and in Him who created and

keeps thee, and such attributes which serve as evidence for every believer, and for the sake of which He pursues justice in order to resemble the Creator in His wisdom and justice ?

13. The Rabbi : That which thou dost express is religion based on speculation and system, the research of thought, but open to many doubts. Now ask the philosophers, and thou wilt find that they do not agree on one action or one principle, since some doctrines can be established by arguments, which are only partially satisfactory, and still much less capable of being proved.

14. Al Khazari : That which thou sayest now, O Jew, seems to be more to the point than the beginning, and I should like to hear more.

15. The Rabbi : Surely the beginning of my speech was just the proof, and so evident that it requires no other argument.

16. Al Khazari : How so ?

17. The Rabbi : Allow me to make a few preliminary remarks, for I see thee disregarding and depreciating my words.

18. Al Khazari : Let me hear thy remarks.

19. The Rabbi : If thou wert told that the King of India was an excellent man, commanding admiration, and deserving his high reputation, one whose actions were reflected in the justice which rules his country and the virtuous ways of his subjects, would this bind thee to revere him ?

20. Al Khazari : How could this bind me, whilst I am not sure if the justice of the Indian people is natural, and not dependent on their king, or due to the king or both ?

21. The Rabbi : But if his messenger came to thee bringing presents which thou knowest to be only procurable in India, and in the royal palace, accompanied by a letter in which it is distinctly stated from whom it comes, and to which are added drugs to cure thy diseases, to preserve thy health, poisons for thy enemies, and other means to fight and kill them without battle, would this make thee beholden to him ?

22. Al Khazari : Certainly. For this would remove my former doubt that the Indians have a king. I should also acknowledge that a proof of his power and dominion has reached me.

23. The Rabbi : How wouldst thou, then, if asked, describe him ?

24. Al Khazari : In terms about which I am quite clear, and to these I could add others which were at first rather doubtful, but are no longer so.

25. The Rabbi : In this way I answered thy first question. In the same strain spoke Moses to Pharaoh, when he told him : ' The God of the Hebrews sent me to thee,' viz. the God of Abraham, Isaac and Jacob. For Abraham was well known to the nations, who also knew that the divine spirit was in contact with the patriarchs, cared for them, and performed miracles for them. He did not say : ' The God of heaven and earth,' nor ' my Creator and thine sent me.' In the same way God commenced His speech to the assembled people of Israel : ' I am the God whom you worship, who has led you out of the land of Egypt,' but He did not say : ' I am the Creator of the world and your Creator.' Now in the same style I spoke to thee, a Prince of the Khazars, when thou didst ask me about my creed. I answered thee as was fitting, and is

fitting for the whole of Israel who knew these things, first from personal experience, and afterwards *through uninterrupted* tradition, which is equal to the former.

26. Al Khazari : If this be so, then your belief is confined to yourselves ?

27. The Rabbi : Yes ; but any Gentile who joins us unconditionally shares our good fortune, without, however, being quite equal to us. If the Law were binding on us only because God created us, the white and the black man would be equal, since He created them all. But the Law was given to us because He led us out of Egypt, and remained attached to us, because we are the pick of mankind.

28. Al Khazari : Jew, I see thee quite altered, and thy words are poor after having been so pleasant.

29. The Rabbi : Poor or pleasant, give me thy attention, and let me express myself more fully.

30. Al Khazari : Say what thou wilt.

31. The Rabbi : The laws of nature comprise nurture, growth, and propagation, with their powers and all conditions attached thereto. This is particularly the case with plants and animals, to the exclusion of earth, stones, metals, and elements.

32. Al Khazari : This is a maxim which requires explanation, though it be true.

33. The Rabbi : As regards the soul, it is given to all animated beings. The result is movement, will power, external as well as internal senses and such like.

34. Al Khazari : This, too, cannot be contradicted.

35. The Rabbi : Intellect is man's birthright above all living beings. This leads to the development of his faculties, his home, his country, from which arise administrative and regulative laws.

36. Al Khazari : This is also true.

37. The Rabbi : Which is the next highest degree ?

38. Al Khazari : The degree of great sages.

39. The Rabbi : I only mean that degree which separates those who occupy it from the physical point of view, as the plant is separated from inorganic things, or man from animals. The differences as to quantity, however, are endless, as they are only accidental, and do not really form a degree.

40. Al Khazari : If this be so, then there is no degree above man among tangible things.

41. The Rabbi : If we find a man who walks into the fire without hurt, or abstains from food for some time without starving, on whose face a light shines which the eye cannot bear, who is never ill, nor ages, until having reached his life's natural end, who dies spontaneously just as a man retires to his couch to sleep on an appointed day and hour, equipped with the knowledge of what is hidden as to past and future : is such a degree not visibly distinguished from the ordinary human degree ?

42. Al Khazari : This is, indeed, the divine and seraphic degree, if it exists at all. It belongs to the province of the divine influence, but not to that of the intellectual, human, or natural world.

43. The Rabbi : These are some of the characteristics of the undoubted prophets through whom God made Himself manifest, and who also made known that there is a God who guides them as He wishes, according to their obedience or disobedience. He revealed to those prophets that which was hidden, and taught them how the world was created, how the generations prior to the Flood followed each other,

and how they reckoned their descent from Adam. He described the Flood and the origin of the 'Seventy Nations' from Shem, Ham and Japheth, the sons of Noah; how the languages were split up, and where men sought their habitations; how arts arose, how they built cities, and the chronology from Adam up to this day.

44. Al Khazari: It is strange that you should possess authentic chronology of the creation of the world.

45. The Rabbi: Surely we reckon according to it, and there is no difference between the Jews of Khazar and Ethiopia in this respect.

46. Al Khazari: What date do you consider it at present?

47. The Rabbi: Four thousand and nine hundred years.[8] The details can be demonstrated from the lives of Adam, Seth and Enōsh to Noah; then Shem and Eber to Abraham; then Isaac and Jacob to Moses. All of them represented the essence and purity of Adam on account of their intimacy with God. Each of them had children only to be compared to them outwardly, but not really like them, and, therefore, without direct union with the divine influence. The chronology was established through the medium of those sainted persons who were only single individuals, and not a crowd, until Jacob begat the Twelve Tribes, who were all under this divine influence. Thus the divine element reached a multitude of persons who carried the records further. The chronology of those who lived before these has been handed down to us by Moses.

48. Al Khazari: An arrangement of this kind removes any suspicion of untruth or common plot. Not

ten people could discuss such a thing without disagreeing, and disclosing their secret understanding ;
nor could they refute any one who tried to establish
the truth of a matter like this. How is it possible
where such a mass of people is concerned ? Finally,
the period involved is not large enough to admit untruth and fiction.

49. The Rabbi : That is so. Abraham himself lived
during the period of the separation of languages. He
and his relatives retained the language of his grandfather Eber, which for that reason is called Hebrew.
Four hundred years after him appeared Moses at a
time when the world was rich in information concerning the heavens and earth. He approached Pharaoh
and the Doctors of Egypt, as well as those of the
Israelites. Whilst agreeing with him they questioned
him, and completely refused to believe that God spoke
with man, until he caused them to hear the Ten Words.
In the same way the people were on his side, not from
ignorance, but on account of the knowledge they possessed. They feared magic and astrological arts, and
similar snares, things which, like deceit, do not bear
close examination, whereas the divine might is like
pure gold, ever increasing in brilliancy. How could
one imagine that an attempt had been made to show
that a language spoken five hundred years previously
was none but Eber's own language split up in
Babel during the days of Peleg ; also to trace the
origin of this or that nation back to Shem or Ham, and
the same with their countries ? Is it likely that any
one could to-day invent false statements concerning
the origin, history, and languages of well-known nations,
the latter being less than five hundred years old ?

50. Al Khazari : This is not possible. How could it be, since we possess books in the handwriting of their authors written five hundred years ago ? No false interpolation could enter the contents of a book which is not above five hundred years of age, such as genea-logical tables, linguistic and other works.

51. The Rabbi : Now why should Moses' speeches remain uncontradicted ? Did not his own people raise objections, not to speak of others ?

52. Al Khazari : These things are handed down well founded and firmly established.

53. The Rabbi : Dost thou think that the languages are eternal and without beginning ?

54. Al Khazari : No ; they undoubtedly had a begin-ning, which originated in a conventional manner. Evi-dence of this is found in their composition of nouns, verbs, and particles. They originated from sounds derived from the organs of speech.

[55. The Rabbi : Didst thou ever see any one who contrived a language, or didst thou hear of him ?]

56. Al Khazari : Neither the one nor the other. There is no doubt that it appeared at some time, but prior to this there was no language concerning which one nation, to the exclusion of another, could come to any agreement.

57. The Rabbi : Didst thou ever hear of a nation which possessed different traditions with regard to the generally acknowledged week which begins with the Sunday and ends with the Sabbath ? How is it pos-sible that the people of China could agree with those of the western islands without common beginning, agreement and convention ?⁹

58. Al Khazari : Such a thing would only have

been possible if they had all come to an agreement. This, however, is improbable, unless all men are the descendants of Adam, of Noah, or of some other ancestor from whom they received the hebdomadal calculation.

59. The Rabbi : That is what I meant. East and West agree on the decimal system. What instinct induced them to keep to the number *ten*, unless it was a tradition handed down by the first one who did so ? [10]

60. Al Khazari : Does it not weaken thy belief if thou art told that the Indians have antiquities and buildings which they consider to be millions of years old ?

61. The Rabbi : It would, indeed, weaken my belief had they a fixed form of religion, or a book concerning which a multitude of people held the same opinion, and in which no historical discrepancy could be found. Such a book, however, does not exist. Apart from this, they are a dissolute, unreliable people, and arouse the indignation of the followers of religions through their talk, whilst they anger them with their idols, talismans, and witchcraft. To such things they pin their faith, and deride those who boast of the possession of a divine book. Yet they only possess a few books, and these were written to mislead the weakminded. To this class belong astrological writings, in which they speak of ten thousands of years, as the book on the Nabataean Agriculture, in which are mentioned the names of Janbūshār, Sagrīt and Roanai.[11] It is believed that they lived before Adam, who was the disciple of Janbūshār, and such like.

62. Al Khazari : If I had supported my arguments by reference to a negro people, i.e. a people not united

upon a common law, thy answer would have been correct. Now what is thy opinion of the philosophers who, as the result of their careful researches, agree that the world is without beginning, and here it does not concern tens of thousands, and not millions, but unlimited numbers of years.

63. The Rabbi: There is an excuse for the Philosophers. Being Grecians, science and religion did not come to them as inheritances. They belong to the descendants of Japheth, who inhabited the north, whilst that knowledge coming from Adam, and supported by the divine influence, is only to be found among the progeny of Shem, who represented the successors of Noah and constituted, as it were, his essence. This knowledge has always been connected with this essence, and will always remain so. The Greeks only received it when they became powerful, from Persia. The Persians had it from the Chaldaeans. It was only then that the famous [Greek] Philosophers arose, but as soon as Rome assumed political leadership they produced no philosopher worthy the name.

64. Al Khazari: Does this mean that Aristotle's philosophy is not deserving of credence?

65. The Rabbi: Certainly. He exerted his mind, because he had no tradition from any reliable source at his disposal. He meditated on the beginning and end of the world, but found as much difficulty in the theory of a beginning as in that of eternity. Finally, these abstract speculations which made for eternity, prevailed, and he found no reason to inquire into the chronology or derivation of those who lived before him. Had he lived among a people with well authenticated and generally acknowledged traditions, he would

have applied his deductions and arguments to establish
the theory of creation, however difficult, instead of
eternity, which is even much more difficult to accept.

66. Al Khazari : Is there any decisive proof ?

67. The Rabbi : Where could we find one for such
a question ?   Heaven forbid that there should be anything in the Bible to contradict that which is manifest
or proved !   On the other hand it tells of miracles
and the changes of ordinary, things newly arising, or
changing one into the other.   This proves that the
Creator of the world is able to accomplish what
He will, and whenever He will.   The question
of eternity and creation is obscure, whilst the arguments are evenly balanced.   The theory of creation
derives greater weight from the prophetic tradition of
Adam, Noah, and Moses, which is more deserving of
credence than mere speculation.   If, after all, a believer in the Law finds himself compelled to admit an
eternal matter and the existence of many worlds prior
to this one, this would not impair his belief that *this*
world was created at a certain epoch,[12] and that Adam
and Noah were the first human beings.

68. Al Khazari : Thus far I find these arguments
quite satisfactory.   Should we continue our conversation, I will trouble thee to adduce more decisive
proofs.   Now take up the thread of thy earlier ex-
position, how the great conviction settled in thy soul,
that the Creator of body and spirit, soul, intellect and
angels—He who is too high, holy and exalted for the
mind still less for the senses to grasp—that He holds
intercourse with creatures made of low and contemptible material, wonderful as this may seem.   For the

smallest worm shows the wonders of His wisdom in a
manner beyond the human mind.

69. The Rabbi : Thou hast forestalled much of my
intended answer to thee. Dost thou ascribe the wisdom
apparent in the creation of an ant (for example) to a
sphere or star, or to any other object, to the exclusion
of the Almighty Creator, who weighs and gives everything its due, giving neither too much, nor too little ?

70. Al Khazari : This is ascribed to the action of
Nature.

71. The Rabbi : What is Nature ?

72. Al Khazari : As far as philosophy teaches, it is
a certain power ; only we do not know what it really
is. No doubt philosophers know.

73. The Rabbi : They know as much as we do.
Aristotle[13] defined it as the beginning and primary
cause through which a thing either moves or rests, not
by accidents, but on account of its innate essence.

74. Al Khazari : This would mean that the thing
which moves or rests on its own account has a cause
through which it moves or rests. This cause is Nature.

75. The Rabbi : This opinion is the result of diligent
research, criticism, and discrimination between accidental and natural occurrences. These things astonish
those who hear them, but nothing else springs from
the knowledge of nature.

76. Al Khazari : All I can see is, that they have
misled us by these names, and caused us to place another
being on a par with God, if we say that Nature is wise
and active. Speaking in their sense, we might even
say : possessed of intelligence.

77. The Rabbi : Certainly ; but the elements, moon,
sun and stars have powers such as warming, cooling,

moistening, drying, etc., but do not merit that wisdom should be ascribed to them, or be reckoned more than a function. Forming, measuring, producing, however, and all that shows an intention, can only be ascribed to the All-wise and Almighty. There is no harm in calling the power which arranges matter by means of heat and cooling, 'Nature,' but all intelligence must be denied it. So must the faculty of *creating* the embryo be denied to human beings, because they only aid matter in receiving human form from its wise Creator. Thou must not deem it improbable that exalted divine traces should be visible in this material world, when this matter is prepared to receive them. Here are to be found the roots of faith as well as of unbelief.

78. Al Khazari : How is this possible ?

79. The Rabbi : These conditions which render man fit to receive this divine influence do not lie within him. It is impossible for him to gauge their quantity or quality, and even if their essence were known, yet neither their time, place, and connexion, nor suitability could be discovered. For this, inspired and detailed instruction is necessary. He who has been thus inspired, and obeys the teaching in every respect with a pure mind, is a believer. Whosoever strives by speculation and deduction to prepare the conditions for the reception of this inspiration, or by divining, as is found in the writings of astrologers, trying to call down supernatural beings, or manufacturing talismans, such a man is an unbeliever. He may bring offerings and burn incense in the name of speculation and conjecture, whilst he is in reality ignorant of that which he should do, how much, in which way, by what means, in which place, by whom,

in which manner, and many other details, the enumera-
tion of which would lead too far.   He is like an ignoramus who enters the surgery of a physician famous for
the curative power of his medicines. The physician
is not at home, but people come for medicines. The
fool dispenses them out of the jars, knowing nothing
of the contents, nor how much should be given to each
person. Thus he kills with the very medicine which
should have cured them. Should he by chance have
effected a cure with one of the drugs, the people will
turn to him and say that he helped them, till they discover that he deceived them, or they seek other advice,
and cling to this without noticing that the real cure
was effected by the skill of the learned physician who
prepared the medicines and explained the proper
manner in which they were to be administered. He
also taught the patients what food and drink, exercise
and rest, etc., was necessary, likewise what air was the
best, and which place of repose   Like unto the patients
duped by the ignoramus, so were men, with few exceptions, before the time of Moses. They were deceived
by astrological and physical rules, wandered from law
to law, from god to god, or adopted a plurality at the
same time. They forgot their guide and master, and
regarded their false gods as helping causes, whilst they
are in reality damaging causes, according to their construction and arrangement. Profitable on its own
account is the divine influence, hurtful on its own
account the absence thereof.

80. Al Khazari : Let us now return to our subject,
and explain to me how your belief grew, how it spread
and became general, how opinions became united after
having differed, and how long it took for the faith to

lay its foundation, and to be built up into a strong and
complete structure. The first element of religion
appeared, no doubt, among single individuals, who
supported one another in upholding the faith which it
pleased God should be promulgated. Their number
increases continually, they grow more powerful, or a
king arises and assists them, also compels his subjects
to adopt the same creed.[14]

81. The Rabbi : In this way only rational religions, of human origin, can arise. When a man
succeeds and attains an exalted position, it is said that
he is supported by God, who inspired him, etc. A
religion of divine origin arises suddenly. It is bidden
to arise, and it is there, like the creation of the world.

82. Al Khazari : Thou surprisest me, O Rabbi.

83. The Rabbi : It is, indeed, astonishing. The
Israelites lived in Egypt as slaves, six hundred thousand men above the age of twenty, descendants of the
Twelve Tribes. Not one of them had separated or
emigrated into another country, nor was a stranger
among them. They looked forward to the promise
given to their ancestors, Abraham, Isaac, and Jacob,
that the land of Palestine should be their inheritance.
At that time it was in the power of seven mighty and
prosperous nations, whilst the Israelites sighed in the
depths of misery under the bondage of Pharaoh, who
caused their children to be put to death, lest they
should increase in number. Notwithstanding their
lowly position as compared to the tyrant in his might,
God sent Moses and Aaron before Pharaoh with signs
and miracles, allowing them even to change the course
of nature. Pharaoh could not get away from them,
nor harm them, neither could he protect himself from

the ten plagues which befel the Egyptians, affecting their streams, land, air, plants, animals, bodies, even their souls. For in one moment, at midnight, died the most precious and most beloved members of their houses, viz. every firstborn male. There was no dwelling without dead, except the houses of the Israel-ites. All these plagues were preceded by warnings and menaces, and their cessation was notified in the same way, so that every one should become convinced that they were ordained by God, who does what He will and when He will, and were not ordinary natural phenomena, nor wrought by constellations or accident. The Israelites left the country of Pharaoh's bondage, by the command of God, the same night and at the same moment, when the firstborn died, and reached the shores of the Red Sea. They were guided by pillars of cloud and fire, and led by Moses and Aaron, the venerated, inspired chiefs, then about eighty years of age. Up to this time they had only a few laws which they had inherited from Adam and Noah. These laws were not abrogated [15] by Moses, but rather increased by him. When Pharaoh pursued the Israelites they did not have recourse to arms, being unskilled in their use. God, however, divided the sea, and they traversed it. Pharaoh and his host were drowned, and the waves washed their corpses towards the Israelites, so that they could see them with their own eyes. It is a long and well-known story.

84. Al Khazari: This is, in truth, divine power, and the commandments connected with it must be accepted. No one could imagine for a moment that this was the result of necromancy, calculation, or phantasy. For had it been possible to procure

belief in any imaginary dividing of the waters, and
the crossing of the same, it would also have been possible to gain credence for a similar imposition concerning their delivery from bondage, the death of
their tormentors, and the capture of their goods and
chattels. This would be even worse than denying
the existence of God.

85. The Rabbi : And later on, when they came to
the desert, which was not sown, he sent them food
which, with the exception of Sabbath, was created
daily for them, and they ate it for forty years.

86. Al Khazari : This also is irrefutable, viz. a
thing which occurred to six hundred thousand people
for forty years. Six days in the week the Manna came
down, but on the Sabbath it stopped. This makes the
observance of the Sabbath obligatory, since divine
ordination is visible in it.

87. The Rabbi : The Sabbatical law is derived
from this circumstance, as well as from the creation of
the world in six days, also from another matter to be
discussed later on.[16] Although the people believed in
the message of Moses, they retained, even after the
performance of the miracles, some doubt as to whether
God really spake to mortals, and whether the Law was
not of human origin, and only later on supported by
divine inspiration. They could not associate speech
with a divine being, since it is something tangible.
God, however, desired to remove this doubt, and commanded them to prepare themselves morally, as well
as physically, enjoining them to keep aloof from their
wives, and to be ready to hear the words of God. The
people prepared and became fitted to receive the
divine afflatus, and even to hear publicly the words of

God. This came to pass three days later, being introduced by overwhelming phenomena, lightning, thunder, earthquake and fire, which surrounded Mount Sinai. The fire remained visible on the mount forty days. They also saw Moses enter it and emerge from it ; they distinctly heard the Ten Commandments, which represent the very essence of the Law. One of them is the ordination of Sabbath, a law which had previously been connected with the gift of the Manna. The people did not receive these ten commandments from single individuals, nor from a prophet, but from God, only they did not possess the strength of Moses to bear the grandeur of the scene. Henceforth the people believed that Moses held direct communication with God, that his words were not creations of his own mind, that prophecy did not (as philosophers assume) burst forth in a pure soul, become united with the Active Intellect (also termed Holy Spirit or Gabriel), and be then inspired. They did not believe Moses had seen a vision in sleep, or that some one had spoken with him between sleeping and waking, so that he only heard the words in fancy, but not with his ears, that he saw a phantom, and afterwards pretended that God had spoken with him. Before such an impressive scene all ideas of jugglery vanished. The divine allocution was followed by the divine writing. For he wrote these Ten Words on two tablets of precious stone, and handed them to Moses. The people saw the divine writing, as they had heard the divine words. Moses made an ark by God's command, and built the Tent over it. It remained among the Israelites as long as prophecy lasted, i.e. about nine hundred years, until the people became disobedient. Then the ark was

hidden, and Nebuchadnezzar conquered and drove
the Israelites into exile.

88. Al Khazari : Should any one hear you relate
that God spoke with your assembled multitude, and
wrote tables for you, etc., he would be blamed for
accusing you of holding the theory of personification.[17]
You, on the other hand, are free from blame, because
this grand and lofty spectacle, seen by thousands,
cannot be denied. You are justified in rejecting [the
charge of] mere reasoning and speculation.

89. The Rabbi : Heaven forbid that I should assume what is against sense and reason. The first of
the Ten Commandments enjoins the belief in divine
providence. The second command contains the prohibition of the worship of other gods, or the association of any being with Him, the prohibition to
represent Him in statues, forms and images, or any
personification of Him. How should we not deem him
exalted above personification, since we do so with
many of His creations, e.g. the human soul, which
represents man's true essence. For that part of Moses
which spoke to us, taught and guided us, was not his
tongue, or heart, or brain. Those were only organs,
whilst Moses himself is the intellectual, discriminating,
incorporeal soul, not limited by place, neither too large,
nor too small for any space in order to contain the
images of all creatures. If we ascribe spiritual elements to it, how much more must we do so to the
Creator of all ? We must not, however, endeavour
to reject the conclusions to be drawn from revelation.
We say, then, that we do not know how the intention
became corporealised and the speech evolved which
struck our ear, nor what new thing God created from

nought, nor what existing thing He employed. He
does not lack the power. We say that He created the
two tables, engraved a text on them, in the same
way as He created the heaven and the stars by His will
alone. God desired it, and they became concrete as He
wished it, engraved with the text of the Ten Words. We
also say that He divided the sea and formed it into
two walls, which He caused to stand on the right and
on the left of the people, for whom He made easy wide
roads and a smooth ground for them to walk on without fear and trouble. This rending, constructing and
arranging, are attributed to God, who required no tool
or intermediary, as would be necessary for human toil.
As the water stood at His command, shaped itself at
His will, so the air which touched the prophet's ear,
assumed the form of sounds, which conveyed the matters
to be communicated by God to the prophet and the
people.

90. Al Khazari : This representation is satisfactory.

91. The Rabbi : I do not maintain that this is exactly how these things occurred ; the problem is no
doubt too deep for me to fathom. But the result was
that every one who was present at the time became
convinced that the matter proceeded from God direct.
It is to be compared to the first act of creation. The
belief in the law connected with those scenes is as
firmly established in the mind as the belief in the
creation of the world, and that He created it in the
same manner in which He—as is known—created the
two tablets, the manna, and other things. Thus
disappear from the soul of the believer the doubts of
philosophers and materialists.

92. Al Khazari : Take care, O Rabbi, lest too great

indulgence in the description of the superiority of thy
people make thee not unbearable, causing thee to over-
look what is known of their disobedience in spite of
the revelation. I have heard that in the midst of it
they made a calf and worshipped it.

93. The Rabbi: A sin which was reckoned all the
heavier on account of their greatness. Great is he
whose sins are counted.[18]

94. Al Khazari: This is what makes thee tedious
and makes thee appear partial to thy people. What
sin could be greater than this, and what deed could
have exceeded this ?

95. The Rabbi: Bear with me a little while that I
show the lofty station of the people. For me it is
sufficient that God chose them as His people from all
nations of the world, and allowed His influence to rest
on all of them, and that they nearly approached being
addressed by Him. It even descended on their women,
among whom were prophetesses, whilst since Adam
only isolated individuals had been inspired till then.
Adam was perfection itself, because no flaw could be
found in a work of a wise and Almighty Creator, wrought
from a substance chosen by Him, and fashioned according to His own design. There was no restraining influence, no fear of atavism, no question of nutrition
or education during the years of childhood and growth ;
neither was there the influence of climate, water, or
soil to consider. For He created him in the form of
an adolescent, perfect in body and mind. The soul
with which he was endowed was perfect ; his intellect
was the loftiest which it is possible for a human being
to possess, and beyond this he was gifted with the
divine power of such high rank, that it brought him

into connexion with beings divine and spiritual, and enabled him, with slight reflection, to comprehend the great truths without instruction. We call him God's son, and we call all those who were like him also sons of God. He left many children, of whom the only one capable of taking his place was Abel, because he alone was like him. After he had been slain by Kain through jealousy of this privilege, it passed to his brother Seth, who also was like Adam, being [as it were] his essence and heart, whilst the others were like husks and rotten fruit. The essence of Seth, then, passed to Enosh, and in this way the divine influence was inherited by isolated individuals down to Noah. They are compared to the heart; they resembled Adam, and were styled sons of God. They were perfect outwardly and inwardly, their lives, knowledge and ability being likewise faultless. Their lives fix the chronology from Adam to Noah, as well as from Noah to Abraham. There were some, however, among them who did not come under divine influence, as Terah, but his son Abraham was the disciple of his grandfather Eber, and was born in the lifetime of Noah. Thus the divine spirit descended from the grandfather to the grandchildren. Abraham represented the essence of Eber, being his disciple, and for this reason he was called *Ibri.*[19] Eber represented the essence of Shem, the latter that of Noah. He inherited the temperate zone, the centre and principal part of which is Palestine, the land of prophecy. Japheth turned towards north, and Ham towards south. The essence of Abraham passed over to Isaac, to the exclusion of the other sons who were all removed from the land, the special inheritance of Isaac. The prerogative of

Isaac descended on Jacob, whilst Esau was sent from
the land which belonged to Jacob. The sons of the
latter were all worthy of the divine influence, as well
as of the country distinguished by the divine spirit.
This is the first instance of the divine influence descending on a number of people, whereas it had previously
only been vouchsafed to isolated individuals. Then
God tended them in Egypt, multiplied and aggrandised
them, as a tree with a sound root grows until it produces perfect fruit, resembling the first fruit from
which it was planted, viz. Abraham, Isaac, Jacob,
Joseph and his brethren. The seed further produced
Moses, Aaron and Miriam, Bezaleel, Oholiab, and the
chiefs of the tribes, the seventy Elders, who were all
endowed with the spirit of prophecy; then Joshua,
Kaleb, Hur, and many others. Then they became
worthy of having the divine light and providence made
visible to them. If disobedient men existed among
them, they were hated, but remained, without doubt,
of the essence inasmuch as they were part of it
on account of their descent and nature, and begat
children who were of the same stamp. An ungodly
man received consideration in proportion to the minuteness of the essence with which he was endowed, for it
reappeared in his children and grandchildren according to the purity of their lineage. This is how we
regard Terah and others in whom the divine afflatus
was not visible, though, to a certain extent, it underlay
his natural disposition, so that he begat a descendant
filled with the essence, which was not the case with all
the posterity of Ham and Japhet. We perceive a
similar phenomenon in nature at large. Many people
do not resemble their father, but take after their grand-

fathers. There cannot, consequently, be any doubt that this nature and resemblance was hidden in the father, although it did not become visible outwardly, as was the nature of Eber in his children, until it reappeared in Abraham.

96. Al Khazari : This is the true greatness, which descended direct from Adam. He was the noblest creature on earth. Therefore you rank above all the other inhabitants of the earth. But what of this privilege at the time when that sin was committed ?

97. The Rabbi : All nations were given to idolatry at that time. Even had they been philosophers, discoursing on the unity and government of God, they would have been unable to dispense with images, and would have taught the masses that a divine influence hovered over this image. which was distinguished by some miraculous feature. Some of them ascribed this to God, even as we to-day treat some particular spots with reverence, going so far as to believe ourselves blessed by their dust and stones.[20] Others ascribed it to the spiritual influence of some star or constellation, or of a talisman, or to other things of that kind. The people did not pay so much attention to a single law as to a tangible image in which they believed. The Israelites had been promised that something visible would descend on them from God which they could follow, as they followed the pillars of cloud and fire when they departed from Egypt. This they pointed out, and turned to it, praising it, and worshipping God in its presence. Thus they also turned towards the cloud which hovered over Moses while God spake with him ; they remained standing and adoring God opposite to it. Now when the people had heard the proclama-

tion of the Ten Commandments, and Moses had ascended the mount in order to receive the inscribed
tables which he was to bring down to them, and then
make an ark which was to be the point towards which
they should direct their gaze during their devotions,*
they waited for his return clad in the same apparel in
which they had witnessed the drama on Sinai, without
removing their jewels or changing their clothes, remaining just as he left them, expecting every moment
to see him return. He, however, tarried forty days,
although he had not provided himself with food, having
only left them with the intention of returning the
same day. An evil spirit overpowered a portion of
the people, and they began to divide into parties and
factions. Many views and opinions were expressed,
till at last some decided to do like the other nations,
and seek an object in which they could have faith,
without, however, prejudicing the supremacy of Him
who had brought them out of Egypt. On the contrary, this was to be something to which they could
point when relating the wonders of God, as the Philistines [21] did with the ark when they said that God dwelt
within it. We do the same with the sky and every
other object concerning which we know that it is set
in motion by the divine will exclusively, and not by
any accident or desire of man or nature. Their sin
consisted in the manufacture of an image of a forbidden
thing, and in attributing divine power to a creation of
their own, something chosen by themselves without

---

* In the original, a clause is inserted which I place here
in order to facilitate the reading : In this was the divine
covenant and God's latest creation, the tablets. To it also
belonged the cloud, the *Urim*, and all miracles by its instrumentality.

the guidance of God. Some excuse may be found for them in the dissension which had broken out among them, and in the fact that out of six hundred thousand souls the number of those who worshipped the calf was below three thousand. For those of higher station who assisted in making it an excuse might be found in the fact that they wished to clearly separate the disobedient from the pious, in order to slay those who would worship the calf. On the other hand, they sinned in causing what was only a sin of intention to become a sin in deed. This sin was not on a par with an entire lapse from all obedience to Him who had led them out of Egypt, as only one of His commands was violated by them. God had forbidden images, and in spite of this they made one. They should have waited and not have assumed power, have arranged a place of worship, an altar, and sacrifices. This had been done by the advice of the astrologers and magicians among them, who were of opinion that their actions based on their ideas would be more correct than the true ones. They resembled the fool of whom we spoke, who entered the surgery of a physician and dealt out death instead of healing to those who came there. At the same time the people did not intend to give up their allegiance to God. On the contrary, they were, in theory, more zealous in their devotion. They there-fore approached Aaron, and he, desiring to make their plan public, assisted them in their undertaking. For this reason he is to be blamed for changing their theo-retical disobedience into a reality. The whole affair is repulsive to us, because in this age the majority of nations have abandoned the worship of images. It appeared less objectionable at that time, because all

nations were then idolators. Had their sin consisted
in constructing a house of worship of their own, and
making a place of prayer, offering and veneration, the
matter would not have been so grave, because nowadays we also build our houses of worship, hold them
in great respect, and seek blessing through their means.
We even say that God dwells in them, and that they
are surrounded by angels. If this were not essential
for the gathering of our community, it would be as
unknown as it was at the time of the kings, when the
people were forbidden to erect places of worship, called
heights. The pious kings destroyed them, lest they
be venerated beside the house chosen by God in which
He was to be worshipped according to His own ordinances. There was nothing strange in the form of the
cherubim made by His command. In spite of these
things, those who worshipped the calf were punished
on the same day, and three thousand out of six hundred
thousand were slain. The Manna, however, did not
cease falling for their maintenance, nor the cloud to
give them shade, nor the pillar of fire to guide them.
Prophecy continued spreading and increasing among
them, and nothing that had been granted was taken
from them, except the two tables, which Moses broke.
But then he pleaded for their restoration; they were
restored, and the sin was forgiven.

98. Al Khazari: The theory I had formed, and the
opinion of what I saw in my dream thou now con-
firmest, viz. that man can only merit divine influence
by acting according to God's commands And even
were it not so, most men strive to obtain it, even astrologers, magicians, fire and sun worshippers, dualists
etc.

99. The Rabbi: Thou art right. Our laws were written in the Tōrāh by Moses, who had them direct from God, and handed them down to the masses assembled in the desert. There was no necessity to quote any older authority with regard to the single chapters and verses, nor with regard to the description of sacrifices, where and in what manner they were to be offered up, and what was to be done with the blood and the limbs, etc. Everything was clearly stated by God, as the smallest matter missing would interfere with the completeness of the whole thing. It is here, as in the formations of nature, which are composed of such minute elements that they defy perception, and if their mutual relation suffered the smallest change, the whole formation would be damaged, that plant or animal, or limb, would be imperfect and non-existing. In the same manner the law prescribes how the sacrificed animal should be dismembered, and what should be done with each limb, what should be eaten and what burnt, who should eat and who burn, and which section [of priests] should have the charge of offering it up, and which dared not. It also prescribed in what condition those who brought the offerings must be, so that they should be faultless, both as regards appearance and apparel, especially the High Priest, who had the privilege of entering the place of Divinity which enclosed God's glory, the ark and the Tōrāh. To this are attached the rules for cleanliness and purity, and the various grades of purification, sanctification, and prayer, the description of which would lead us too far. In all these matters they had to rely on the reading of the Tōrāh, combined with the traditions of the Rabbis, based on God's communica-

tions to Moses. In the same manner the form of the Tabernacle was shown to Moses on the mountain, viz. the tabernacle, the interior, the candlestick, the ark, and the surrounding court, with its pillars, coverings, and all appurtenances, were caused by God to appear to him in their real shape, in the form in which He commanded to have them executed. In the same way was the temple of Solomon built according to the model revealed to David. So also will the last sanctuary promised us be shaped and arranged according to the details seen by the prophet Ezekiel. In the service of God there is no arguing, reasoning, and debating Had this been possible, philosophers with their wisdom and acumen would have achieved even more than Israel.

100. Al Khazari : Thus the human mind can accept the Law cheerfully and unhesitatingly, without doubting that a prophet would come to the oppressed and enslaved people, and promise them that they would at an appointed time, thus and without delay, be delivered from bondage. Moses led them to Palestine against seven nations, each of which was stronger than they were, assigned to each tribe its portion of the land before they reached it. All this was accomplished in the shortest space of time, and accompanied by miraculous events. This proves the omnipotence of the Sender as well as the greatness of the Messenger, and the high station of those who alone received this message. Had he said : [22] ' I was sent to guide the whole world in the right path,' and would only have partially fulfilled his task, his message would have been deficient, since the divine will would not have been carried out completely. The perfection of his work was marred

by the fact that his book was written in Hebrew,[23] which made it unintelligible to the peoples of Sind, India, and Khazar. They would, therefore, be unable to practise his laws till some centuries had elapsed, or they had been prepared for it by changes of conquest, or alliance, but not through the revelation of that prophet himself, or of another who would stand up for him, and testify to his law.

101. The Rabbi: Moses invited only *his* people and those of his own tongue to accept his law, whilst God promised that there should at all times be prophets to expound his law. This He did so long as they found favour in His sight, and His presence was with them.

102. Al Khazari: Would it not have been better or more commensurate with divine wisdom, if all mankind had been guided in the true path?

103. The Rabbi: Or would it not have been best for all animals to have been reasonable beings? Thou hast, apparently, forgotten what we said previously concerning the genealogy of Adam's progeny, and how the spirit of divine prophecy rested on one person, who was chosen from his brethren, and the essence of his father. It was he in whom this divine light was concentrated. He was the kernel, whilst the others were as shells which had no share in it. The sons of Jacob were, however, distinguished from other people by godly qualities, which made them, so to speak, an angelic caste. Each of them, being permeated by the divine essence, endeavoured to attain the degree of prophecy, and most of them succeeded in so doing. Those who were not successful strove to approach it by means of pious acts, sanctity, purity, and inter-

course with prophets. Know that he who converses
with a prophet experiences spiritualization during the
time he listens to his oration. He differs from his
own kind in the purity of soul, in a yearning for the
[higher] degrees and attachment to the qualities of
meekness and purity. This was a manifest proof to
them, and a clear and convincing sign [24] of reward
hereafter. For the only result to be expected from
this is that the human soul becomes divine, being detached from material senses, joining the highest world,
and enjoying the vision of the divine light, and hearing
the divine speech. Such a soul is safe from death,
even after its physical organs have perished. If thou,
then, findest a religion the knowledge and practice of
which assists in the attainment of this degree, at the
place pointed out and with the conditions laid down
by it, this is beyond doubt the religion which insures
the immortality of the soul after the demise of the body.

104. Al Khazari : The anticipations of other churches
are grosser and more sensuous than yours.

105. The Rabbi : They are none of them realized
till after death, whilst during this life nothing points
to them.

106. Al Khazari : May be ; I have never seen any
one who believed in these promises desire their speedy
fulfilment. On the contrary, if he could delay them
a thousand years, and remain in the bonds of this life
in spite of the hardship of this world, he would prefer
it.

107. The Rabbi : What is thy opinion concerning
him who witnessed those grand and divine scenes ?

108. Al Khazari : That he, no doubt, longs for the
perpetual separation of his soul from his material

senses, in order to enjoy that light. It is such a person who would desire death.

109. The Rabbi: Now all that our promises imply is that we shall become connected with the divine influence by means of prophecy, or something nearly approaching it, and also through our relation to the divine influence, as displayed to us in grand and awe-inspiring miracles. Therefore we do not find in the Bible: 'If you keep this law, I will bring you after death into beautiful gardens and great pleasures.' On the contrary it is said: ' You shall be my chosen people, and I will be a God unto you, who will guide you. Whoever of you comes to me, and ascends to heaven, is as those who, themselves, dwell among the angels,[25] and my angels shall dwell among them on earth. You shall see them singly or in hosts, watching you and fighting for you without your joining in the fight. You shall remain in the country which forms a stepping-stone to this degree, viz. the Holy Land. Its fertility or barrenness, its happiness or misfortune, depend upon the divine influence which your conduct will merit, whilst the rest of the world would continue its natural course. For if the divine presence is among you, you will perceive by the fertility of your country, by the regularity with which your rainfalls appear in their due seasons, by your victories over your enemies in spite of your inferior numbers, that your affairs are not managed by simple laws of nature, but by the divine Will. You also see that drought, death, and wild beasts pursue you as a result of disobedience, although the whole world lives in peace. This shows you that your concerns are arranged by a higher power than mere nature.'

All this, the laws included, is closely connected with
the promises, and no disappointment is feared. All
these promises have one basis, viz. the anticipation of
being near God and His hosts. He who attains this
degree need not fear death, as is clearly demonstrated
in our Law. The following parable will illustrate this :
One of a company of friends who sought solicitude in
a remote spot, once journeyed to India, and had honour
and rank bestowed on him by her king, who knew that
he was one of these friends, and who had also known
their fathers, former comrades of his own. The king
loaded him with presents for his friends, gave him
costly raiment for himself, and then dismissed him,
sending members of his own retinue to accompany
him on his return journey. No one knew that they
belonged to the court, nor that they travelled into the
desert. He had received commissions and treaties,
and in return he had to swear fealty to the king. Then
he and his Indian escort returned to his companions,
and received a hearty welcome from them. They
took pains to accommodate them and to show them
honour. They also built a castle and allowed them
to dwell in it. Henceforth they frequently sent ambassadors to India to wait upon the king, which was
now more easy of accomplishment, as the first messengers guided them the shortest and straightest route.
All knew that travelling in that country was rendered
easier by swearing allegiance to his king and respecting his ambassadors. There was no occasion to inquire why this homage was necessary, because it was
patent that by this means he came into connexion
with the monarch—a most pleasing circumstance.
Now these companions are the Children of Israel, the

first traveller is Moses, the later travellers are the prophets, whilst the Indian messengers are the Shekinah and the angels. The precious garments are the spiritual light which dwelt in the soul of Moses on account of his prophetship, whilst the visible light appeared on his countenance. The presents are the two tables with the Ten Commandments. Those in possession of other laws saw nothing of this, but were told : ' Continue in obedience to the King of India as this company of friends, and you will after death become the associates of the king, otherwise he will turn you away, and punish you after death.' Some might say : No one ever returned to inform us whether, after death, he dwelt in paradise or in hell. The majority were satisfied with the arrangement, which coincided with their views. They obeyed willingly, and allowed themselves to entertain a faint hope, which to all appearance was a very strong one, as they commenced to be proud and to behave haughtily towards other people. But how can they boast of expectations after death to those who enjoy the fulfilment already in life ? Is not the nature of the prophets and godly men nearer to immortality than the nature of him who never reached that degree ?

110. Al Khazari : It does not agree with common sense that when man perishes, body and soul should disappear at the same time, as is the case with animals, and that the philosophers alone will—as they believe —escape. The same applies to the statement made by believers in other faiths—that man, by the pronunciation of one word alone, may inherit paradise, even if, during the whole of his life, he knew no other word than this, and of this did not even understand

the great significance, viz. that one word raised him
from the ranks of a brute to that of an angel. He who
did not utter this word would remain an animal, though
he might be a learned and pious philosopher, who
yearned for God all his life.

111. The Rabbi : We do not deny that the good
actions of any man, to whichever people he may belong,
will be rewarded by God. But the priority belongs
to people who are near God during their life, and we
estimate the rank they occupy near God after death
accordingly.

112. Al Khazari : Apply this also in the other direction, and judge their degree in the next world according
to their station in this world.

113. The Rabbi : I see thee reproaching us with
our degradation and poverty, but the best of other
religions boast of both. Do they not glorify Him who
said : He who smites thee on the right cheek, turn to
him the left also ; and he who takes away thy coat, let
him have thy shirt also.[27] He and his friends and
followers, after hundreds of years of contumely, flog-
ging and slaying, attained their well-known success,
and just in these things they glorify. This is also
the history of the founder of Islam and his friends,
who eventually prevailed, and became powerful. The
nations boast of these, but not of these kings whose
power and might are great, whose walls are strong, and
whose chariots are terrible. Yet our relation to God
is a closer one than if we had reached greatness already
on earth.

114. Al Khazari : This might be so, if your humility
were voluntary ; but it is involuntary, and if you had
power you would slay.

115. The Rabbi : Thou hast touched our weak spot, O King of the Khazars. If the majority of us, as thou sayest, would learn humility towards God and His law from our low station, Providence would not have forced us to bear it for such a long period. Only the smallest portion thinks thus. Yet the majority may expect a reward, because they bear their degradation partly from necessity, partly of their own free will. For whoever wishes to do so can become the friend and equal of his oppressor by uttering one word, and without any difficulty. Such conduct does not escape the just Judge. If we bear our exile and degradation for God's sake, as is meet, we shall be the pride of the generation which will come with the Messiah, and accelerate the day of the deliverance we hope for. Now we do not allow any one who embraces our religion theoretically by means of a word alone to take equal rank with ourselves, but demand actual self-sacrifice, purity, knowledge, circumcision, and numerous religious ceremonies. The convert must adopt our mode of life entirely. We must bear in mind that the rite of circumcision is a divine symbol, ordained by God to indicate that our desires should be curbed, and discretion used, so that what we engender may be fitted to receive the divine Influence. God allows him who treads this path, as well as his progeny, to approach Him very closely. Those, however, who become Jews do not take equal rank with born Israelites, who are specially privileged to attain to prophecy, whilst the former can only achieve something by learning from them, and can only become pious and learned, but never prophets. As regards the promises at which thou art so astonished, our sages, long ago, gave de-

scriptions of paradise and hell, their length and width,[28]
and depicted the enjoyments and punishments in
greater detail than is given in any later religions. From
the very beginning I only spoke to thee of what is
contained in the books of the Prophets.[29] They, however, do not discuss the promises of after-life with so
much diffuseness as is done in the sayings of the Rabbis.
Nevertheless the prophetic books allude to the return
of the dust of the human body to the earth, whilst the
spirit returns to the Creator who gave it.[30] They
also mention the resurrection of the dead at some
future time, the sending of a prophet called Elijah
AlKhidr,[31] who had already been sent once, but who
was taken away by God in the same way as another said that he never tasted death. The
Torāh contains the prayer of one who was specially
privileged to become a prophet, and he prayed that his
death might be made easy, and his end be as the end
of the Children of Israel.[32] After the death of Samuel
King Saul invoked his aid, and he prophesied for
him concerning all that would happen to him in
the same way as he had prophesied to him whilst
living.[33] Although this action of Saul, viz. consulting
the dead, is forbidden in our law, it shows that the
people at the time of the prophets believed in the
immortality of the soul after the decay of the body.
For this reason they consulted the dead. All educated
people, including women, know by heart the opening
prayer of our morning liturgy, which runs as follows :
O Lord, the spirit which Thou hast breathed into me
is hallowed ; Thou hast created it, Thou guardest it,
and Thou wilt after a time take it from me, but wilt
restore it to me in the other world. As long as it is

within me, I praise Thee, and am grateful to Thee, O
Lord of the universe. Praise be to Thee who restoreth
the spirit unto the dead.[34] The notion of ' Paradise '
itself, of which people often speak, is derived from the
Tōrāh, being the exalted abode which was intended
for Adam. Had he not been disobedient, he would
have remained in it for ever. Similarly ' Gēhinnōm '
was nothing but a well-known place near the Holy
House, a trench in which the fire was never extinguished, because unclean bones, carrion and other
impurities used to be burned there. The word is a
compound Hebrew one.[35]

116. Al Khazari : If that is so, then there has been
nothing new since your religion was promulgated,
except certain details concerning paradise and hell,
their arrangement, and the repetition and enlargement
of these.

117. The Rabbi : Even this is not new either. The
Rabbis have said so much on the subject that there is
nothing thou couldst hear concerning it which could
not be found in their writings, if thou didst but search
for it.

PART TWO

1. AFTER this the Khazari, as is related in the history of the Khazars, was anxious to reveal to his Vezier in the mountains of Warsān the secret of his dream and its repetition, in which he was urged to seek the God-pleasing deed. The king and his Vezier travelled to the deserted mountains on the sea shore, and arrived one night at the cave in which some Jews used to celebrate the Sabbath. They disclosed their identity to them, embraced their religion, were circumcised in the cave, and then returned to their country, eager to learn the Jewish law. They kept their conversion secret, however, until they found an opportunity of disclosing the fact gradually to a few of their special friends. When the number had increased, they made the affair public, and induced the rest of the Khazars to embrace the Jewish faith. They sent to various countries for scholars and books, and studied the Tōrāh. Their chronicles also tell of their prosperity, how they beat their foes, conquered their lands, secured great treasures ; how their army swelled to hundreds of thousands, how they loved their faith, and fostered such love for the Holy House that they erected a Tabernacle in the shape of that built by Moses. They also honoured and cherished those born Israelites who lived

among them. While the king studied the Tōrāh and
the books of the prophets, he employed the Rabbi as
his teacher, and put many questions to him on Hebrew
matters. The first of these questions referred to the
names and attributes ascribed to God and their anthro-
pomorphistic forms, which are unmistakeably objectionable alike both to reason and to law.

2. Said the Rabbi: All names of God, save the
Tetragrammaton, are predicates and attributive descriptions, derived from the way His creatures are affected
by His decrees and measures. He is called *merciful*, if
he improves the condition of any man whom people
pity for his sorry plight. They attribute to Him mercy
and compassion, although this is, in our conception,
surely nothing but a weakness of the soul and a quick
movement of nature. This cannot be applied to God,
who is a just Judge, ordaining the poverty of one individual and the wealth of another. His nature remains quite unaffected by it. He has no sympathy
with one, nor anger against another. We see the same
in human judges to whom questions are put. They
decide according to law, making some people happy,
and others miserable. He appears to us, as we observe
His doings, sometimes a 'merciful and compassionate
God,' (Exod. xxxiv. 6), sometimes 'a jealous and
revengeful God' (Nahum i. 2), whilst He never changes
from one attribute to the other. All attributes (excepting the Tetragrammaton) are divided into three
classes, viz. *creative*, *relative* and *negative*. As regards
the *creative* attributes, they are derived from acts
emanating from Him by ways of natural medium,[1] e.g.
making poor and rich, exalting or casting down, 'merciful
and compassionate,' 'jealous and revengeful,' 'strong and

almighty,' and the like. As regards the *relative attri-*
butes, viz. 'Blessed, praised, glorified, holy, exalted,
and extolled,' they are borrowed from the reverence
given to Him by mankind. However numerous these
may be, they produce no plurality, as far as He is concerned, nor do they affect his Unity. As regards the
negative attributes, such as 'Living, Only, First and
Last,' they are given to Him in order to negative their
contrasts, but not to establish them in the sense we
understand them. For we cannot understand life
except accompanied by sensibility and movement.
God, however, is above them. We describe Him as
living in order to negative the idea of the rigid and
dead, since it would be an *a priori* conclusion that that
which does not live is dead. This cannot, however,
be applied to the intellect. One cannot, e.g. speak of
time as being endowed with life, yet it does not
follow that it is dead, since its nature has nothing to
do with either life or death. In the same way one
cannot call a stone ignorant, although we may say
that it is not learned. Just as a stone is too low to
be brought into connexion with learning or ignorance,
thus the essence of God is too exalted to have anything
to do with life or death, nor can the terms light or
darkness be applied to it. If we were asked whether
this essence is light or darkness, we should say light
by way of metaphor, for fear one might conclude that
that which is not light must be darkness. As a matter
of fact we must say that only material bodies are subject to light and darkness, but the divine essence is no
body, and can consequently only receive the attributes
of light or darkness by way of simile, or in order to
negative an attribute hinting at a deficiency. Life

and death are, therefore, only applicable to material
bodies, whilst the divine essence is as much exempt
from both as it is highly extolled above them. The
' life ' of which we speak in this connexion is not like
ours, and this is what I wish to state, since we cannot
think of any other kind of life but ours. It is as if
one would say : We know not what it is. If we say
' living God ' and ' God of life ' (Ps. cvi. 28), it is but
a relative expression placed in opposition to the gods
of the Gentiles, which are ' dead gods ' from which no
action emanates. In the same way we take the term
One, viz. to negative plurality, but not to establish
unity as we understand it. For we call a thing one,
when the component parts are coherent and of the
same materials, e.g. *one* bone, *one* sinew, one water, one
air. In a similar way time is compared to a compact
body, and we speak of one day, and one year. The
divine essence is exempt from complexity and divisibility, and ' one ' only stands to exclude plurality. In
the same way [we style Him] ' First ' in order to
exclude the notion of any later origin, but not to assert
that He has a beginning ; thus also ' Last ' stands to
repudiate the idea that His existence has no end, but
not to fix a term for Him. All these attributes neither
touch on the divine essence, nor do they lead us to
assume a multiplicity. The attributes which are connected with the Tetragrammaton are those which
describe His power of creating without any natural
intermediaries, viz. Creator, Producer, Maker, ' To
Him who alone doeth great wonders (Ps. cxxxvi. 4),'
which means that [He creates] by His bare intention
and will, to the exclusion of any assisting cause. This
is perhaps meant in the word of the Bible : 'And I

appeared unto Abraham . . . as *El Shaddāi*' (Exod.
vi. 3), viz. in the way of power and dominion, as is
said : 'He suffered no man to do them wrong ; yea, He
reproved kings for their sake' (Ps. cv. 14). He did
not, however, perform any miracle for the patriarchs
as He did for Moses, saying : 'but my name J H W H
was I not known to them' (Exod. l. c). This means
by My name J H W H , since the *bēth* in *beēl shaddāi*
refers to the former. The wonders done for Moses and
the Israelites left no manner of doubt in their souls that
the Creator of the world also created these things which
He brought into existence immediately by His will, as
the plagues of Egypt, the dividing of the Red Sea, the
manna, the pillar of a cloud, and the like. The
reason of this was not because they were higher than
the Patriarchs, but because they were a multitude, and
had nourished doubt in their souls, whilst the patriarchs
had fostered the utmost faith and purity of mind. If
they had all their lives been pursued by misfortune,
their faith in God would not have suffered. Therefore
they required no signs. We also style Him wise of
heart, because He is the essence of intelligence, and
intelligence itself ; but this is no attribute. As to
'Almighty,' this belongs to the creative attributes.

3. Al Khazari : 'How dost thou explain those attributes which are even of a more corporeal nature than
those, viz. seeing, hearing, speaking, writing the tablets,
descending on mount Sinai, rejoicing in His works,
grieved in His heart.'

4. The Rabbi : Did I not compare him with a just
judge in whose qualities no change exists, and from
whose decrees result the prosperity and good fortune
of people, so that they say that he loves them and

takes pleasure in them ?   Others, whose fate it is to
have their houses destroyed and themselves be annihi-
lated, would describe Him as filled with hate and wrath.
Nothing, however, that is done or spoken escapes Him,
' He sees and hears ' ; the air and all bodies came into
existence by His will, and assumed shape by His
command, as did heaven and earth. He is also described as ' speaking and writing.' Similarly from the
aethereal and spiritual substance, which is called ' holy
spirit,' arose the spiritual forms called ' glory of God '
(Exod. xix. 20).   Metaphorically He is called J H W H
(ibid.) who descended on the mount Sinai.   We
shall discuss this more minutely when treating on
metaphysics.[2]

5. Al Khazari : Granting that thou hast justified
the use of these attributes, so that no idea of plurality
need of necessity follow, yet a difficulty remains as
regards the attribute of Will with which thou dost
invest Him, but which the philosopher denies.[3]

6. The Rabbi : If no other objection is raised,
except the Will, we will soon vindicate ourselves.
We say : O philosophers, what is it which in thy
opinion made the heavens revolve continually, the
uppermost sphere carrying the whole, without place
or inclination in its movement, the earth firmly
fixed in the centre without support or prop ; which fashioned the order of the universe in quantity, quality,
and the forms we perceive ? Thou canst not help
admitting this, for things did neither create themselves nor each other.   Now the same adapted the
air to giving the sound of the Ten Commandments, and
formed the writing engraved in the tables, call it will,
or thing, or what thou wilt.

7. Al Khazari : The secret of the attributes is now clear, and I understand the meaning of ' The Glory of God,' ' Angel of God,' and Shekhinah. They are names applied by the prophets to things perceptible, as ' Pillar of Cloud,' ' Consuming Fire,' ' Cloud,' ' Mist, Fire, Splendour,' as it is said of the light in the morning, in the evening, and on cloudy days that the rays of light go forth from the sun, although it is not visible. Yet we say that the rays of light are inseparable from the sun, although in reality this is not so. It is the terrestrial bodies which, being opposite to it, are affected by it, and reflect its light.

8. The Rabbi : Even so does the glory of God, which is only a ray of the divine light, benefit His people in His country.

9. Al Khazari : I understand what thou meanest by ' His people,' but less intelligible is what thou sayest about ' His country.'

10. The Rabbi : Thou wilt have no difficulty in perceiving that one country may have higher qualifications than others. There are places in which particular plants, metals, or animals are found, or where the inhabitants are distinguished by their form and character, since perfection or deficiency of the soul are produced by the mingling of the elements.

11. Al Khazari : Yet I never heard that the inhabitants of Palestine were better than other people.

12. The Rabbi : How about the hill on which you say that the vines thrive so well ? If it had not been properly planted and cultivated, it would never produce grapes. Priority belongs, in the first instance, to the people which, as stated before, is the essence and kernel [of the nations]. In the second instance, it

would belong to the country], on account of the religious acts connected with it, which I would compare to the cultivation of the vineyard. No other place would share the distinction of the divine influence, just as no other mountain might be able to produce good wine.

13. Al Khazari : How could this be ? In the time between Adam and Moses were not prophetic visions in other places granted to Abraham in Ur of the Chaldaeans, Ezekiel and Daniel at Babylon, and Jeremiah in Egypt ?

14. The Rabbi : Whosoever prophesied did so either in the [Holy] Land, or concerning it, viz. Abraham in order to reach it, Ezekiel and Daniel on account of it. The two latter had lived during the time of the first Temple, had seen the Shekhinah, through the influence of which each one who was duly prepared became of the elect, and able to prophesy. Adam lived and died in the land. Tradition tells us that in the cave [of Machpelāh] were buried the four pairs : Adam and Eve, Abraham and Sarah, Isaac and Rebeccah, Jacob and Leah.[4] This is the land which bore the name ' before the Lord,' and of which it is stated that ' the eyes of the Lord thy God are always upon it ' (Deut. xi. 12). It was also the first object of jealousy and envy between Cain and Abel, when they desired to know which of them would be Adam's successor, and heir to his essence and intrinsic perfection ; to inherit the land, and to stand in connexion with the divine influence, whilst the other would be a nonentity. Then Abel was killed by Cain, and the realm was without an heir. It is stated that ' Cain ' went out of the presence of Lord (Gen. iv. 16), which means that he left the land, saying : ' Behold, Thou hast driven me out this day

from the face of the earth, and from Thy face shall I
be hid' (ib. v. 14). In the same way is it said : 'But
Jonah rose up to flee unto Tarshish from the presence
of the Lord' (Jonah i. 3), but he only fled from the
place of prophecy. God, however, brought him back
there out of the belly of the fish, and appointed him
prophet in the land. When Seth was born he was
like Adam, as it is said : 'He begat in his own likeness, after his image' (Gen. v. 3), and took Abel's place,
as it is said : For God has appointed me another seed,
instead of Abel, whom Cain slew (ib. iv. 25). He
merited the title : 'Son of God,' like Adam, and he had
a claim on the land, which is the next step to paradise.
The land was then the object of jealousy between Isaac
and Ishmael, till the latter was rejected as worthless,
although it was said concerning him : 'Behold, I have
blessed him, and will multiply him exceedingly' (ib.
xvii. 20) in worldly prosperity ; but immediately after
it is said : 'My covenant will I establish with Isaac'
(v. 21), which refers to his connexion with the divine
influence and happiness in the world to come. Neither
Ishmael nor Esau could boast of a covenant, although
they were otherwise prosperous. Jealousy arose between
Jcoob and Esau for the birthright and blessing, but Esau
was rejected in favour of Jacob, in spite of his strength
and the latter's weakness. Jeremiah's prophecy concerning Egypt was uttered in Egypt itself. This was also
the case with Moses, Aaron and Miriam. Sinai and
Parān are reckoned as belonging to Palestine, because
they are on this side of the Red Sea, as it is said : 'And
I will set thy bounds from the Red Sea, even unto the
sea of the Philistines, and from the desert unto the
river' (Exod. xxiii. 31). The 'desert' is that of

Parūn, ' that great and terrible wilderness ' (Deut. i. 19),
being the southern border. 'The fourth river is
Euphrates' (Gen. ii. 14), designates the northern
border, where there were the altars of the Patriarchs,
who were answered by fire from heaven and the divine
light. The 'binding' of Isaac took place on a desolate
mountain, viz. Moriah. Not till the days of David,
when it was inhabited, was the secret revealed that it
was the place specially prepared for the Shekhinah.
Araunah, the Jebusite, tilled his land there. Thus it
is said : 'And Abraham called the name of the place,
The Lord shall see, as it is said to this day, in the mount
of the Lord it shall be seen ' (ib. xxii. 14). In the Book
of the Chronicles it is stated more clearly that the
Temple was built on mount Moriah. These are, without doubt, the places worthy of being called the gates
of heaven. Dost thou not see that Jacob ascribed the
vision which he saw, not to the purity of his soul, nor
to his belief, nor to true integrity, but to the place, as
it is said : 'How awful is this place ' (ib. xxviii. 17).
Prior to this it is said : 'And he lighted upon a certain
place ' (ver. 11), viz. the chosen one. Was not Abraham
also, and after having been greatly exalted, brought
into contact with the divine influence, and made the
heart of this essence, removed from his country to the
place in which his perfection should become complete ?
Thus the agriculturer finds the root of a good tree in a
desert place. He transplants it into properly tilled
ground, to improve it and make it grow ; to change it
from a wild root into a cultivated one, from one which
bore fruit by chance only to one which produced a
luxuriant crop. In the same way the gift of prophecy
was retained among Abraham's descendants in Pales-

tine, the property of many as long as they remained in the land, and fulfilled the required conditions, viz. purity, worship, and sacrifices, and, above all, the reverence of the Shekhinah. For the divine influence, one might say, singles out him who appears worthy of being connected with it, such as *prophets and pious men*, and is their God. Reason chooses those whose natural gifts are perfect, viz. *Philosophers* and those whose souls and character are so harmonious that it can find its dwelling among them. The spirit of life, pure and simple, is to be found in beings which are endowed with ordinary primary faculties, and particularly adapted to higher vitality—viz. *animals*. Finally, organic life finds its habitat in a mixture of harmonious elements, and produces—*plant*.

15. Al Khazari : These are the general rules of a science which must be classified. This does not concern us now, and I will ask thee about it when we speak on the subject. Continue thy discourse on the special advantages of the Land of Israel.

16. The Rabbi : It was appointed to guide the world, and apportioned to the tribes of Israel from the time of the confusion of languages, as it is said : ' When the Most High divided among the nations their inheritance ' (Deut. xxxii. 8). Abraham was not fit to gain the divine influence, and to enter into a mutual compact, until he had, in Palestine, made the covenant with Him ' between the pieces ' (Gen. xv. 17). What is now thy opinion of a select community which has merited the appellation ' people of God,' and also a special name called ' the inheritance of God,' and of seasons fixed by Him, not merely agreed upon or settled by astronomical calculations, and therefore styled

' feasts of the Lord.' The rules regarding purity and worship, prayers and performances, are fixed by God, and therefore called ' work of God ' and ' service of the Lord.'

17. Al Khazari : In such an arrangement the ' glory of God' was bound to become apparent.

18. The Rabbi : Dost thou not see that even the land was given its Sabbaths, as it is said : ' Sabbath of the land' (Lev. xxv. 6), and ' The land shall keep a Sabbath unto the Lord ' (ibid. 2). It is forbidden to sell it for ever, as it is said : ' For Mine is the land ' (ver. 23). Observe that the ' feasts of the Lord ' and the ' Sabbaths of the land ' belong to the ' land of the Lord.'

19. Al Khazari : Was not the day primarily calculated as dawning first in China, because it forms the eastern commencement of the inhabited earth ?

20. The Rabbi : The beginning of the Sabbath must be calculated from Sinai, or rather Alush,[5] where the Mannah first descended. Consequently Sabbath does not come in till the sun has set behind Sinai, and so on to the remote west, and round the globe to China, which is the extreme end of the inhabited earth. Sabbath begins in China eighteen hours later than in Palestine, since the latter lies in the centre of the world.[6] Sunset in Palestine, therefore, concurs with midnight in China, and midday in Palestine concurs with sunset in China. This is the problem of the system based on the *eighteen hours* in the [Talmudical] rule : If the conjunction of the moon takes place before midday, the new moon becomes visible near sunset.[7]

This refers to Palestine, the place where the law was given, and where Adam at the end of Sabbath was transferred from paradise. It is there where the

calendar began after the six days of creation. Adam,
then, began to name the days, as he did with all that
dwelt on earth, and the following generations continued counting in the same way. This is the reason
why there is no difference among mankind about the
seven days of the week,[8] which commenced at the hour
when the inhabitants of the extreme west held noon.
This was the hour of sunset for Palestine,[9] and at this
moment the first light was created,[10] the sun being
created later on. This first light was but an illumina-
tion, which soon passed away, leaving the world in
darkness. The established order was then that night
preceded day, as it is written: ' It was evening and
it was morning.' In the same manner the Tōrāh
ordained: ' From evening unto evening ' (Lev. xxiii. 32).
Do not quote against me those recent astronomers, the
thieves of science, though their theft was unintentional. They found, however, their science in a precarious condition, since the eye of prophecy was stricken
with blindness; so they had recourse to speculation,
and composed books on the strength of it. In contradistinction to the Tōrāh, they considered China as
the original home of the calculation of the days. The
contrast is not, however, complete, because they agree
with the Jewish theory in assuming the beginning of
the break of the day to have taken place in China.
The difference between our theory and theirs consists
chiefly in the circumstance that we count the night
before the day. The ' eighteen ' hours must, consequently, be made the basis of the nomination of the
days of the week. For there are six hours between
Palestine, where the nomination of the days began,
and the place of the sun at the time when nomination

began.   Thus the name of Sabbath, e.g. was employed
for the beginning of the day on which the sun rose for
the extreme west, whilst it set for Adam in Palestine.
It kept the name ' beginning of Sabbath ' till the sun
culminated for him eighteen hours later, when it was
evening in China, and also beginning of the Sabbath.
This was the extreme limit for the day to be called
Sabbath,[11] because the region further on[12] is only
called east of the place where the days began to be
counted.   A place must, however, exist which is at the
same time extreme west and the beginning of east.   This
is, for Palestine, the beginning of the inhabited world,
not only from the point of view of the law, but also
from that of natural science.   For it would be impossible for the days of the week to have the same names
all over the world unless we fix one place which marks
the beginning, and another one not far off, not that
the one be merely an eastern point for the other, but
that the one should be east absolute, and the other
west absolute.   If this were not so the days could not
have definite names, since every point of the equator
can be east or west at the same time.   China would
thus be east for Palestine, but west for the antipodal
side.   The latter would be east for China, but west for
[what we call] west, and the last-named would be east
for the antipodal side, but west for Palestine, and there
would be neither east, nor west, nor beginning, nor
end, nor definite names for the days.   Adam, however,
did give definite names to the days, taking Palestine
for his starting-point, but each name spreads over a
certain geographical latitude, because it is impossible
to fix the horizon for every single point on earth
Jerusalem itself would have many east and west points ;

the east of Zion would not be also the east of the Temple,
and their horizons, strictly speaking, different, though
not noticeable to the eye. This would be the case in
a greater degree between Damascus and Jerusalem,
and we could not deny that in the former place Sabbath commenced earlier than it does in the latter, and
in Jerusalem sooner than it does in Egypt. A certain
latitude must, therefore, be allowed. But the latitude
in which differences in the nomination of the day become apparent amounts to eighteen hours, neither
more nor less. The inhabitants of one meridian still call
the day Sabbath, whilst those of another are past it,
and so on till eighteen hours after the time when the
Sabbath [13] began, and the sun culminated in Jerusalem. It is then when the name Sabbath comes to
an end. Therefore no one exists who would call the
day Sabbath, but uses the name of the next day. This
is meant by the words: If the conjunction takes place
before noon, it is understood that the new moon is
visible at sunset. In other words: If the Mōlād takes
place before noon on the Sabbath in Jerusalem, it is
understood that the new moon is visible on the Sabbath at sunset. This is because the name Sabbath is
retained for eighteen hours after the reason for so
calling it had departed from the place where it had
begun, and the sun a day and a night later culminates
again in Palestine. The new moon is, therefore, bound
to appear at the eastern border of China in the twilight
of the Sabbath. This agrees with the rule of the sages:
A night and a day are reckoned to the month. The
name Sabbath gives place everywhere to Sunday,
although Palestine had before that left Sabbath, and
was in the midst of Sunday. The intention of [this

rule] was that the name of the same day of the week should hold good all over the world, and the question could be put both to the inhabitants of China and the West : ' On which day did you celebrate the New Year ? ' The answer would be : ' On Sabbath.' This notwithstanding that the latter people had finished the feast, whilst the former, according to the geographical position of their country towards Palestine, were still celebrating it. With regard to the name of the days of the week, they had both kept the same day.

Thus does the knowledge of the ' *Sabbath of the Lord* ' and the ' *Festivals of the Lord* ' depend upon the land which is the ' inheritance of the Lord,' and has, as thou didst read, the other names of ' His holy mountain ' (Ps. xcix. 9,), ' His footstool,' *ib.* 5 ' Gate of heaven ' (Gen. xxviii. 7). ' For the law shall go forth from Zion ' (Micah iv. 2). [Thou didst also read] how the Patriarchs endeavoured to live in the country whilst it was in the hands of the pagans, how they yearned for it, and had their bones carried into it, as did Jacob and Joseph. Moses prayed to see it, and when this was denied to him, he considered it a misfortune. Thereupon it was shown to him from the summit of Pisgah, which was to him an act of grace. Persians, Indians, Greeks, and children of other nations begged to be allowed to offer up sacrifices, and to be prayed for in the holy Temple ; they spent their wealth at the place, though they believed in other laws not recognized by the Tōrāh. They honour it to this day, although the Shekhinah no longer appears there. All nations make pilgrimages to it, long for it, excepting we ourselves, because we are punished and in disgrace.

All the Rabbis tell of its great qualities would take too long to relate.

21. Al Khazari : Let me hear a few of their observations.

22. The Rabbi : One sentence is : All roads lead up to Palestine, but none from it.[14] Concerning a woman who refuses to go there with her husband, they decreed that she is divorced, and forfeits her marriage settlement.[15] On the other hand, if the husband refuses to accompany his wife to Palestine, he is bound to divorce her and pay her settlement. They further say : It is better to dwell in the Holy Land, even in a town mostly inhabited by heathens, than abroad in a town chiefly peopled by Israelites ; for he who dwells in the Holy Land is compared to him who has a God, whilst he who dwells abroad is compared to him who has no God. Thus says David : ' For they have driven me out this day from abiding in the inheritance of the Lord, saying, Go, serve other gods ' (1 Sam. xxvi. 19), which means that he who dwells abroad is as if he served strange gods.[16] To Egypt they ascribed a certain superiority over other countries on the basis of a syllogism in the following way : If Egypt, with regard to which a covenant was made,[17] is a forbidden land, other countries are still more so. Another saying is : To be buried in Palestine is as if buried beneath the altar.[18] They praise him who is in the land more than him who is carried thither dead. This is expressed thus : He who embraces it when alive is not like him who does so after his death.[19] They say concerning him who could live there, but did not do so, and only ordered his body to be carried thither after his death : While you lived you made

Mine inheritance an abomination, but in death 'you come and contaminate my country' [20] (Jer. ii. 1). It is told that R. Hananyah, when asked whether it was lawful for a person to go abroad in order to marry the widow of his brother, said : His brother married a pagan woman ; praised be God who caused him to die ; now this one follows him.[21] The sages also forbade selling estates or the remains of a house to a heathen,[22] or leaving a house in ruins. Other sayings are : Fines can only be imposed in the land itself ; [23] no slave must be transported abroad,[24] and many similar regulations. Further, the atmosphere of the Holy Land makes wise.[25] They expressed their love of the land as follows : He who walks four yards in the land is assured of happiness in the world to come,[26] R. Zērā said to a heathen who criticized his foolhardiness in crossing a river without waiting to reach a ford, in his eagerness to enter the land : How can the place which Moses and Aaron could not reach, be reached by me ? [27]

23. Al Khazari : If this be so, thou fallest short of the duty laid down in thy law, by not endeavouring to reach that place, and making it thy abode in life and death, although thou sayest : 'Have mercy on Zion, for it is the house of our life,' [28] and believest that the Shekhinah will return thither. And had it no other preference than that the Shekhinah dwelt there five hundred years, this is sufficient reason for men's souls to retire thither and find purification there, as happens near the abodes of the pious and the prophets. Is it not ' the gate of heaven ' ? All nations agree on this point. Christians believe that the souls are gathered there and then lifted up to heaven. Islām teaches that it is the

place of the *ascent*,[29] and that prophets are caused to
ascend from there to heaven, and, further, that it is
the place of gathering on the day of Resurrection. Everybody turns to it in prayer and visits it in pilgrimage.
Thy bowing and kneeling in the direction of it is either
mere appearance or thoughtless worship. Yet your
first forefathers chose it as an abode in preference to
their birth-places, and lived there as strangers, rather
than as citizens in their own country. This they did
even at a time when the Shekhinah was yet visible, but
the country was full of unchastity, impurity, and
idolatry. Your fathers, however, had no other desire
than to remain in it. Neither did they leave it in times
of dearth and famine except by God's permission.
Finally, they directed their bones to be buried there.

24. The Rabbi : This is a severe reproach, O king of
the Khazars. It is the sin which kept the divine promise with regard to the second Temple, viz. : Sing and
rejoice, O daughter of Zion ' (Zech. ii. 10), from being
fulfilled. Divine Providence was ready to restore everything as it had been at first, if they had all willingly
consented to return. But only a part was ready to do
so, whilst the majority and the aristocracy remained in
Babylon, preferring dependence and slavery, and un-
willing to leave their houses and their affairs. An allusion to them might be found in the enigmatic words of
Solomon : I sleep, but my heart waketh (Song v. 2–4).
He designates the exile by *sleep*, and the continuance
of prophecy among them by the wakefulness of the
heart. ' It is the voice of my beloved that knocketh '
means God's call to return ; ' My head is filled with
dew ' alludes to the Shekhinah which emerged from the
shadow of the Temple. The words : ' I have put off

my coat,' refer to the people's slothfulness in consenting
to return. The sentence : ' My beloved stretcheth forth
his hand through the opening' may be interpreted as
the urgent call of Ezra, Nehemiah, and the Prophets,
until a portion of the people grudgingly responded to
their invitation. In accordance with their mean mind
they did not receive full measure. Divine Providence
only gives man as much as he is prepared to receive ;
if his receptive capacity be small, he obtains little, and
much if it be great. Were we prepared to meet the
God of our forefathers with a pure mind, we should find
the same salvation as our fathers did in Egypt. If we
say : ' Worship his holy hill—worship at His footstool
—He who restoreth His glory to Zion' (Ps. xcix. 9, 5), and
other words, this is but as the chattering of the starling
and the nightingale. We do not realise what we say
by this sentence, nor others, as thou rightly observest,
O Prince of the Khazars.

25. Al Khazari : Enough on this subject. Now I
should like an explanation of what I read about the
sacrifices. Reason cannot accept such expressions as :
My offering, My bread for My sacrifices made by fire,
'for a sweet savour unto Me' (Num. xxviii. 2), employed
in connexion with the sacrifices, describing them as
being God's offering, bread, and incense.

26. The Rabbi : The expression : *By My fires* removes
all difficulty. It states that offering, bread and sweet
savour, which are ascribed to Me, in reality belong to
My fires, i.e. to the fire which was kindled at God's
behest, and fed by the offerings. The remaining pieces
were food for the priests. The deeper signification of
this was to create a well arranged system, upon which
the King should rest in an exalted, but not local

sense. As a symbol of the Divine Influence, consider the reasoning soul which dwells in the perishable
body. If its physical and nobler faculties are properly
distributed and arranged, raising it high above the animal
world, then it is a worthy dwelling for King Reason, who
will guide and direct it, and remain with it as long as
the harmony is undisturbed. As soon, however, as this
is impaired, he departs from it. A fool may imagine
that Reason requires food, drink, and scents, because he
sees himself preserved as long as these are forthcoming,
but would perish if deprived of them. This is not the
case. The Divine Influence is beneficent, and desirous
of doing good to all. Wherever something is arranged
and prepared to receive His guidance, He does not refuse
it, nor withhold it, nor hesitate to shed light, wisdom,
and inspiration on it. If, however, the order is disturbed, it cannot receive this light, which is, then, lost.
The Divine Influence is above change or damage. All
that is contained in the ' order of sacrificial service,' its
proceedings, offerings, burning of incense, singing, eating, drinking, is to be done in the utmost purity and
holiness. It is called : ' Service of the Lord,' ' the bread
of thy God ' (Num. viii. 11 ; Lev. xxi. 8), and similar
terms which relate to his pleasure in the beautiful harmony prevailing among the people and priesthood. He,
so to say, accepts their hospitality and dwells among
them in order to show them honour. He, however, is
most Holy, and far too exalted to find pleasure in their
meat and drink. It is for their own benefit, as is also
the proper working order of the digestion in the stomach
and liver. The nobler ingredients of the food go to
strengthen the heart ; the best of all, the spirit. Not only
are heart, mind, and brain regenerated by means of this

food, but also the digestive organs and all other organs through the strengthening matter which reaches them through the arteries, nerves and sinews. Altogether, this is so arranged and prepared, as to become fit to receive the guidance of the reasoning soul, which is an independent substance, and nearly approaches the angelic, of which it is stated : ' Its dwelling is not with flesh ' (Dan. ii. 11). It inhabits the body as ruler and guide, not in the sense of space, nor does it partake of this food, because it is exalted above it. The Divine Influence only dwells in a soul which is susceptible to intellect, whilst the soul only associates with the warm vital breath. The latter must needs have a mainspring to which it is attached, as is the flame to the top of the wick. The heart is compared to the wick, and is fed by the flow of blood. Blood is produced by the digestive organs, and therefore requires the stomach, the liver, and lower organs. The heart, in the same way, requires the lungs, throat, nose, the diaphragm, and the muscles which move the muscles of the chest for breathing, as well as to keep in balance the temperature of the heart between the air which enters, and that which is expelled. It further requires for the removal of the food, refuse expelling forces, viz. the excretory and urinary organs. In this way the body is formed from all the component parts mentioned. It also requires organs of motion from place to place, in order to procure its wants, to avoid that which is harmful, and to attract and to repel. It requires hands and feet, advisers who distinguish, warning against what is to be feared, and advising what is to be hoped for ; who keep account of what has taken place, and record what has passed, in order to recommend care or hope for future events.

It requires the internal and external senses, the seat of
which is in the head, and which are assisted by the
functions of the heart. The whole body is thus harmoniously arranged, but under the control of the heart,
which forms the primary home of the soul. Its localiza-
tion in the brain is of secondary importance, the heart
remaining its regulator. In exactly the same way is
the living, godly people arranged, as Joshua said : ' Here-
by shall ye know that the living God is among you '
(iii. 10). The fire was kindled by the will of God, when
the people found favour in His sight, being a sign that
He accepted their hospitality and their offerings. For
the fire is the finest and noblest element beneath the
sphere of the moon. Its seat is the fat and vapour of
sacrifices, the smoke of the incense and oil, as it is the
nature of fire to cling to fat and oil. So also does
natural heat cling to the finest fatty globules of the
blood. God commanded the construction of the altar
burnt offerings, the Altar of Incense, and the candlestick ; their holocausts, incense, and the lamp oil. As
regards the altar of burnt offerings, it was destined to
bear the visible fire, whilst the Golden Altar was re-
served for the invisible and finer fire. The candlestick
was to bear the light of wisdom and inspiration ; the
table that of abundance and material provisions. The
sages say : He who wishes to be wise must turn to the
south ; he who wishes to be rich must turn to the
north.[30] All these implements stood in the service of
the Holy Ark and the Cherubim which occupied the
place of the heart, and the lungs above it. The vessels,
such as the laver and its foot, tongs, firepans, dishes,
spoons, bowls, pots, and forks, etc., were all required.
A place was wanted to house them, viz. the Tabernacle,

tent and cover, and the court of the Tabernacle with its appurtenances, as an enclosure for the whole. As bearers of the entire household God appointed the Levites, because they were nearest to Him, especially after the affair of the golden calf, as it is said : ' And all the sons of Levi gathered themselves together unto Him ' (Exod. xxxii. 26). From among them He chose Elazar, the finest and noblest of them, as it is said : ' And to the office of Elazar the son of Aaron the priest [pertaineth] the oil for the light, and the sweet incense, and the daily meat offering, and the anointing oil ' (Numb. iv. 16)— things to which the finer fire clings. The light of wisdom, however, and inspiration was attached to the *Urim* and *Tummim*, as well as to the most select section of Levites, viz. the family of Kohāth, who carried the appurtenances of the internal service : the Ark, Table, Candlestick, Altars, and the Holy Vessels ' with which they served.' With regard to them it is said : ' Because the service of the sanctuary belonged unto them, they should bear upon their shoulders ' (Num. vii. 9)—just as the internal organs of the body are without bones which help to carry them, but are, themselves, borne by the innate powers in conjunction with all that belongs to them. Another branch of the children of Gershōn bore the more delicate external appurtenances, viz. the carpets of the Tabernacle, the Tent and its cover, and the covering of badgers' skin that was above it. The lower section of the B'nē Merāri bore the grosser utensils, viz. its hooks,[31] boards, bars, pillars, and sockets. The last two sections were aided in carrying their burden by having chariots, as it is said : ' Two wagons for the Gershoni and four wagons for Merāri according to their service ' (Num. vii. 7–8). All this was systematically arranged

by God. I do not, by any means, assert that the
service was instituted in the order expounded by me,
since it entailed something more secret and higher, and
was based on a divine law. He who accepts this completely without scrutiny or argument, is better off than
he who investigates and analyses. He, however, who
steps down from the highest grade to scrutiny, does well
to turn his face to the latent wisdom, instead of leading
it to evil opinions and doubts which lead to corruption.

27. Al Khazari : Rabbi, thy symbolization was excellent, but the head and its senses, as well as the anointing oil were left unconsidered.

28. The Rabbi : Quite so. The root of all knowledge
was deposited in the Ark which took the place of the
heart, viz. the Ten Commandments, and its branch is
the Tōrāh on its side, as it is said : ' Put it in the side
of the ark of the covenant of the Lord your God ' (Deut.
xxxi. 26). From there went forth a twofold knowledge,
firstly, the scriptural knowledge, whose bearers were
the priests ; secondly, the prophetic knowledge which
was in the hands of the prophets. Both classes were,
so to speak, the people's watchful advisers, who compiled the chronicles. They, therefore, represent the
head of the people.

29. Al Khazari : So you are to-day a body without
either head or heart.

30. The Rabbi : Thou sayest rightly, but we are not
even a body, only scattered limbs, like the ' dry bones '
which Ezekiel saw [in his vision] (chap. xxxvii.). These
bones, however, O king of the Khazars, which have retained a trace of vital power, having once been the seat
of a heart, brain, breath, soul, and intellect, are better
than certain bodies formed of marble and plaster, en-

dowed with heads, eyes, ears, and all limbs, in which never dwelt the spirit of life, nor ever can dwell in them, since they are but imitations of man, not man in reality.

31. Al Khazari : It is as thou sayest.

32. The Rabbi : The 'dead' nations which desire to be held equal to the 'living' people can obtain nothing more than an external resemblance. They built houses for God, but no trace of Him was visible therein. They turned hermits and ascetics in order to secure inspiration, but it came not. They, then, deteriorated, became disobedient, and wicked ; yet no fire fell down from heaven upon them, nor rapid pestilence, as a manifest punishment from God for their disobedience. Their heart, I mean the house in which they used to meet, was destroyed, but otherwise their status was not affected. This could only take place in accordance with the largeness or smallness of their number, with their strength or weakness, disunion or unity, following upon natural or accidental causes. We, however, since our heart, I mean the Holy House, was destroyed, were lost with it. If it be restored, we, too, will be restored, be we few or many, or in whichever way this may happen. For our master is the living God, our King, Who keeps us in this our present condition in dispersion and exile.

33. Al Khazari : Certainly. A similar dispersion is not imaginable in any other people, unless it became absorbed by another, especially after so long a period. Many nations which arose after you have perished without leaving a memory, as Edōm, Mōāb, Ammōn, Aran, the Philistines, Chaldaeans, Medians, Persians, and Javān, the Brahmans, Sabaeans, and many others.

34. The Rabbi : Do not believe that I, though agree-

ing with thee, admit that we are dead. We still hold
connexion with that Divine Influence through the laws
which He has placed as a link between us and Him.
There is circumcision, of which it is said :' My covenant
shall be in your flesh for an everlasting covenant' (Gen.
xvii. 13). There is further the Sabbath, 'It is a sign
between me and you throughout your generations'
(Exod. xxxi. 13). Besides this there is 'the covenant of
the Fathers,' and the covenant of the law, first granted
on Hōreb, and then in the plains of Moab in connexion
with the promises and warnings laid down in the section :
'When thou shalt beget children and grandchildren'
(Deut. iv. 25). Compare further the antithesis : 'If
any of thine be driven out unto the utmost parts of
heaven' (chap. xxx. 10) ; 'Thou shalt return unto the
Lord thy God' (ibid. 2), finally, the song : 'Give ear'
(chap. xxxii. 1) ; and other places. We are not like
dead, but rather like a sick and attenuated person who
has been given up by the physicians, and yet hopes for
a miracle or an extraordinary recovery, as it is said :
'Can these bones live ?' (Ezek. xxxvii. 3). Compare
also the simile in the words : 'Behold my servant shall
prosper' ; 'He has no form nor comeliness,' 'Like one
from whom men hid their faces' (Is. lii. 13 ; which
means that he is, on account of his deformity and
repulsive visage, compared to an unclean thing,
which man only beholds with disgust, and turns
away ; 'Despised and rejected of men,' 'A man of
sorrows and acquainted with grief' liii. 3).

35. Al Khazari : How can this serve as a comparison
for Israel, as it is said : 'Surely he has borne our
griefs ?' That which has befallen Israel has come to
pass on account of its sins.

36. The Rabbi : Israel amidst the nations is like the heart amidst the organs of the body ; it is at one and the same time the most sick and the most healthy of them.

37. Al Khazari : Make this a little clearer.

38. The Rabbi : The heart is exposed to all sorts of diseases, and frequently visited by them, such as sadness, anxiety, wrath, envy, enmity, love, hate, and fear. Its temperament changes continually, undulating between excess and deficiency, and moreover influenced by inferior nourishment, by movement, exertion, sleep, or wakefulness. They all affect the heart whilst the limbs rest.

39. Al Khazari : Now I understand how it can be the most sick and most healthy of all organs simultaneously.

40. The Rabbi : Is it possible that it could suffer from swelling, or a cancer, or boils, a wound, weakness, and asthma, as is possible in other organs ?

41. Al Khazari : Impossible. For the smallest trace of these would bring on death. Its extreme sensibility, caused by the purity of its blood, and its great intelligence causes it to feel the slightest symptom, and expels it as long as it is able to do so. The other organs lack this fine sensibility, and it is therefore possible that they can be affected by some strange matter which produces illness.

42. The Rabbi : Thus its sensibility and feeling expose it to many ills, but they are at the same time the cause of their own expulsion at the very beginning, and before they have time to take root.

43. Al Khazari : Quite so.

44. The Rabbi : Our relation to the Divine Influence

is the same as that of the soul to the heart. For this
reason it is said : ' You only have I known of all the
families of the earth, therefore I will punish you for all
your inquities ' (Amos iii. 2). These are the illnesses.
As regards its health, it is alluded to in the words of the
sages : He forgives the sins of his people, causing the
first of them to vanish first.[32] He does not allow our
sins to become overwhelming, or they would destroy us
completely by their multitude. Thus he says : ' For
the iniquity of the Amorites is not yet full ' (Gen. xv.
16). He left them alone till the ailment of their sins
had become fatal.   Just as the heart is pure in substance and matter, and of even temperament, in order
to be accessible to the intellectual soul, so also is Israel
in its component parts. In the same way as the heart
may be affected by disease of the other organs, viz. the
lusts of the liver, stomach and genitals, caused through
contact with malignant elements ; thus also is Israel
exposed to ills originating in its inclinings towards the
Gentiles. As it is said : ' They were mingled among
the heathens and learned their works ' (Ps. cvi. 35).
Do not consider it strange if it is said in the same sense :
' Surely, he has borne our griefs and carried our sorrows '
(Is. liii. 4). Now we are burdened by them, whilst the
whole world enjoys rest and prosperity. The trials
which meet us are meant to prove our faith, to cleanse
us completely, and to remove all taint from us. If we
are good, the Divine Influence is with us in this world.
Thou knowest that the elements gradually evolved
metals, plants, animals, man, finally the pure essence of
man. The whole evolution took place for the sake of
this essence, in order that the Divine Influence should
inhabit it. That essence, however, came into existence

for the sake of the highest essence, viz. the prophets and pious. A similar gradation can be observed in the prayer : ' Give thy fear, O Lord our God, over all Thy works.' Then : ' Give glory to Thy people ' ; finally : ' The pious shall see and rejoice,' [33] because they are the purest essence.

45. Al Khazari : Thy interesting comparison has completely riveted my attention. But I should expect to see more hermits and ascetics among you than among other people.

46. The Rabbi : I regret that thou hast forgotten those fundamental principles in which thou didst concur. Did we not agree that man cannot approach God except by means of deeds commanded by him ? Dost thou think that this can be gained by meekness, humility, etc., alone ?

47. Al Khazari : Certainly, and rightly so. I think I read in your books as follows : ' What doth the Lord thy God require of thee, but to fear the Lord thy God ' (Deut. x. 12) and ' What doth the Lord require of thee ' (Mic. vi. 8), and many similar passages ?

48. The Rabbi : These are the rational laws, being the basis and preamble of the divine law, preceding it in character and time, and being indispensable in the administration of every human society. Even a gang of robbers must have a kind of justice among them if their confederacy is to last. When Israel's disloyalty had come to such a pass that they disregarded rational and social principles (which are as absolutely necessary for a society as are the natural functions of eating, drinking, exercise, rest, sleeping, and waking for the individual), but held fast to the sacrificial worship and other divine laws, He was satisfied with even less. It was told to

them : ' Haply you might observe those laws which
rule the smallest and meanest community, such as refer
to justice, good actions, and recognition of God's bounty.'
For the divine law cannot become complete till the social
and rational laws are perfected.   The rational law demands justice and recognition of God's bounty.   What
has he, who fails in this respect, to do with offerings,
Sabbath, circumcision, etc., which reason neither demands, nor forbids ?   These are, however, the ordinations especially given to Israel as a corollary to the
rational laws.   Through this they received the advantage of the Divine Influence, without knowing how it
came to pass that the ' Glory of God ' descended upon
them, and that ' the fire of God ' consumed their offerings ; how they heard the allocution of the Lord ; and
how their history developed.   These are matters which
reason would refuse to believe if they were not guaranteed
by irrefutable evidence.   In a similar sense it was said
to them : ' What doth the Lord thy God require of
thee ? ' (Deut. x. 12) and ' Add your burnt offerings '
(Jer. vii. 21), and similar verses.   Can it be imagined
that the Israelites observe ' the doing of justice and the
love of mercy;' but neglect circumcision, Sabbath, and
the other laws, and felt happy withal ?

49. Al Khazari : After what thou hast said I should
not think so.   In the opinion of philosophers, however,
he becomes a pious man who does not mind in which
way he approaches God, whether as a Jew or a Christian,
or anything else he chooses.   Now we have returned to
reasoning, speculating and dialectics.   According ot
this everyone might endeavour to belong to a creed
dictated by his own speculating, a thing which would
be absurd.

50. The Rabbi : The divine law imposes no asceticism
on us. It rather desires that we should keep the equi-
poise, and grant every mental and physical faculty its
due, as much as it can bear, without overburdening one
faculty at the expense of another. If a person gives
way to licentiousness he blunts his mental faculty ; he
who is inclined to violence injures some other faculty.
Prolonged fasting is no act of piety for a weak person
who, having succeeded in checking his desires, is not
greedy. For him feasting is a burden and self-denial.
Neither is diminution of wealth an act of piety, if
it is gained in a lawful way, and if its acquisition does
not interfere with study and good works, especially for
him who has a household and children. He may spend
part of it in almsgiving, which would not be displeasing
to God ; but to increase it is better for himself. Our
law, as a whole, is divided between *fear, love,* and *joy,*
by each of which one can approach God. Thy contrition on a fast day does nothing the nearer to God than
thy joy on the Sabbath and holy days, if it is the outcome of a devout heart. Just as prayers demand devotion, so also is a pious mind necessary to find pleasure
in God's command and law ; that thou shouldst be
pleased with the law itself from love of the Lawgiver.
Thou seest how much He has distinguished thee, as if
thou hadst been His guest invited to His festive board.
Thou thankest Him in mind and word, and if thy joy
lead thee so far as to sing and dance, it becomes worship
and a bond of union between thee and the Divine Influence. Our law did not consider these matters optional, but
laid down decisive injunctions concerning them, since it
is not in the power of mortal man to apportion to each
faculty of the soul and body its right measure, nor to

decide what amount of rest and exertion is good, or to determine how long the ground should be cultivated till it
finds rest in the years of release and jubilee,or the amount
of tithe to be given, etc. God commanded cessation of
work on Sabbath and holy days, as well as in the culture
of the soil, all this ' as a remembrance of the exodus from
Egypt,' and ' remembrance of the work of creation.'
These two things belong together, because they are the
outcome of the absolute divine will, but not the result
of accident or natural phenomena. It is said : ' For
ask now of the days that are past—Did ever a people
hear the voice of God—Or hath God assayed,' etc.
(Deut. iv. 32 sqq.). The observance of the Sabbath is
itself an acknowledgment of His omnipotence, and at
the same time an acknowledgment of the creation by
the divine word. He who observes the Sabbath because
the work of creation was finished on it acknowledges the
creation itself. He who believes in the creation believes
in the Creator. He, however, who does not believe in
it falls a prey to doubts of God's eternity and to doubts
of the existence of the world's Creator. The observance
of the Sabbath is therefore nearer to God than monastic
retirement and ascetism. Behold how the Divine Influence attached itself to Abraham, and then to all those
who shared his excellence and the Holy Land. This Influence followed him everywhere, and guarded his posterity, preventing the detachment of any of them, it
brought them to the most sheltered and best place, and
caused them to multiply in a miraculous manner, and
finally raised them to occupy a degree worthy of such
excellence. He is, therefore, called : ' God of Abraham '
(Gen. xxviii. 13),'God of the land' (1 Sam.iv.4),'Dwelling
between the Cherubim ' (Ps. ix. 12), ' Dwelling in Zion '

(Ps. cxxxv. 21), ' Abiding in Jerusalem ' (Ps. cxxiii. 1),
these places being compared to heaven, as it is said :
' Dwelling in heaven ' (Ps. cxxiii. 1). His light shines in
these places as in heaven, although through mediums
which are fit to receive this light. He sheds it upon
them, and this it is that is called *love*. It has been taught
us, and we have been enjoined to believe in it, as
well as to praise and thank Him in the prayer : " With
eternal love Thou lovest us " ; so that we should bear in
mind that it originally came from Him, but not from us.
To give an instance, we do not say that an animal
created itself, but that God formed and fashioned it,
having selected the proper matter for it. In the same
manner it was He who initiated our delivery from Egypt
to be His people and to acknowledge Him as king, as He
said : ' I am the Lord your God who led you out of the
land of Egypt to be unto you a God ' [34] (Lev. xxii. 33,
Num. xv. 41). He also says : ' O Israel, in whom I will
be glorified ' (Is. xlix. 3).

51. Al Khazari : This sentence seems to go too far,
and is overbold in expressing that the Creator is glorified
through mortal man.

52. The Rabbi : Wouldst thou find this less strange
in the creation of the sun ?

53. Al Khazari : Certainly, on account of its great
power. Next to God it is the cause of being. By its
means night and day and the seasons of the year are
determined ; minerals, metals, plants, and animals were
developed through its instrumentality. Its light produced sight and colours. Wherefore should not the
action of such a thing be an object of glory among men ?

54. The Rabbi : Are not the intellectual faculties
much finer than the light that is seen ? Or were not

the inhabitants of the earth prior to the Israelites in
blindness and error excepting those few whom I mentioned ? [35]   Some people said that there was no Creator ;
that no part of the world was more worthy of being
created than being creator, the universe being eternal.
Others say that the spheres are eternal and creative.
They consequently adore them.   Others again assert
that the fire is the essence of light and all the miraculous
products of its power ; it must, therefore, be worshipped.
The soul also is fire.   Others worship different things,
viz. sun, moon, stars, and animal forms, which are in
connexion with special phenomena.   Other people
adore their kings and sages.   They all, however, agree
that there is nothing in the world which is contrary to
nature, nor is there any Providence.   Even philosophers
who, with their refined intuition and clear view, acknowledge a Prime Cause different from earthly things and
unparalleled, are inclined to think that this Prime Cause
exercises no influence on the world, and certainly not on
individuals, as he is too exalted to know them, much
less to make them the basis of a new entity.   The community was at last considered sufficiently pure for the
light to dwell on it, to be worthy of seeing miracles
which changed the course of nature, and to understand
that the world had a King who watched and guarded it,
who knew both great and small, rewarded the good and
the wicked, and directed the hearts.   All who came
after these philosophers could not detach themselves
from their principles, so that to-day the whole civilized
world acknowledges that God is eternal, and that the
world was created.   They look upon the Israelites and
all that befell them as a proof of this.

55. Al Khazari : This is glory indeed, and an extra-

ordinary proof. It is justly written : ' To make Himself
an everlasting name ' (Is. lxiii. 12), ' So didst Thou get
Thee a name as it is this day ' (Neh. ix. 10), and ' In
praise, in name, and in honour ' (Deut. xxvi. 19).

56. The Rabbi : Didst thou not see how David intro-
duces the praise of the Tōrāh, when he first speaks of
the sun in the words : ' The heavens declare the glory
of God ' (Ps. xix. 2). He describes how ubiquitous its
light, how pure its body, how steady its path, and beautiful its countenance. This is followed by the words :
' The law of the Lord is perfect ' (ver. 7), etc., as if he
wished to convey that one should not wonder at such a
description. For the Tōrāh is more pure, more resplendent, more widely known, more exalted, and more useful still. If there were no Israelites there would be no
Tōrāh. They did not derive their high position from
Moses, but Moses received his for their sake. The
divine love dwelt among the descendants of Abraham,
Isaac, and Jacob. The choice of Moses, however, was
made in order that the good fortune might come to
them through his instrumentality. We are not called
the people of Moses, but the people of God, as it is said :
' The people of the Lord ' (Ezek. xxxvi. 20) and ' The
people of the God of Abraham ' (Ps. xlvii. 10). Proof
of the Divine Influence is not found in well chosen words,
in raising the eyebrows, closing the eyes during prayers,
contrition, movement, and talk behind which there are
no deeds ; but a pure mind, illustrated by corresponding
actions which, by their very nature, are difficult to perform, and are yet performed with the utmost zeal and
love. It is to be found in one who, wherever he may,
strives to reach the chosen place three times a year, and
bearing with the greatest pleasure and joy all fatigues

and expenses connected therewith. He pays the 'first
tithe,' and the 'second tithe,' and the 'poor tithe,' and
the expenses connected with his apparel for the Temple.
He renounces the harvest in the years of release and
jubilee, incurs expense for a tabernacle, holy days, and
abstention from work ; gives the first fruits, the first-
born animals, priests' emoluments, the first of the shear-
ing, and the first of the dough, apart from vows and
free gifts, and fines connected with intentional and unintentional sins, and peace offerings. Further offerings
due on account of private happenings, impurity, child-
bed, issue, leprosy, and many other things. All this is
regulated by divine command, without [human] speculation. It is not possible for man to determine the
relative importance of each, and he need not fear
any deterioriation in them. It is as if He assessed
Israel, and measured them as well as the harvests of
Palestine as regards vegetable and animal life. He also
considered the tribe of Levi, and ordained these asses-
ments in the desert, because he knew that, as long as
they were not infringed, Israel would retain its surplus,
and the Levite would not be in want. It never could
come to such a pass that a tribe or family would be
reduced to poverty, because he ordained the return of the
whole property in the year of jubilee in the same status
as it was in the first year of the distribution of the land.
The details of these regulations would fill volumes. He
who studies them carefully will see that they are not of
human origin. Praised be He who has contrived them :
'He hath not dealt so with any nation ; they are judgments which they knew not' (Ps. cxlvii. 20). This
arrangement lasted during the periods of both Temples
for about 1,300 years, and had the people remained in

the straight path, it would have been ' as the days of
the heaven on earth ' (Deut. xi. 20).

57. Al Khazari : At present you are in great confusion
concerning those heavy duties. What nation could
observe such regulations ?

58. The Rabbi : The community whose guardian and
compensator is always in its midst—I mean God. Joshua
said : ' You cannot serve the Lord, for He is an holy
God ' (chap. xxiv. 19). Notwithstanding this, his community was so zealously observing that, in the matter of
the trespass of ' the devoted thing of Jericho,' not more
than the one, Achan, was found disobedient among more
than six hundred thousand. The punishment followed
immediately, just as it did in the case of Miriam, who
was afflicted with leprosy ; also in the cases of Uzzah,
Nadab and Abihu, and the people of Beth-Shemesh, who
were punished because they had ' looked into the ark
of the Lord ' (1 Sam. vi. 19). It was one of the wonderful traits of God that His displeasure for minor transgressions was shown on the walls of houses and in the
clothes, whilst for more grievous sins the bodies were
more or less severely stricken. The priests were appointed to study this profound science and to discover
to what extent these trials were God's punishment (this
often took them weeks to find out, as was the case with
Miriam), or how much was simply constitutionally cur-
able or incurable. This is an abstruse science to which
God pointed in the words : ' Take heed in the plague of
leprosy, that thou observe diligently and do according
to all that the priests, the Levites, shall teach you '
(Deut. xxiv. 8).

59. Al Khazari : Hast thou a satisfactory argument
on the matter ?

60. The Rabbi : I told thee that there is no comparison to be made between our intelligence and the Divine
Influence, and it is proper that we leave the cause of
these important things unexamined. I take, however,
the liberty of stating—though not with absolute cer-
tainty—that leprosy and issue are occasionally the consequence of contamination by corpses. A dead body
represents the highest degree of malignancy, and a
leprous limb is as if dead. It is the same with lost
σπέρμα, because it had been endowed with living power,
capable of engendering a human being. Its loss, therefore, forms a contrast to the living and breathing, and
on account of its ideal potentiality only affects noble
minds and highly strung souls which incline towards
the divine, prophetic, visionary, and towards genuine
imagination. There are people who feel depressed as
long as they have not purified themselves after such an
accident. Experience has taught them that their touch
deteriorates such fine things as pearls and wine. Most
of us feel influenced by the vicinity of dead bodies and
graves, and our spirits are depressed as long as we find
ourselves in a house in which there is a corpse. Those
of coarser mould remain untouched. We see the same
in intellectual matters. He who seeks purity of thought
in philosophic studies, or purity of soul in prayer, feels
uncomfortable in the association with women and scof-
fers, or during the recitation of jocular or love songs.

61. Al Khazari : This explains to me why the physical
birthright, viz. the σπέρμα, contaminates, though being
wholly spiritual, whilst other excreta do not do so, in
spite of their repulsive aspect, odour, and quantity.
Now I should still like to hear the explanation of the
leprosy of the garment and the house.

62. The Rabbi : I mentioned that as one of the cha-racteristics of the Shekhinah, that it occupies in Israel the same place as the spirit of life in the human body. It granted them a divine life, and allowed them to find lustre, beauty, and light in their souls, bodies, disposi-tions, and houses. When it was absent from them, their intelligence waned, their bodies deteriorated, and their beauty faded. The effect of the disappearance of the divine light became noticeable in every individual. One can easily see how the breath of a person is sud-denly lost through fear and sorrow, whereby the body also suffers. On women and boys who go out at night one may sometimes see black and green marks, the result of their weak nerves. This is attributed to demons, but diseases of body and mind are often pro-duced by the sight of people who have died or were killed.

63. Al Khazari : I perceive that your law comprises all sorts of profound and strange sciences, ·not to be found in other codes.

64. The Rabbi : The members of the Synhedrion were bound not to let any science, real and fictitious, or conventional, escape their knowledge, magic and lan-guage included. How was it possible at all times to find seventy scholars unless learning was common among the people ? If one elder died, another of the samestampsucceeded him. This could not be otherwise, as all branches of science were required for the practice of the law. Natural sciences was wanted for agriculture, in order to recognise ' mingled seed,' to be careful with the produce of the seventh year and of newly planted trees, to distinguish the various kinds of plants, that their nature might be preserved, and one species be not mixed

up with another. It is difficult enough to know whether
chondros is a kind of barley, or spelt, a kind of wheat,
or *brassica* is a kind of cabbage ; to study the
powers of their roots and how far they spread in the
ground ; how much of it remains for the following year,
and how much does not remain ; how much space and
time is to be left between each species. Further, the
distinction of the various species of animals served
various purposes, among which is to know which com-
municates poison and which not.[36] With this is connected the knowledge of injuries which make an animal
unlawful for food. This is even more profound than
what Aristotle wrote on the subject, viz. how to know
which injuries are fatal and thus to deter people from
eating carrion. The small remnant of this knowledge
which has remained makes us wonder. Add to this
the acquaintance with the blemishes which disqualify
priests from taking part in the Temple service, as well
as of the blemishes which prohibit the offering up of
certain animals as sacrifices. Then there is the knowledge of the various kinds of issue and of the period of
purification. All this requires instruction. Man is not
able to determine these matters by reflection alone, without divine assistance.[37] The same is the case with the
knowledge of the revolutions of the spheres, of which
the yearly calendar is but one fruit. The excellence of
the calculation of the calendar is famous, and it is well
known what deep root it has taken among these people,
few in number, yet excellently equipped with model institutions. Could it be otherwise ? On account of the smallness, humbleness, and dispersion of the people it is hardly
noticed among the other nations, yet those relics of the
Divine made it into one firmly established organization.

The calendar, based on the rules of the revolution of the moon, as handed down by the House of David, is truly wonderful. Though hundreds of years [38] have passed, no mistake has been found in it, whilst the observations of Greek and other astronomers are not faultless. They were obliged to insert corrections and supplements every century, whilst our calendar is always free from error, as it rests on prophetic tradition. Had there been the smallest flaw in a fundamental rule this would to-day have assumed serious proportions, on account of the time difference between the conjunction of the moon and the moment when she becomes visible. In the same manner our sages were, without doubt, acquainted with the movements of the sun and astronomy in general. Music was the pride of a nation which distributed their songs in such a way that they fell to the lot of the aristocracy of the people, viz. the Levites, who made practical use of them in the holy house and in the holy season. For their maintenance they were satisfied with the tithes, as they had no occupation but music. As an art it is highly esteemed among mankind, as long as it is not abused and degraded, and as long as the people preserves its original nobleness and purity. David and Samuel were its great masters. Dost thou think that they understood it well or not ?

65. Al Khazari : There can be no doubt that *their* art was most perfect, and touched the souls, as people say that it changes the humour of a man's soul to a different one. It is impossible that it should now reach the same high level. It has deteriorated, and servants and half-crazy people are its patrons. Truly, Rabbi, it sank from its greatness, as you have sunk in spite of your former greatness.

66. The Rabbi : What is thy opinion of Solomon's accomplishments ? Did he not, with the assistance of divine, intellectual, and natural power, converse on all sciences ? The inhabitants of the earth travelled to him, in order to carry forth his learning, even as far as India. Now the roots and principles of all sciences were handed down from us first to the Chaldaeans, then to the Persians and Medians, then to Greece, and finally to the Romans.[39] On account of the length of this period, and the many disturbing circumstances, it was forgotten that they had originated with the Hebrews, and so they were ascribed to the Greeks and Romans. To Hebrew, however, belongs the first place, both as regards the nature of the languages, and as to fullness of meanings.

67. Al-Khazari : Is Hebrew superior to other languages ? Do we not see distinctly that the latter are more finished and comprehensive ?

68. The Rabbi : It shared the fate of its bearers, degenerating and dwindling with them. Considered historically and logically, its original form is the noblest. According to tradition it is the language in which God spoke to Adam and Eve, and in which the latter conversed. It is proved by the derivation of Adam from *adāmāh*, *ishshāh* from *ish* ; *ḥayyāh* from *ḥayy* ; *Cain* from *qānithī* ; *Shēth* from *shāth*, and *Nōah* from *yᵉnaḥ*, *mēnū*. This is supported by the evidence of the Tōrāh. The whole is traced back to Eber, Nōah and Adam. It is the language of Eber after whom it was called *Hebrew*,[40] because after the confusion of tongues it was he who retained it. Abraham was an Aramaean of *Ur Kasdim*, because the language of the Chaldaeans was Aramaic. He employed Hebrew as a specially holy language and

Aramaic for everyday use. For this reason Ishmael
brought it to the Arabic speaking nations, and the
consequence was that Aramaic, Arabic and Hebrew are
similar to each other in their vocabulary, grammatical
rules, and formations. The superiority of Hebrew is
manifest from the logical point of view if we consider
the people who employed it for discourses, particularly
at the time when prophecy was rife among them, also
for preaching, songs and psalmody. It is conceivable
that their rulers such as for instance, Moses, Joshua,
David, and Solomon lacked the words to express what
they wished, as it is the case with us to-day, because it
is lost to us ? Dost thou not see how the Tōrāh, when
describing the Tabernacle, Ephōd and breastplate and
other objects, always finds the most suitable word for
all these strange matters ? How beautifully is this
description composed ? It is just the same with the
names of people, species of birds and stones, the diction
of David's Psalms, the lamentations of Job, and his
dispute with his friends, the addresses of Isaiah, etc.

69. Al-Khazari : Thou wilt only succeed in placing
it on a par with other languages thus. But where is its
pre-eminence ? Other languages surpass it in songs
metrically constructed and arranged for tunes.[41]

70. The Rabbi : It is obvious that a tune is independent of the metre, or of the lesser or greater
number of syllables. The verse *hōdū la'dōnāi ki tōb* can,
therefore, be sung to the same tune as *l'ōsē niflāōth
g'dōlōth l'baddō*. This is the rule in sentences in which
the tune must follow the grammatical construction.
Rhymed poems, however, which are recited, and in
which a good metre is noticeable, are neglected for something higher and more useful.

71. Al-Khazari : And what may that be ?

72. The Rabbi : The faculty of speech is to transmit
the idea of the speaker into the soul of the hearer. Such
intention, however, can only be carried out to perfection by means of oral communication.   This
is better than writing. The proverb is : ' From the
mouths of scholars, but not from the mouth of books.'
Verbal communication finds various aids either in
pausing or continuing to speak, according to the requirements of the sentence, by raising or lowering the voice,
in expressing astonishment, question, narrative, desire,
fear or submission by means of gestures, without which
speech by itself would remain inadequate. Occasionally
the speaker even has recourse to movements of eyes,
eyebrows, or the whole head and hands, in order to
express anger, pleasure, humility or haughtiness to the
degree desired.   In the remnant of our language which
was created and instituted by God, are implanted subtle
elements calculated to promote understanding, and to
take the place of the above aids to speech. These are the
accents with which the holy text is read. They denote
pause and continuation, they separate question from
answer, the beginning from the continuation of the
speech, haste from hesitation, command from request,
on which subject books might be written. He who
intends to do this must omit poetry, because it can only
be recited in one way. For it mostly connects when it
should stop and stops where it should go on. One
cannot avoid this except with great trouble.

73. Al-Khazari : It is but proper that mere beauty
of sound should yield to lucidity of speech. Harmony
pleases the ear, but exactness makes the meaning clear.
I see, however, that you Jews long for a prosody, in

imitation of other peoples, in order to force the Hebrew language into their metres.

74. The Rabbi : This is because we remained and are froward. Instead of being satisfied with the superiority mentioned above, we corrupted the structure of our language, which is built on harmony, and created discord.

75. Al-Khazari : How so ?

76. The Rabbi : Didst thou not see that a hundred persons read the Tōrāh as one person, stopping in one moment, and continuing simultaneously ?

77. Al-Khazari I have, indeed, observed this, and never saw the like of it either among Persians or Arabs. It is impossible in the recitation of a poem. Now I should like to know how the Hebrew language obtained that advantage, and how the metre interferes with it.

78. The Rabbi : The reason is that you can put together two [vowelless] consonants,[42] but not three vowels,[43] except in rare cases.[44] This not only gives the speech a rest, but enables it to obtain that advantage, viz. consonance and fluency in reading. This makes learning by heart and the grasping of the meaning easy. The first thing which destroys metrical reading is the relation of those two consonants.[45] Correct accentuation becomes impossible, so that *ŏkhlāh* (food) is read like *ōkhᵉlāh* [46] (she is eating) ; *ŏmrō* (his word) and *āmerū* (they have spoken) have metrically the same value as *ōmēr* (speaking) and *ōmer* (word). Thus also the time difference between *shábti*, which is past tense, and *wᵉ shabtí*, which is future, lost. We might find a way out of this difficulty if we followed the ways of the *Piyyūt* [47] which does not interfere with the lan-

guage, and merely employs the rhyme. But in matters
of poetry, the same befell us which befell our forefathers,
concerning whom it is written : ' They mingled among
the gentiles and learned their works '(Ps. cvi. 35).

79. Al-Khazari : I should like to ask whether thou
knowest the reason why Jews move to and fro when
reading the Bible ?

80. The Rabbi : It is said that it is done in order to
arouse natural heat. My personal belief is that it
stands in connexion with the subject under discussion.
As it often happened that many persons read at the
same time, it was possible that ten or more read from
one volume. This is the reason why our books are so
large. Each of them was obliged to bend down in his
turn in order to read a passage, and to turn back again.
This resulted in a continual bending and sitting up, the
book lying on the ground. This was one reason. Then
it became a habit through constant seeing, observing
and imitating, which is in man's nature. Other people
read each out of his own book, either bringing it near
to his eyes, or, if he pleased, bending down to it without
inconveniencing his neighbour. There was, therefore,
no necessity of bending and sitting up. We will now
discuss the importance of the accents, the orthographic
value of the seven principal vowel signs, the grammatical accuracy resulting from them as well as from
the distinction between Qāmes, Pataḥ, Ṣere and Sĕgōl.
They influence the meaning of grammatical forms and
assist in distinguishing between past and future
tenses e.g., שַׂמְתִּי and וְשַׂמְתִּי and וַאֲבָרְכֵהוּ and וָאֲבָרְכֵהוּ
(Is. li. 2, and Gen. xxvii, 33) ; or between a verb and an
adjective, e.g. חָכַם and חָכָם ; between the interro-
gative *Hē* and the article, as in הַעוֹלָה הִיא לְמַעְלָה

(Eccl. iii. 21), and other cases. The euphony and
structure of speech is increased by the sequence of two
vowelless consonants, which enables a whole congregation to read Hebrew simultaneously without mistakes.[48]
Other rules apply to the musical acents. For the vowel
sounds are divided in Hebrew into three classes,[49]
viz. U-sound, A-sound, and I-sound; or in another
division: great U-sound, or *Qāmeṣ*, medium U-sound,
or *Ḥōlem*; little U-sound, or *Shūreq*; great A-sound, or
Pataḥ,; little A-sound or *Segōl*; great I-sound or
Sērē; little I-sound, or *Ḥireq*. Shewā [50] is sounded with
all these [vowels] under certain conditions. It is
vowel absolute,[51] because any addition would require
a vowelless consonant to follow. *Qāmeṣ* is followed
by a long closed syllable, but not by dāgēsh in the first
form.[52] Dagēsh can only follow, if demanded by the
exigencies of the second or third forms, the syllable
being long, by one of the vowel letters *alef* or *hē*, as
in ברא and קנה. A syllable of this kind can also
end in a vowelless consonant, as in קאם (Hos. x. 14).[53]
Ḥōlem also can be followed by a vowel letter which is
wāw or *alef* as in לא and לו, or a syllable of this kind
can be closed by a consonant as שׁור and שׂמאל. The
vowel letters after *Sērē* are [54] *alef* or *yōd* as in יוצא and
יואי. *Hē*, however, only in the second form, but
not in the first.[55] *Shūreq* is free [56] for all three forms. It
can be followed by a vowel letter, or dāgēsh, or vowelless
consonant. Its long vowel is expressed by *wāw* only
as, ללון, לו and לקח. *Ḥireq* follows the rule of
Shūreq as in לין, לי and לבי. *Pataḥ*, and *Segōl* are
not followed by a vowel letter in the first form, but are
lengthened by the second form, either for the sake of
emphasis,[57] or on account of the accent, or in the pause

at the end of a sentence.[58] The rules of the *first form*
are obtained by considering the formation of each word
separately, without any relation to the construction
of the sentence with its variety of combination and
separation, and long and short words.   Then are
obtained the seven principal vowels in their original,
unchanged form and the simple Shewā without *ga'yā*.
The *second form* deals with euphony in the construction
of sentences. Occasionally elements of the first form
are altered to please the second. The *third form* concerns the accents, and sometimes reacts on both preceding ones.   In the first form three consecutive
vowels without an intervening consonant or dāgesh are
possible, but three, or more, short vowels may follow
each other as in Arabic. This, however, is impossible
in the second form. As soon as three vowels follow
each other in the first form, the second one lengthens
one of them to the quantity of a long vowel as in מִשְׁכָּנִי,
רצפת, לִשְׁכָּנִי (Ps. xxxi. 12 ; Esth. i. 6).   For Hebrew
does not allow three consecutive [59] vowels, except when
a consonant is either repeated as in שררך [60] (Cant. vii. 3),
or in the case of gutturals as in נהרי and נחלי, the
reader being at liberty to read [the first syllable] long
or short. In the same way the first form allows the
sequence of two long closed syllables. The second
form, however, to prevent clumsiness of speech, shortens
one long syllable as in שמתי and ושמתי. It is obvious
that the pronunciation of פעל and similar forms is
contrary to its vocalisation, the second syllable being
lengthened in spite of the Pataḥ, whilst the first is
read short in spite of the Qāmes. The heightening of the
second syllable is due to the tone, but not to make
it slightly longer. Words as אמר-לי and עשה-לי (Gen.

xx. 5; xxi. 6) remain therefore in the first form,
because the smaller word has the tone. We also find
פָּעַל with two Qāmeṣ though in the past tense. The
cause of this is to be found in the *athnaḥ* or *sōf pāsūq*, [61]
and we say that this is possible in the second form on
account of the pause. We follow this up till we find
even פָּעַל with two Qāmeṣ and zāqēf.[62] The reason
of this we find in a virtual pause, the word being entitled
to *athnaḥ* or *sōf pāsūq*, but other cogent reasons made
athnaḥ and *sōf pāsūq* in this case impossible. On the
other hand we find these two accents with two pataḥs,
however strange this may be, e.g. וַתִּשְׁבַּרְנָה, וְזָקַנְתִּי, וַיֹּאמֶר,
וַיֵּלַךְ. The reason of pataḥ in וַיֹּאמֶר is found in
examining its meaning, as it cannot stand in pause,
and is necessarily connected with the following com-
plement of the sentence.[63] There are only a few exceptions as כַּאֲשֶׁר אָמָר, (Gen. xxi. 1), because the
verb completes the sentence logically, and can take
Qāmeṣ because of the pause.

As regards, however, וילך and ותשברנה, they should
originally be וַיֵּלֵךְ and ותשברנה; but the transformation of the I-sound with great Pataḥ,[64] without any
intermediate element, was too awkward, and therefore Pataḥ stepped in. The form זקנתי belongs
probably to the same class, because the root is זָקֵן, the
Ṣērē being changed into Pataḥ at the end of a sentence.
We marvel why the פָּעַל forms have the accent on the
first syllable which is read long, although it has Sēgōl.
We must, however, consider that, if the first syllable
remained short, Hebrew phonology would require the
second syllable to be read long and with accent, and a
slight quiescent would creep in between the second and
third radicals. This would be inelegant, which is not the

case in the first syllable, which must have this quiescent
and has also room for it. This lengthening of the
penultima corresponds to עֵל פֶּן, but not to עֵל פֻּן.
For when the word has athnaḥ, or sōf pāsūq, it is פֶּעֵל
corresponding to עֵל פָּאן. This shows the necessity
of lengthening the vowel in שמתי and שָׁמְתִי. We
consider forms like שער and נער likewise strange,
because the Pataḥ of the first syllable is read long.
We soon discover, however, that they are פֶּעֵל forms
with Pataḥ on account of the guttural. For this reason they undergo no change in the *status constructus*,
as do נהר and קהל (Gen. xv. 18; Exod. xii. 6),
which are formed like דָּבָר. Then we find אעשה,
יעשה, אבנה and אקנה with Segōl and vowel letters.
If we consider the first instance, we find it to be a form
יפעל, אפעל, the second radical not being long, but
always forming a closed syllable with Pataḥ. We are
now to read אעשֶׁה instead of Pataḥ, because no A-
sound can precede a silent *hē*, unless it be Qāmeṣ.
Qāmeṣ is long, whilst the second radical of a verb can
never have a long vowel, except when read with a vowel,
or when followed by Alef as in אצא. It is for this
reason that אעשׂה is read with Segōl which is the shortest
vowel imaginable, but interchanges with Ṣērē when
the second form requires to replace the one by the other
at the ends of sentences. There is almost no necessity
for the hē of אעשה except in the pause or with the
accent, and is eased by dāgesh as in אעשה־לך and אבנה־לי,
(Exod. xxxiii. 5), in which cases the hē has no function.
This is not the case [with א] in אצא, אבא. In בא־לי,
there is no dāgesh, the א being preceded by Ṣērē and
being a radical. Hē, however, is considered to be so
weak that it is both graphically and phonetically

omitted in ויקן ,ויבן and ויעש. How could it, then,
close a syllable vocalized by Ṣērē ?[65] It was, therefore,
left to Sēgōl, the slightest vowel, at all events, in the
first form. The second form changed it into Ṣērē, when
standing in pause.[66] It appears likewise strange that
מראה ,מעשה ,מקנה and similar forms have Ṣērē in the
construct state, but Sēgōl in the absolute. We should
think the reverse to be correct.[67] But if we consider
that the third radical, viz. a silent *Hē* is treated as
altogether absent, and those nouns have the forms of
מרא ,מעש ,מקן, nothing but Sēgōl will serve till some circumstances bring it out with a long vowel as in מראֶה,
מעשֶה ,מראיהן and מעשיהן. Sēgōl becomes Ṣērē to take
the place of [small] Pataḥ in מראֶם and מעשֹם. Words
of the first form can be altered by the second as
to the vowels, but not as to the pronunciation. The
word בן has Ṣērē in the absolute state, Sēgōl in the
construct. Occasionally the latter is lengthened by
the tone as in בן־יאיר (Esth. ii. 5) with the Sēgōl of
the first form In other cases the tone precipitates
it, although it has Ṣērē according to the first form,
as in בן אחר (Gen. xxx. 24). In segolate forms with
the accent on the last syllable Ṣērē is no longer per-
plexing. The author of this profound science held
secrets which are unknown to us. We may have
discovered some by means of which he intended to
stimulate our investigation as we have said above, with
regard to העולה היא למעלה. Or we might find out the
rules of distinguishing between past and future, in-
finitive and participle of the passive voice, e.g. נאסף אל עמי
(Gen. xlix. 29), with Qāmeṣ, and נאשר נאסף (Num. xxvii.
13) with Pataḥ. The masoretic text vocalizes three
times וישחט (Lev. viii. 15, 19, 23), with Qāmeṣ, although

syntactically speaking the words stand only virtually in pause. There are many instances that the
Sēgōl after Zarqā has the force of Athnaḥ, or sōf
pasūk, or Zākēf, causing an alteration of the first form.
If I wished to enlarge on the subject, the book would
become too lengthy. I only desired to give thee a taste
of this profound study, which is not built on hap-hazard,
but on fixed rules.

81. Al Khazari: This is sufficient to enlighten me
on the wonderful character of the Hebrew language.
Now I desire the description of a servant of God according to your conception. Afterwards I will ask thee for
thy arguments against the Karaites. Then I should
like to hear the principal articles of faith and religious
axioms. Finally I wish to know which branches of
ancient study have been preserved among you.

Finished is the second part, and we begin—

PART THREE

THE RABBI: According to our view a servant of God is not one who detaches himself from the world, lest he be a burden to it, and it to him; or hates life, which is one of God's bounties granted to him, as it is written: 'The number of thy days I will fulfil'; 'Thou shalt live long' (Exod. xxiii. 26). On the contrary, he loves the world and a long life, because it affords him opportunities of deserving the world to come. The more good he does the greater is his claim to the next world. He even reaches the degree of Enoch, concerning whom it is said: 'And Enoch walked with God' (Gen. v. 24); or the degree of Elijah, freed from worldly matters, and to be admitted to the realm of angels. In this case he feels no loneliness in solitude and seclusion, since they form his associates. He is rather ill at ease in a crowd, because he misses the divine presence which enables him to dispense with eating and drinking. Such persons might perhaps be happier in complete solitude; they might even welcome death, because it leads to the step beyond which there is none higher. Philosophers and scholars also love solitude to refine their thoughts, and to reap the fruits of truth from their researches, in order that all remaining doubts be dispelled by truth. They only desire the society of disciples who stimulate their re-

search and retentiveness, just as he who is bent upon
making money would only surround himself with persons with whom he could do lucrative business. Such
a degree is that of Socrates and those who are like him.
There is no one nowadays who feels tempted to strive
for such a degree, but when the Divine Presence was
still in the Holy Land among the people capable of prophecy, some few persons lived an ascetic life in deserts
and associated with people of the same frame of mind.
They did not seclude themselves completely, but they
endeavoured to find support in the knowledge of the
Law and in holy and pure actions which brought them
near to that high rank. These were the disciples of
prophets. He, however, who in our time, place, and
people, ' whilst no open vision exists ' (1 Sam. iii. 1), the
desire for study being small, and persons with a natural
talent for it absent, would like to retire into ascetic
solitude, only courts distress and sickness for soul and
body. The misery of sickness is visibly upon him, but
one might regard it as the consequence of humility and
contrition. He considers himself in prison as it were,
and despairs of life from disgust of his prison and pain,
but not because he enjoys his seclusion. How could it
be otherwise ? [1]   He has no intercourse with the divine
light, and cannot associate himself with it as the prophets. He lacks the necessary learning to be absorbed
in it and to enjoy it, as the philosophers did, all the rest
of his life. Suppose he is God-fearing, righteous, desires to meet his God in solitude, standing, humbly and
contritely, reciting as many prayers and supplications
as he possibly can remember, all this affords him satis-
faction for a few days as long as it is new. Words frequently repeated by the tongue lose their influence on

the soul, and he cannot give to the latter humbleness or submission. Thus he remains night and day, whilst his soul urges him to employ its innate powers in seeing, hearing, speaking, occupation, eating, cohabitation, gain, managing his house, helping the poor, upholding the law with money in case of need. Must he not regret those things to which he has tied his soul, a regret which tends to remove him from the Divine Influence, which he desired to approach ?

2. Al Khazari : Give me a description of the doings of one of your pious men at the present time.

3. The Rabbi : A pious man is, so to speak, the guardian of his country, who gives to its inhabitants provisions and all they need. He is so just that he wrongs no one, nor does he grant anyone more than his due. Then, when he requires them, he finds them obedient to his call. He orders, they execute ; he forbids, they abstain.

4. Al Khazari : I asked thee concerning a pious man, not a prince.

5. The Rabbi : The pious man is nothing but a prince who is obeyed by his senses, and by his mental as well as his physical faculties, which he governs corporeally, as it is written : ' He that ruleth his spirit [is better] than he that taketh a city ' (Prov. xvi. 32). He is fit to rule, because if he were the prince of a country he would be as just as he is to his body and soul. He subdues his passions, keeping them in bonds, but giving them their share in order to satisfy them as regards food, drink, cleanliness, etc. He further subdues the desire for power, but allows them as much expansion as avails them for the discussion of scientific or mundane views, as well as to warn the evil-minded. He allows the

senses their share according as he requires them for the
use of hands, feet, and tongue, as necessity or desire
arise. The same is the case with hearing, seeing, and
the kindred sensations which succeed them ; imagination, conception, thought, memory, and will power,
which commands all these ; but is, in its turn, sub-
servient to the will of intellect. He does not allow any
of these limbs or faculties to go beyond their special
task, or encroach upon another. If he, then, has satisfied each of them (giving to the vital organs the necessary amount of rest and sleep, and to the physical ones
waking, movements, and worldly occupation), he calls
upon his community as a respected prince calls his dis-
ciplined army, to assist him in reaching the higher or
divine degree which is to be found above the degree of
the intellect. He arranges his community in the same
manner as Moses arranged his people round Mount Sinai.
He orders his will power to receive every command
issued by him obediently, and to carry it out forthwith.
He makes faculties and limbs do his bidding without
contradiction, forbids them evil inclinations of mind and
fancy, forbids them to listen to, or believe in them, until
he has taken counsel with the intellect. If he permits
they can obey him, but not otherwise. In this way
his will power receives its orders from him, carrying them
out accordingly. He directs the organs of thought and
imagination, relieving them of all worldly ideas mentioned above, charges his imagination to produce, with
the assistance of memory, the most splendid pictures
possible, in order to resemble the divine things sought
after. Such pictures are the scenes of Sinai, Abraham
and Isaac on Moriah, the Tabernacle of Moses, the
Temple service, the presence of God in the Temple, and

the like. He, then, orders his memory to retain all
these, and not to forget them ; he warns his fancy and
its sinful prompters not to confuse the truth or to trouble
it by doubts ; he warns his irascibility and greed not to
influence or lead astray, nor to take hold of his will, nor
subdue it to wrath and lust. As soon as harmony is
restored, his will power stimulates all his organs to obey
it with alertness, pleasure, and joy. They stand without fatigue when occasion demands, they bow down
when he bids them to do so, and sit at the proper
moment. The eyes look as a servant looks at his
master, the hands drop their play and do not meet, the
feet stand straight, and all limbs are as frightened and
anxious to obey their master, paying no heed to pain or
injury. The tongue agrees with the thought, and does
not overstep its bounds, does not speak in prayer in a
mere mechanical way as the starling and the parrot,
but every word is uttered thoughtfully and attentively.
This moment forms the heart and fruit of his time,
whilst the other hours represent the way which leads to
it. He looks forward to its approach, because while it
lasts he resembles the spiritual beings, and is removed
from merely animal existence. Those three times of
daily prayer are the fruit of his day and night, and the
Sabbath is the fruit of the week, because it has been
appointed to establish the connexion with the Divine
Spirit and to serve God in joy, not in sadness, as has
been explained before. All this stands in the same
relation to the soul as food to the human body. Prayer
is for his soul what nourishment is for his body. The
blessing of one prayer lasts till the time of the next,
just as the strength derived from the morning meal lasts
till supper. The further his soul is removed from the

time of prayer, the more it is darkened by coming in contact with worldly matters. The more so, as necessity brings it into the company of youths, women, or wicked people; when one hears unbecoming and soul-darkening words and songs which exercise an attraction for his soul which he is unable to master. During prayer he purges his soul from all that passed over it, and prepares it for the future. According to this arrangement there elapses not a single week in which both his soul and body do not receive preparation. Darkening elements having increased during the week, they cannot be cleansed except by consecrating one day to service and to physical rest. The body repairs on the Sabbath the waste suffered during the six days, and prepares itself for the work to come, whilst the soul remembers its own loss through the body's companionship. He cures himself, so to speak, from a past illness, and provides himself with a remedy to ward off any future sickness. This is almost the same as Job did with his children every week, as it is written : ' It may be that my sons have sinned ' (Job i. 5). He, then, provides himself with a monthly cure, which is ' the season of atonement for all that happened during this period,' viz. the duration of the month, and the daily events, as it is written : ' Thou knowest not what a day may bring forth ' (Prov. xxvii. 1) He further attends the Three Festivals and the great Fast Day, on which some of his sins are atoned for, and on which he endeavours to make up for what he may have missed on the days of those weekly and monthly circles. His soul frees itself from the whisperings of imagination, wrath, and lust, and neither in thought or deed gives them any attention. Although his soul is unable to atone for sinful thoughts—the re-

sult of songs, tales, etc., heard in youth, and which
cling to memory—it cleanses itself from real sins,
confesses repentance for the former, and undertakes to
allow them no more to escape his tongue, much less to
put them into practice, as it is written : ' I am pur-
posed that my mouth shall not transgress ' (Ps. xvii. 3).
The fast of this day is such as brings one near to the
angels, because it is spent in humility and contrition,
standing, kneeling, praising and singing. All his physical faculties are denied their natural requirements, being
entirely abandoned to religious service, as if the animal
element had disappeared. The fast of a pious man is
such that eye, ear, and tongue share in it, that he regards
nothing except that which brings him near to God.
This also refers to his innermost faculties, such as mind
and imagination. To this he adds pious works.

6. Al Khazari : Dost thou refer to deeds generally
known ?

7. The Rabbi : The social and rational laws are those
generally known. The divine ones, however, which
were added in order that they should exist in the people
of the ' Living God ' who guides them, were not known
until they were explained in detail by Him. Even those
social and rational laws are not quite known, and though
one might know the gist of them, their scope remains
unknown. We know that the giving of comfort and the
feeling of gratitude are as incumbent on us as is chasten-
ing of the soul by means of fasting and meekness ; we
also know that deceit, immoderate intercourse with
women, and cohabitation with relatives are abominable ;
that honouring parents is a duty, etc. The limitation
of all these things to the amount of general usefulness
is God's. Human reason is out of place in matters of

divine action, on account of its incapacity to grasp
them.   Reason must rather obey, just as a sick person
must obey the physician in applying his medicines and
advice.   Consider how little circumcision has to do with
philosophy, and how small is its social influence.   Yet
Abraham, in spite of the hardship the very nature of
this command must have seemed at his age, subjected
his person and children to it, and it became the sign of
the covenant, of the attachment of the Divine Influence
to him, as it is written : ' And I will establish My covenant between me and thee and thy seed after them in
their generations, for an everlasting covenant, to be a
God unto thee . . . ' (Gen. xvii. 7).

8. Al Khazari : You accepted this command in a
proper manner indeed, and you perform it publicly with
the greatest zeal and readiness, praising it and expressing its root and origin in the formula of blessing.   Other
nations may desire to imitate you, but they only have
the pain without the joy [1a] which can only be felt by him
who remembers the cause for which he bears the pain.

9. The Rabbi : Even in other instances of imitation
no people can equal us at all.   Look at the others who
appointed a day of rest in the place of Sabbath.   Could
they contrive anything which resembles it more than
statues resemble living human bodies ?

10. Al Khazari : I have often reflected about you
and come to the conclusion that God has some secret
design in preserving you, and that He appointed the
Sabbath and holy days among the strongest means of
preserving your strength and lustre.   The nations broke
you up and made you their servants on account of your
intelligence and purity.   They would even have made
you their warriors were it not for those festive seasons

observed by you with so much conscientiousness, because they originate with God, and are based on such causes as ' Remembrance of the Creation,' ' Remembrance of the exodus from Egypt,' and ' Remembrance of the giving of the Law.' These are all divine commands, to observe which you are charged. Had these not been, not one of you would put on a clean garment ; you would hold no congregation to remember the law, on account of your everlasting affliction and degradation. Had these not been, you would not enjoy a single day in your lives. Now, however, you are allowed to spend the sixth part of life in rest of body and soul. Even kings are unable to do likewise, as their souls have no respite on their days of rest. If the smallest business calls them on that day to work and stir, they must move and stir, complete rest being denied to them. Had these laws not been, your toil would benefit others, because it would become their prey. Whatever you spend on these days is your profit for this life and the next, because it is spent for the glory of God.

11. The Rabbi : The observant among us fulfils those divine laws, viz. circumcision, Sabbath, holy days, and the accessories included in the divine law. He refrains from forbidden marriages, using mixtures in plants, clothes and animals, keeps the years of release and jubilee, avoids idolatry and its accessories, viz. discovering secrets only accessible by means of the Urim and the Thummim, or dreams. He does not listen to the soothsayer, or astrologer, or magician, augur or necromancer. He keeps the regulations concerning issue, of eating and touching unclean animals and lepers ; abstains from partaking of blood and forbidden fat, because they form part of the ' five offerings of the Lord.'

He observes the sacrifices ordained for intentional and unintentional transgressions ; the duty of redeeming the first-born of man and beast. He brings the offerings for every child born to him, and whenever he is purged from issue and leprosy ; pays the various kinds of tithes, visits the Holy Land three times in the year ; observes the rules of the Paschal lamb with all accessories, as it is ' a sacrifice of the Lord ' incumbent upon every freeborn Israelite. He observes the laws of the tabernacle, the palm branch and Shofar, and takes care of the holy and pure implements required for the offerings. He observes the sacrifices for his own purification, as also the regulation of the corner, the ' Orlah,' and [the fruits] holy to praise the Lord therewith. In short, he observes as many of the divine commands as to justify him in saying : ' I have not transgressed one of Thy commands, nor forgotten ' (Deut. xxvi. 13). There are further to be added vows and free gifts, peace offerings and self-denials. These are the religious laws, most of which are performed in connexion with the priestly service. The social laws are such as the following : ' Thou shalt not murder,' ' Thou shalt not commit adultery, steal, give false testimony against thy neighbour,' ' Honouring thy parents,' ' You shall love the stranger,' ' You shall not speak untruth and not lie ' ; such as concern the avoidance of usury, the giving of correct weights and measures ; the gleanings to be left, such as the forgotten grapes, the corners, etc. The ethical laws are : ' I am the Lord thy God,' ' Thou shalt have no other God,' and ' Thou shalt not take the name of thy God in vain,' with its corollary that God is all present, and penetrates all the secrets of man, as well as his actions and words, that he requites good and evil, and ' that the eyes of the Lord

run to and fro'(2 Chron. xvi. 9), etc. The religious person
never acts, speaks or thinks without believing that he
is observed by eyes which see and take note, which reward and punish and call to account for everything
objectionable in word and deed. In walking or sitting
he is like one afraid and timid, who is at times ashamed
of his doings ; but on the other hand he is glad and
rejoices, and his soul exults whenever he has done a good
action, as if he had shown some attention to the Lord in
enduring hardships in obedience to God. Altogether he
believes in and bears in mind the following words :
' Consider three things, and thou wilt commit no sin ;
understand what is above thee, an all-seeing eye and a
hearing ear, and all thine actions are written in a book '
(Abōth. ii. 1). He further recalls the convincing proof
adduced by David : 'He that planted the ear, shall He
not hear ; He that formed the eye, shall He not see ? '
(Ps. xciv. 9). There is also the Psalm beginning : ' O
Lord, Thou hast searched me and knowest me ' (Ps.
cxxxiv.). [When reading it,] he remembers that all his
limbs are placed with consummate wisdom, in proper
order and proportion. He sees how they obey his will,
though he know not which part of them should move.
If, for example, he wishes to rise, he finds that his limbs
have, like obedient helpers, raised his body, although he
does not even know [the nature of] these limbs. It is
the same when he wishes to sit, walk, or assumes any
position. This is expressed in the words : ' Thou
knowest my downsitting and mine uprising . . . Thou
searchest out my path and my lying down, and art
acquainted with all my ways ' (ver. 2–3). The organs of
speech are much finer and more delicate than these.
The child, as thou seest, repeats everything he hears,

without knowing with which organ, nerve, muscle he must speak. The same is the case with the organs of breathing in singing melodies. People reproduce them quite harmoniously without being aware how it was done; as if their Creator produced them ever anew and placed them in man's service. Such, indeed, is the case; at least it nearly approaches it. One must not consider the work of creation in the light of an artisan's craft. When the latter, e.g. has built a mill, he departs, whilst the mill does the work for which it was constructed. The Creator, however, creates limbs and endows them continually with their faculties. Let us imagine His solicitude and guidance removed only for one instant, and the whole world would suffer. If the religious person remembers this with every movement he first acknowledges the Creator's part in them, for having created and equipped them with the assistance necessary for their permanent perfection. This is as if the Divine Presence were with him continually, and the angels virtually accompanied him. If his piety is consistent, and he abides in places worthy of the Divine Presence, they are with Him in reality, and he sees them with his own eyes occupying a degree just below that of prophecy. Thus the most prominent of the Sages, during the time of the Second Temple, saw a certain apparition and heard a kind of voice [*Bath Qōl*]. This is the degree of the pious, next to which is that of prophets The pious man derives from his veneration of the Divine Influence, near to him, what the servant derives from his master who created him, loaded him with gifts, and watches him in order to reward or to punish him. Thou wilt not, then, find any exaggeration in the words he utters when retiring into a private

chamber : ' With your permission, O honoured ones,' in
reference to the Divine Presence ! And when he returns he recites the blessing : ' He that has created man
in wisdom.' How sublime is this formula of blessing ;
what deep meaning is in its wording for him who considers it in the right spirit ? Beginning with ' wisdom '
and concluding with the words : ' Healer of all flesh and
doer of wonders,' it furnishes a proof for the miraculous-
ness visible in the creation of living beings, endowed
with the faculties of expelling and retaining. The words
' all flesh ' encompass all living beings. In this way he
connects his mind with the Divine Influence by various
means, some of which are prescribed in the written Law,
others in tradition. He wears the phylacteries on his
head on the seat of the mind and memory, the straps
falling down on his hand, where he can see them at
leisure. The hand phylactery he wears above the mainspring of his faculties, the heart. He wears the Zīzith
lest he be entrapped by worldly thoughts, as it is
written : ' That ye may not go astray after your heart
and after your eyes ' (Num. xv. 39). Inside the phylacteries are written [verses describing His] unity, reward,
punishment, and ' the remembrance of the exodus from
Egypt,' because they furnish the irrefutable proof that
the Divine Influence is attached to mankind, and that
Providence watches them and keeps record of their deeds.
The pious man, then, examines his sensations, and devotes part of them to God. Tradition teaches that the
smallest measure of praise which it is man's duty to
offer to God, consists in a hundred blessings daily. First
among these are the ordinary ones, then he supplements them in the course of the day by the blessings
which accompany the savouring of odours, eatables and

things heard and seen. Whatever he does beyond those
is a gain, and brings him nearer to God, as David says :
' My mouth shall show forth Thy righteousness, Thy
salvation all the day, for I know not the numbers thereof ' (Ps. lxxi. 15). He means to say : Thy glory is not
comprehended by numbers, but I will devote myself to
it all my life and never be free from it. Love and fear
no doubt enter the soul by these means, and are measured with the measure of the law, lest the joy felt on
Sabbaths and holy days outstep its bounds and develop
into extravagance, debauchery and idleness, and neglect
of the hours of prayer. Fear, on the other hand, should
not go so far as to despair of forgiveness, and make him
spend all his life in dread, causing him to transgress the
command given him to feel pleasure in all that sustains
him, as it is written : ' Thou shalt rejoice in every good
thing ' (Deut. xxvi. 11). It would also diminish his
gratitude for God's bounties ; for gratitude is the effect
of joy. He, however, will be as one alluded to in the
words : ' Because thou didst not serve the Lord thy God
in joy . . . thou shalt serve thine enemies' (Deut. xxviii.
47, 49 ; Lev. xix. 17). Zeal in reproving ' thy neighbour,' and in study should not pass into wrath and
hatred, disturbing the purity of his soul during prayer.
He is deeply convinced of the ' justice of God's judgment.' He finds in it protection and solace from sorrow
and the troubles of life if he is convinced of the justice
of the Creator of all living creatures ; He who sustains
and guides them with a wisdom which the human intellect is only capable of grasping in a general way, but
not in detail. See how wonderfully conceived is the
nature of the creatures ; how many marvellous gifts
they possess which show forth the intention of an all-

wise Creator, and the will of an omniscient all-powerful
Being. He has endowed the small and the great with
all necessary internal and external senses and limbs.
He gave them organs corresponding to their instincts.
He gave the hare and stag the means of flight required
by their timid nature ; endowed the lion with ferocity
and the instruments for robbing and tearing. He who
considers the formation, use and relation of the limbs to
the animal instinct, sees wisdom in them and so perfect
an arrangement that no doubt or uncertainty can remain in his soul concerning the justice of the Creator.
When an evil thought suggests that there is injustice in
the circumstance that the hare falls a prey to the lion
or wolf, and the fly to the spider, Reason steps in warning him as follows : How can I charge the all-Wise with
injustice when I am convinced of His justice, and that
injustice is quite out of the question ? If the lion's
pursuit of the hare and the spider's of the fly were mere
accidents, I should assert the necessity of accident. I
see, however, that this wise and just Manager of the
world equipped the lion with the means for hunting,
with ferocity, strength, teeth and claws ; that He furnished the spider with cunning and taught it to weave a
net which it constructs without having learnt to do so ;
how He equipped it with the instruments required, and
appointed the fly as its food, just as many fishes serve
other fishes for food. Can I say aught but that this is
the fruit of a wisdom which I am unable to grasp, and
that I must submit to Him who is called : ' The Rock
whose doing is perfect ' (Deut. xxxii. 4). Whoever
reflects on this will do as did Nahum of Gimzō, of whom
it is related that no matter what happened to him, he
always said : ' This, too, is for the best.' [2] He will, then,

always live happily, and all tribulations will fall lightly
upon him. He will even welcome them if he is conscious of having transgressed, and will be cleansed
through them as one who has paid his debt, and is glad
of having eased his mind. He looks joyfully forward
to the reward and retribution which await him ; nay,
he enjoys affording mankind a lesson of patience and
submission to God, not less than gaining a good reputation. Thus it is with [his own troubles, and also with [3]]
those of mankind at large. If his mind is disturbed by
the length of the exile and the diaspora and degradation
of his people, he finds comfort first in ' acknowledging
the justice of the decree,' as said before ; then in being
cleansed from his sins ; then in the reward and recom-
pense awaiting him in the world to come, and the attachment to the Divine Influence in this world. If an evil
thought make him despair of it, saying : ' Can these
bones live ? ' (Ezek. xxxvii. 3)—our traces being
thoroughly destroyed and our history decayed, as it is
written : they say : ' our bones are dried ' (ibid 11)—let
him think of the manner of the delivery from Egypt and
all that is put down in the paragraph : ' For how many
favours do we owe gratitude to God ? ' [4] He will, then,
find no difficulty in picturing how we may recover our
greatness, though only one of us may have remained.
For it is written : ' Worm of Jacob '—what can remain of a man when he has become a worm in his
grave ?

12. Al Khazari : In this manner he lives a happy
life even in exile ; he gathers the fruit of his faith in this
world and the next. He, however, who bears the exile
unwillingly, loses his first and his last rewards.

13. The Rabbi : His pleasure is strengthened and

enhanced by the duty of saying blessings over everything he enjoys or which happens to him in this world.

14. Al Khazari : How can that be, are not the blessings
an additional burden ?

15. The Rabbi : Is it not beseeming that a perfect
man should find more pleasure in that which he par-
takes than a child or an animal ; even as an animal
enjoys it more than does a plant though the latter is
continually taking nourishment ?

16. Al Khazari : This is so because he is favoured
with the consciousness of enjoyment. If a drunken
person were given all he desires, whilst being completely
intoxicated, he would eat and drink, hear songs, meet
his friends, and embrace his beloved. But if told of it
when sober, he would regret it and regard it as a loss
rather than a gain, since he had all these enjoyments
whilst he was incapable of appreciating them.

17. The Rabbi : Preparing for a pleasure, experiencing
it and looking forward to it, double the feeling of enjoyment. This is the advantage of the blessings for him
who is used to say them with attention and devotion.
They produce in his soul a kind of pleasure and grati-
tune towards the Giver. He was prepared to give
them up ; now his pleasure is all the greater, and he says :
' He has kept us alive and preserved us.' He was prepared for death, now he feels gratitude for life, and
regards it as gain. Should sickness and death over-
take thee, they will be light, because thou hast communed
with thyself and seen that thou gainest with thy
Lord. According to thy nature thou art well fitted to
abjure enjoyment, since thou art dust. Now He has
presented thee with life and desire ; thou art grateful to
Him. If He takes them away, thou sayest : ' The Lord

has given, the Lord has taken.' (Job i. 21). Thus thy
whole life is one enjoyment. Whoever is unable to
pursue such a course, consider not his pleasure a human
pleasure, but a brutish one, which he does not perceive,
any more than the drunkard alluded to above. The
godly person fully grasps the meaning of each blessing,
and knows its purpose in every connexion. The blessing,
' He who created the lights,' places before his eye the
order of the upper world, the greatness of the heavenly
bodies and their usefulness, that in the eyes of their
Creator they are no greater than worms, though they
appear to us immense on account of the profit we
derive from them. The proof that He is their Creator
may be found in the circumstance already mentioned,
that His wisdom and power observable in the creation
of the ant and bee is not less than in that of the sun
and its sphere. The traces of this providence and
wisdom are finer and more wonderful in the ant and bee,
because, in spite of their minuteness, He put faculties
and organs into them. This he bears in mind lest the
light appear to him too great, and an evil genius lead
him to adopt some views of worshippers of spirits, and
make him believe that the sun and moon are able to
help or injure independently, whilst they can only
assist to do so indirectly, like the wind and fire. It is
written : ' If I behold the sun when it shines . . . and
my heart has been secretly enticed ' (Job xxxi. 26, 27).
At the blessing beginning : ' with eternal love,' he, in a
similar manner, bears in mind the attachment of the
Divine Influence to the community which was prepared to
receive it, as a smooth mirror receives the light, and that
the Law is the outcome of His will in order to establish
His sway on earth ; as it is in heaven. His wisdom did

not demand of Him to create angels on earth, but mortals
of flesh and blood, in whom natural gifts and certain
characteristics prevail according to favourable or un-
favourable influences, as this is explained in the ' Book
of Creation.'[5]   Whenever some few, or a whole community, are sufficiently pure, the divine light rests on
them and guides in an incomprehensible and miraculous
manner which is quite outside the ordinary course of
the natural world. This is called ' Love and joy."
The Divine Influence, however, found next to the stars
and spheres none who accepted his commands and who
adhered to the course He had dictated, with the exception of a few between Adam and Jacob. When
they had become a people, the Divine Influence rested
upon them out of love, 'in order to be a God unto
them.'   In the desert he arranged them in the manner
of the sphere in four standards, corresponding to the four
quarters of the sphere, and in twelve tribes, corresponding to the twelve signs of the zodiac, the camp of the
Levites being in the centre, just as it is stated in the
' Book of Creation.'   ' The holy Temple is exactly in
the centre, but God carries them all.'   All this points
to ' love ' for the sake of which the blessing is recited.
In the reading of the Shema, which then follows, he
accepts the obligations of the Law, as in the piece
beginning ' True and certain,' which expresses the firm
resolution to observe the Tōrāh. This is as if, after
having clearly and unmistakably imbibed all that
preceded, he binds his soul and testifies that the children
should submit to the Law for ever, just as the forefathers
had done, according to the words : ' Upon our fathers,
and upon us, and our children and our (coming)
generations . . . a good word, firmly established, that

never passes away.' To this he attaches these articles
of creed which complete the Jewish belief, viz. the
recognition of God's sovereignty, His eternity, and the
providential care which He bestowed on our forefathers ;
that the Tōrāh emanated from Him, and that the proof
for all this is to be found in the delivery from Egypt.
This is alluded to in the words : ' It is true that Thou art
the Lord our God ; truly from everlasting is Thy name
. . . the help of our fathers . . . from Egypt didst Thou
redeem us.' He who unites all this in pure thought is a
true Israelite and worthy of aspiring to the Divine
Influence which among all nations was exclusively connected with the children of Israel. He finds no difficulty in standing before the Divine Presence, and he
receives an answer as often as he asks. The prayer of
the ' Eighteen Benedictions ' must follow the blessing
' He has redeemed Israel' immediately and promptly,
standing upright for this prayer in the condition described previously, when we discussed the blessings which
relate to the whole Israelitish nation. Prayers of more
individual character are voluntary and not incumbent,
and they have their place in the paragraph ending, ' He
who hears the prayer.' In the first paragraph, entitled,
' Fathers,' [5a] the worshipper remembers the piety of the
Patriarchs, the establishment of the covenant with them
on the part of God for all times, which never ceases,
as is expressed in the words : ' He brings the Redeemer
to their children's children.' The second blessing,
known as ' Mighty Deeds,' teaches that God's is the
eternal rule of the world, not however, as natural
philosophers assert, that this is done by natural and
empirical means. The worshipper is further reminded
that He ' revives the dead ' whenever He desires, how-

ever far this may be removed from the speculation of
natural philosophers. Similar ideas prevail in the
words : ' He causes the wind to blow, and the rain to
descend.' According to His desire He ' delivers those in
bondage,' as may be established by instances from the
history of Israel. Having read these paragraphs which
enlighten him in the belief that God keeps up a connexion
with this material world, the worshipper extols and
sanctifies Him by the declaration that no corporeal
attitude appertains to Him. This is done in the paragraph beginning : ' Thou art holy,' a blessing which
inculcates belief in the attributes of sublimity and
holiness commented upon by philosophers. This paragraph follows the others in which the absoluteness of
God's sovereignty is laid down. They convince us that
we have a King and Lawgiver, and without them we
had lived in doubt, the theories of philosophers
and materialists. The paragraphs of ' Fathers ' and
' Mighty Deeds,' must therefore precede that of the
' sanctification of God.' After this the worshipper
begins to pray for the wants of the whole of Israel, and
it is not permissible to insert other prayers except in
the place of voluntary supplications. A prayer, in
order to be heard, must be recited *for* a multitude, or
in a multitude or, for an individual who could take the
place of a multitude. None such, however, is to be found
in our age.

18. Al Khazari : Why is this ? If every one read
his prayers for himself, would not his soul be purer
and his mind less abstracted ?

19. The Rabbi : Common prayer has many advantages. In the first instance a community will never
pray for a thing which is hurtful for the individual,

whilst the latter sometimes prays for something [to
the disadvantage of other individuals, or some of them
may pray for something] [6] that is to *his* disadvantage.
One of the conditions of prayer, craving to be heard, is
that its object be profitable to the world, but not hurtful
in any way.   Another is that an individual rarely
accomplishes his prayer without slips and errors.   It
has been laid down, therefore, that the individual
recite the prayers of a community, and if possible in a
community of not less than ten persons, so that one
makes up for the forgetfulness or error of the other.   In
this way [a complete prayer is gained, read with un-
alloyed devotion.   Its blessing rests on everyone] [7]
each receiving his portion.   For the Divine Influence
is as the rain which waters an area (if deserving of it),
and includes some smaller portion which does not
deserve it, but shares the general abundance.   On the
other hand, the rain is withheld from an area which does
not deserve it, although some portion is included which
did deserve it, but suffers with the majority.   This is
how God governs the world.   He reserves the reward of
every individual for the world to come ; but in this
world He gives him the best compensation, granting
salvation in contradiction to His neighbours.   There
are but few who completely escape the general retribution.   A person who prays but for himself is like
him who retires alone into his house, refusing to assist
his fellow-citizens in the repair of their walls.   His
expenditure is as great as his risk.   He, however, who
joins the majority spends little, yet remains in safety,
because one replaces the defects of the other.   The city
is in the best possible condition, all its inhabitants enjoying its prosperity with but little expenditure, which all

share alike.   In a similar manner, Plato styles that which
is expended on behalf of the law, ' the portion of the
whole.' [7a]   If the individual, however, neglects this
' portion of the whole ' which is the basis of the welfare
of the commonwealth of which he forms a part, in the
belief that he does better in spending it on himself,
sins against the commonwealth, and more against himself.   For the relation of the individual is as the relation
of the single limb to the body.   Should the arm, in case
bleeding is required, refuse its blood, the whole body,
the arm included, would suffer.   It is, however, the
duty of the individual to bear hardships, or even death,
for the sake of the welfare of the commonwealth.   He
must particularly be careful to contribute his ' portion
of the whole,' without fail.   Since ordinary speculation
did not institute this, God prescribed it in tithes, gifts,
and offerings, etc., as a ' portion of the whole ' of
worldly property.   Among *actions* this is represented
by Sabbath, holy days, years of release and jubilee
and similar institutions ; among *words* it is prayers,
blessings and thanksgivings ; among *abstract* things
it is love, fear and joy.   The first place [of the second
group of blessings] is very appropriately given to the
prayer for intelligence and enlightenment to obey God.
Man prays to be brought near to his Master.   He,
therefore, says first :[8] ' Thou graciously givest reason to
man,' which is immediately followed by ' He who takes
delight in repentance.'   Thus ' wisdom,' ' knowledge '
and ' intelligence ' move in the path of the Law and
worship in the words : ' Restore us, O our Father, to
Thy Law.'   Since mortal man cannot help sinning, a
prayer is required for forgiveness of transgressions in
thought and deed.   This is done in the formula end-

ing : ' the Merciful who forgiveth much.' To this paragraph he adds the result and sign of forgiveness, viz. the redemption from our present condition. He begins : ' Behold our misery,' and concludes : ' Redeemer of Israel.' After this he prays for the health of body and soul, and for the bestowal of food to keep up the strength in the blessing of the ' years.' Then he prays for the reunion of the scattered, in the paragraph ending : ' He who gathers together the scattered of His people of the house of Israel.' With this is connected the re-appearance of justice and restoration of the former condition [of the people] in the words : ' Rule over us Thou alone.' He, then, prays against evil and the destruction of the thorns in the paragraph of the ' heretics.' This is followed by the prayer for the preservation of the pure essence in : ' The just.' He, then, prays for the return to Jerusalem which again is to form the seat of the Divine Influence, and with this is connected the prayer concerning the Messiah, the son of David. This concludes all worldly wants. He now prays for the acceptance of his prayer, as well as for the visible revelation of the Shekhinah, just as appeared to the prophets, pious, and those who were delivered from Egypt, in the paragraph ending : ' O Thou who hearest prayer.' Then he prays : ' Let mine eye behold,' and concludes : ' He who restores His Shekhinah to Zion.' He imagines the Shekhinah standing opposite to him and bows down with the words : ' We give thanks,' which contain the acknowledgment and gratitude for God's mercy. The whole concludes with the paragraph : ' He maketh peace,' in order to take leave from the Shekhinah in peace.

20. Al Khazari : There is nothing to criticise, as I see how settled and circumspect all these arrangements are.

There was one point to be mentioned, viz. that your prayers say so little of the world to come. But thou hast already proved to me that he who prays for attachment to the Divine Light, and the faculty of seeing it with his own eyes in this world, and who, nearly approaching the rank of prophets, is thus engaged in prayer—and nothing can bring man nearer to God than this—has without doubt prayed for more than the world to come. He gains it with the other. He whose soul is in contact with the Divine Influence, though still exposed to the accidents and sufferings of the body, it stands to reason that it will gain a more intimate connexion with the former, when it has become free and detached from this unclean vessel.

21. The Rabbi : I can explain this better to thee by a parable. A man visited the king. The latter accorded him his most intimate friendship, and permitted him to enter his presence whenever he wished. He became so familiar with the king that he invited him to his house and table. The king not only consented, but sent his noblest veziers to him and did to him what he had done to no one else. Whenever he had neglected something, or had done something wrong, and the king kept aloof from him, he only entreated him to return to his former custom, and not to forbid his veziers to come and see him. The other inhabitants of the country only craved the king's protection when they undertook a journey, against robbers, wild beasts, and the terrors of the road. They were confident that the king would assist and take care of them during their journey, although he had never done so as long as they remained at home. Each of them boasted that the king cared for him more than for anybody else, thinking he had honoured the

king more than anybody else.   The stranger, however,
thought little of his departure, nor did he ask for a guard.
When the hour arrived he was told that he would perish
in the dangers of the journey since he had no one to take
care of him.   ' Who gave you companions ? ' asked he.
' The king ' said they, ' whom we have petitioned for
assistance ever since we have been in this city ; ' but
we have not seen thee do likewise.'   ' You fools,'
answered he ; ' is a person who called on him in the hour
of safety not more entitled to expect his assistance in
the hour of danger, though he did not open his mouth ?
Will he refuse his assistance to a man in the time of need
after having responded to him during his prosperity ?
If you boast that he takes care of you because you have
shown him honour, has anyone of you done so much
in this respect, took so much trouble in the execution of
his commands, in keeping aloof from dishonour, in
respecting his name and code as I did ?   Whatever I
did, I did at his command and instruction.   As to you,
you honour him according to your own conception and
fancy, yet he fails you not.   How can he, now, leave me,
if I am in need, during my journey, because, trusting his
justice, I did not speak to him of it as you have done.'
This parable is only meant for those who depart from the
right course, and do not accept the words of the Sages.[8]
But apart from this, our prayers are full of allusions of
the world to come, and the utterances of the Sages, which
are handed down from the Prophets, are studded with
descriptions of Paradise and Gehinnōm, as explained
before.[9]   Now I have sketched out to thee the conduct of
a religious person in the present time, and thou canst
imagine what it was like in that happy time and that
divine place amidst the people whose roots were

Abraham, Isaac and Jacob. They represent the
essence of the latter, men and women distinguished by
virtue, suffering nothing unbecoming to pass their
lips. The godly man moves about among them, but
his soul is not polluted by the improper words which he
may hear, nor does any impurity adhere to his garment
or dress from issue, or vermin, or corpses, or leprosy,
etc., because they all live in holiness and purity. This
is in a greater measure the case in the land of the
Shekhinah, where he only meets people who occupy the
degree of holiness, as Priest, Levites, Nazirites, Sages,
Prophets, Judges and Overseers. Or he sees ' a multitude that kept holiday with the voice of joy and praise '
(Ps. xlii. 5), on the ' three festivals in the year.' He
only hears the ' Song of the Lord,' only sees the ' Work
of the Lord,' particularly if he is a priest or Levite who
lives on the bread of the Lord and, like Samuel, lives
in the ' House of the Lord ' from his infancy. He
need not seek any livelihood, as his whole life is devoted
to the ' Service of the Lord.' How does his work and
the purity and excellence of his soul appear to
thee ?

22. Al Khazari : This is the highest degree, above
which there is none but the angelic one. Such a mode
of life entitles man to the prophetic afflatus, particularly
there where the Shekhinah dwells. A religion of this
kind can do without ascetic or monastic retirement.
Now I request thee to give me an outline of the doctrine
of the Karaites. For I see that they are much more
zealous believers than the Rabbanites, and their arguments are, as I perceive, more striking and in harmony
with the Tōrāh.

23. The Rabbi : Did we not state before that specu-

lation, reasoning and fiction on the Law do not lead to
the pleasure of God ?   Otherwise dualists, materialists,
worshippers of spirits, anchorites, and those who burn
their children are all endeavouring to come near to God ?
We have, however, said, that one cannot approach God
except by His commands. For he knows their com-
prehensiveness, division, times, and places, and consequences in the fulfilment of which the pleasure of God
and the connexion with the Divine Influence are to
be gained. Thus it was in the building of the Tabernacle. With every item it is said : ' And Bezaleel made
the ark . . ., the lid . . ., the carpets . . . ,' and
concerning each of them is stated : ' Just as the Lord
had commanded Moses.' This means neither too much
nor too little, although our speculation cannot
bear on works of this kind.   Finally it is said :
' And Moses saw the whole work, and behold they
had performed it just as the Lord had commanded,
thus they worked, and Moses blessed them ' (Exod.
xxxix. 43). The completion of the Tabernacle was
followed by the descent of the Shekhinah, the two
conditions which form the pillars of the Law having
been fulfilled, viz., firstly, that the Law originated
with God ; secondly, that the people conformed with
it in a pure mind. God commanded the building
of the Tabernacle, and the whole people obeyed
—as it is said ' Of every man that giveth it willingly
with his heart, shall ye take My offering ' (chap. xxv.
2)—with the greatest zeal and enthusiasm. The result was equally perfect, viz. the appearance of the
Shekhinah, as it is said : ' And I will dwell in their midst.'
I gave thee the example of the creation of the plant and
animal, and told thee that the form which distinguishes

one plant from another and one animal from another is
not a natural force [but a work of God, called nature by
philosophers.   As a matter of fact the powers of nature][10]
are capable of favouring such a development according
to the proportion of heat and cold, moisture and dryness.   One thing would, then, become a plant, another
a vine, this a horse, that a lion.   We are unable to
determine these proportions, and could we do it, we
might produce blood or milk, etc. from liquids mixed
by our own calculations.   We might, eventually, create
living beings, endowed with the spirit of life.   Or we
might produce a substitute for bread from ingredients
which have no nourishing powers, simply by mixing the
right proportions of heat and cold, moisture and dryness,
and particularly if we knew the spherical constellations and their influences which, in the opinion of
astrologers, assist to bring forth of anything that is
desired in this world.   We have seen, however, that
all alchymists and necromancers who have tried those
things, have been put to shame.   Do not raise the
objection that these people are able to produce animals
and living beings, as bees from flesh and gnats from
wine.   These are not the consequences of their calculations and agency, but of experiments.   It was found
that cohabitation was followed by the birth of a
child ; man, however, does but plant the seed in
the soil prepared to receive and develop it.   The
calculation of proportions which give the human form
belongs exclusively to the Creator.   In the same
manner is the determination of the living people
worthy to form the seat of the Divine Influence God's
alone.   This calculating and weighing must be learnt
from Him, but we should not reason about His word, as

it is written : ' There is no wisdom nor understanding
nor counsel against the Lord ' (Prov. xxi. 30). What
dost thou think we should adopt in order to become
like our fathers, to imitate them, and not to speculate
about the Law ?

24. Al Khazari : We can only accomplish this through
the medium of their traditional teachings, by the support
of their deeds, and by endeavouring to find one who is
regarded as an authority by one generation, and capable
of handing down the history of another.   The latter
generation, however, cannot, on account of the multitude of its individuals, be suspected of having made a
general agreement to carry the Law with its branches
and interpretations unaltered from Moses downward
either in their memories or in a volume.

25. The Rabbi : What wouldst thou think if difference were found in one or two copies ?

26. Al Khazari : [One must study several copies,[11]]
the majority of which cannot be faulty. The minority
can, then, be neglected. The same process applies to
traditions. If the minority differs, we turn to the
majority.

27. The Rabbi : Now, what is thy opinion if in
the manuscripts a letter were found which is in contrast to common sense, e.g. *ṣādū* (Lam. iv. 18), where
we should expect *ṣārū*,[12] and *nafshī* (Ps. xxiv. 4), where
we should read *nafshō* ?

28. Al Khazari : Common sense would in these and
other cases alter in all volumes, first the letters, then the
words, then the construction, then the vowels and accents, and consequently also the sense. There are many
verses to which the reader can give an opposite meaning
by altering the place of any of these appositives.

29. The Rabbi : In which form did Moses leave his
book to the Israelites in thy opinion ?

30. Al Khazari : Undoubtedly without either vowels
or accents, just as our scrolls are written. There was as
little agreement possible among the people [13] on this
point, as on the unleavened bread, or Passover, or other
laws which were given as a ' remembrance of the delivery
from Egypt.' These laws confirm in the minds of the
Israelites the historical truth of the exodus from Egypt
by means of the recurring ceremonies, which could
not possibly be the result of common agreement without
causing contradiction.

31. The Rabbi : There is, therefore, no doubt that the
Book was preserved in memory with all its vowels,
divisions of syllables and accents : by the priests, because they required them for the Temple service, and in
order to teach the people ; by the kings, because they
were commanded : ' And it shall be with him and he
shall read therein all the days of his life ' (Deut. xvii. 19).
The judges had to know it to enable them to give judgment ; the members of the Sanhedrion, because they were
warned : ' Keep therefore and do them, for this is your
wisdom and understanding ' (Deut. iv. 6) ; the pious, in
order to receive reward ; and, finally, the hypocrites, to
acquire a good name. The seven vowels and accents
were appointed as signs for forms which were regarded
as Mosaic tradition. Now, how have we to judge those
persons who first divided the text into verses, equipped
it with vowel signs, accents, and masoretic signs, concerning full or defective orthography ; and counted the
letters with such accuracy that they found out that the
gimel of *gāhōn* [14] (Lev. xi. 42) stood right in the middle
of the Tōrāh, and kept a record of all irregular vowels ?

Dost thou consider this work either superfluous or idle, or dutiful zeal ?

32. Al Khazari : The latter no doubt. It was to serve as a fence round the law in order to leave no room for alterations. Moreover, it is a great science. The system of vowel signs and accents reveals an order which could only emanate from divinely-instilled notions, quite out of proportion to our knowledge. It can only have been received from a community of favoured ones or a single individual of the same stamp. In the latter case it must have been a prophet, or a person assisted by the Divine Influence. For a scholar who lacks this assistance can be challenged by another scholar to adopt his views in preference.

33. The Rabbi : The acknowledgment of tradition is therefore incumbent upon us as well as upon the Kara- ites, as upon anyone who admits that the Tōrāh, in its present shape and as it is read, is the Tōrāh of Moses.

34. Al Khazari : This is exactly what the Karaites say. But as they have the complete Tōrāh, they con- sider the tradition superfluous.

35. The Rabbi : Far from it. If the consonantic text of the Mosaic Book requires so many traditional classes of vowel signs, accents, divisions of sentences and masoretic signs for the correct pronunciation of words, how much more is this the case for the comprehension of the same ? The meaning of a word is more comprehensive than its pronunciation. When God revealed the verse : ' This month shall be unto you the beginning of months ' (Exod. xii. 2), there was no doubt whether He meant the calendar of the Copts—or rather the Egyptians— among whom they lived, or that of the Chaldæans who were Abraham's people in Ur-Kasdim ; or solar [or

lunar months], [16] or lunar years, which are made to
agree with solar years, as is done in embolismic years.
I wish the Karaites could give me a satisfactory answer
to questions of this kind. I would not hesitate to adopt
their view, as it pleases me to be enlightened. I further
wish to be instructed on the question as to what makes
an animal lawful for food; whether 'slaughtering'
means cutting its throat or any other mode of killing;
why killing by gentiles makes the flesh unlawful; what
is the difference between slaughtering, skinning, and the
rest of it. I should desire an explanation of the forbidden fat, seeing that it lies in the stomach and entrails
close to the lawful fat, as well as of the rules of cleansing
the meat. Let them draw me the line between the fat
which is lawful and that which is not, inasmuch as there is
no difference visible. Let them explain to me where the
tail of the sheep, which they declare unlawful, ends.
One of them may possibly forbid the end of the tail
alone, another the whole hind part. I desire an explanation of the lawful and unlawful birds, excepting
the common ones, such as the pigeon and turtle dove.
How do they know that the hen, goose, duck, and par-
tridge are not unclean birds ? I further desire an explanation of the words : ' Let no man go out of his place
[on the seventh day]' (Exod. xvi. 29). Does this refer to
the house or precincts, estate—where he can have many
houses—territory, district, or country. For the word
place can refer to all of these. I should, further, like to
know where the prohibition of work on the Sabbath
commences ? Why pens and writing material are not ad-
missible in the correction of a scroll of the Law (on this
day), but lifting a heavy book, or a table, or eatables,
entertaining guests and all cares of hospitality should

be permitted, although the guests would be resting, and
the host be kept employed ? This applies even
more to women and servants, as it is written : ' That
thy manservant and thy maidservant rest as well as
thou ' (Deut. v. 14). Wherefore it is forbidden to ride
[on the Sabbath] horses belonging to gentiles, or to
trade. Then, again, I wish to see a Karaite give judgment between two parties according to the chapters
Exodus xxi. and Deuteronomy xxi. 10 sqq. For that
which appears plain in the Tōrāh, is yet obscure, and
much more so are the obscure passages, because the oral
supplement was relied upon. I should wish to hear the
deductions he draws from the case of the daughters of
Zelophehād to questions of inheritance in general. I want
to know the details of circumcision, fringes and tabernacle ;
why it is incumbent on him to say prayers ; whence
he derives his belief in reward and punishment in the
world after death ; how to deal with laws which interfere
with each other, as circumcision or Paschal lamb with
Sabbath, which must yield to which, and many other matters which cannot be enumerated in general, much less in
detail. Hast thou ever heard, O King of the Khazars,
that the Karaites possess a book which contains a fixed
tradition on one of the subjects just mentioned, and
which allows no differences on readings, vowel signs,
accents, or lawful or unlawful matters, or decisions ?

36. Al Khazari : I have neither seen anything of the
kind, nor heard about it. I see, nevertheless, that they
are very zealous.

37. The Rabbi : This, as I have already told thee,
belongs in the province of speculative theory. Those
who speculate on the ways of glorifying God for the
purpose of His worship, are much more zealous than

those who practise the service of God exactly as it is
commanded. The latter are at ease with their tradition, and their soul is calm like one who lives in a town,
and they fear not any hostile opposition. The former,
however, is like a straggler in the desert, who does not
know what may happen. He must provide himself with
arms and prepare for battle like one expert in warfare.
Be not, therefore, astonished to see them so energetic,
and do not lose courage if thou seest the followers of
tradition, I mean the Rabbanites, falter. The former
look for a fortress where they can entrench themselves,
whilst the latter lie down on their couches in a place
well fortified of old.

38. Al Khazari : All thou sayest is convincing, because the Law enjoins that there shall be ' one Tōrāh
and one statute.' Should Karaite methods prevail there
would be as many different codes as opinions. Not
one individual would remain constant to one code.
For every day he forms new opinions, increases his knowledge, or meets with someone who refutes him with some
argument and converts him to his views. But whenever we find them agreeing, we know that they follow
the tradition of one or many of their ancestors. In such
a case we should not believe their views, and say : ' How
is it that you agree concerning this regulation, whilst
reason allows the word of God to be interpreted in
various ways ? ' If the answer be that this was the
opinion of Anan,[17] or Benjamin,[18] Saul,[19], or others,
then they admit the authority of tradition received from
people who lived before them, and of the best tradition,
viz. that of the Sages. For they were many, whilst
those Karaite teachers were but single individuals. The
view of the Rabbis is based on the tradition of the Pro-

phets; the other, however, on speculation alone. The
Sages are in concord, the Karaites in discord. The
sayings of the Sages originate with 'the place which
God shall choose,' and we must therefore accept even
their individual opinions. The Karaites have nothing of
the kind. I wish I knew their answer regarding the calculation of the new moon.[20] I see that their authorities
follow Rabbanite practice in the intercalation of Adar.
Nevertheless they taunt the Rabbanites, when the Tishri
new moon appears, with the question: ' How could it
happen that you [once] kept the fast of the day of
Atonement on the *ninth* of Tishri ? ' [21] Are they not
ashamed not to know, when intercalating, whether the
month is Ellul or Tishri; or Tishri or Marḥeshwān, if
they do not intercalate ? They ought rather to say:
' I am drowning, but fear not the wet ! ' [22] We do not
know whether the month is Tishri, Marḥeshwān, or
Ellul. How can we criticise those in whose steps we
follow, and whose teachings we adopt,[23] and ask: Do you
fast on the ninth or tenth of Tishri ?

39. The Rabbi: Our law is linked to the ' ordination
given to Moses on Sinai,' or sprung ' from the place
which the Lord shall choose ' (Is. ii. 3), ' for from Zion
goes forth the Law, and the word of God from Jerusalem.' Its mediators were the Judges, Overseers,
Priests, and the members of the Synhedrion. It is
incumbent upon us to obey the Judge appointed for the
time being, as it is written: ' Or to the judge who will
be in those days . . . and thou shalt inquire, and they
shall tell thee the sentence of judgment, and thou shalt
do according to the word which they tell thee . . .
from the place which the Lord shall choose . . . and
thou shall take heed to do according to all they teach

thee' (Deut. xvii. 9 sqq.). Further : 'The man who
doeth presumptuously not to listen to the priest . . .
this man shall die, and thou shalt remove the evil from
thy midst.' Disobedience to the Priest or Judge is
placed on a par with the gravest transgressions, in the
words : 'Thou shalt remove the evil from thy midst.'
This concludes with the words : 'And all the people
shall hear and fear, and do no more presumptuously.'
This refers to the time when the order of the Temple
service and the Synhedrion, and the sections [of the
Levites], who completed the organization, were still
intact, and the Divine Influence was undeniably among
them either in the form of prophecy or inspiration, as
was the case during the time of the second Temple.
Among these persons no agreement or convention was
possible. In a similar manner arose the duty of reading
the Book of Esther on Purim, and the ordination of
Ḥanuccah, and we can say : 'He who has commanded
us to read the Megillāh' and 'to kindle the light of
Ḥanuccah,' or 'to complete' or 'to read' the Hallēl,[24]
'to wash the hands,' 'the ordination of the Erūb,' and
the like. Had our traditional customs arisen after the
exile, they could not have been called by this name, nor
would they require a blessing, but there would be a
regulation or rather a custom. The bulk of our laws,
however, derives its origin from Moses, as an 'ordination given to Moses from Sinai.' This also explains how
a people obtained during forty years sufficient food and
clothing, in spite of their large number. Moses was with
them, and the Shekhinah did not forsake them, giving
them general as well as special laws. Is it not absurd
to assume that they refrained from inquiring occasionally
into the details, and handing down their explanations

and subdivisions ?   Take the verse : ' And I will make
known the laws of God and His statutes ' (Exod. xviii. 16),
which is supplemented by the other : ' For this is your
wisdom and understanding in the eyes of the nations,
which shall hear all these laws, and they will say, surely
this great nation is a wise and understanding people '
(Deut. iv. 6).   He who wishes to gainsay this verse may
look at the Karaites ; but he who desires to confirm it,
let him behold the branches of knowledge embodied in
the Talmud, which form only a small portion of the
natural, metaphysical, mathematical, and astronomical
studies [in which the Sages indulged].   He will, then,
see that they deserve praise above all nations for their
learning.   Some of our laws originate, in certain circumstances mentioned before, ' from the place which
the Lord shall choose.'   Prophecy lasted about forty
years of the second Temple.[25]   Jeremiah, in his prophetic speeches, commended the people of the second
Temple for their piety, learning, and fear of God (chap.
xxix. 10 sqq.).   If we did not rely on men like these, on
whom should we rely ?   We see that prescriptions given
after Moses' death became law.   Thus Solomon hallowed :
' The middle of the court ' (1 Kings viii. 64 sq.), slaugh-
tered sacrifices on a place other than the altar, and
celebrated ' the feast seven days and seven days.'
David and Samuel appointed the order of the Temple
choir, which became a fixed law.   Solomon added to
the sanctuary built in the desert, and omitted from it.[26]
Ezra imposed the tax of one-third of a shekel on the
community of the second Temple (Neh. x. 33).   A
stone paving was put in the place of the Ark, hiding
it behind a curtain, because they knew that the Ark had
been buried there.[27]

40. Al Khazari : How·could this be made to agree with the verse : ' Thou shalt not add thereto, nor diminish from it ? ' (Deut. xiii. 1).

41. The Rabbi : This was only said to the masses, that they should not conjecture and theorise, and contrive laws according to their own conception, as the Karaites do. They were recommended to listen to the post-Mosaic prophets, the priests and judges, as it is written : ' I will raise them up a prophet . . . and he shall speak unto them all that I shall command him ' (Deut. xviii. 18). With regard to the priests and judges it is said that their decisions are binding. The words : ' You shall not add,' etc., refer to ' that which I commanded you through Moses ' and any ' prophet from among thy brethren ' who fulfils the conditions of a prophet. They further refer to regulations laid down in common by priests and judges ' from the place which thy Lord shall choose.' For they have divine assistance, and would never, on account of their large number, concur in anything which contradicts the Law. Much less likelihood was there of erroneous views, because they had inherited vast learning, for the reception of which they were naturally endowed. The members of the Synhedrion, as is known by tradition, had to possess a thorough acquaintance with all branches of science.[28] Prophecy had scarcely ceased, or rather the *Bath Qōl*, which took its place. Now, suppose we allow the Karaite interpretation of the sentence ' From the morrow of the Sabbath till the morrow of the Sabbath ' (Lev. xxiii. 11, 15, 16) to refer to the Sunday. But we reply that one of the judges, priests, or pious kings, in agreement with the Synhedrion and all Sages, found that this period was fixed with the intention of creating

an interval of fifty days between ' the first fruits of the
harvest of barley and the harvest of wheat,' and to
observe ' seven weeks,' which are ' seven complete
Sabbaths.' The first day of the week is only mentioned
for argument's sake in the following manner : should
the day of ' putting the sickle to the corn ' be a Sunday,
you count till Sunday. From this we conclude that
should the beginning be on a Monday, we count till
Monday. The date of putting the sickle, from which
we count, is left for us to fix. This was fixed for the
second day of Passover, which does not contradict the
Tōrāh, since it originated with ' the place which the
Lord shall choose ' on the conditions discussed before.
Perhaps this was done under the influence of divine
inspiration. It was quite possible, and it saves us from
the confusion of those who endeavour to cause confusion.

42. Al Khazari : With these broad and irrefutable
declarations thou hast cut off, O Rabbi, some minor
points which I had in my mind to urge on behalf of the
Karaite interpretation, by which I hoped to silence
thee.

43. The Rabbi : If the general principles are obvious
to thee do not mind minor details. The latter are often
subject to error, and owing to their wide ramification,
know no bounds, and lead astray those who regard them
from different points of view. A person who is convinced of the justice of the Creator and His all-embracing
wisdom will pay no attention to apparent cases of injustice on earth, as it is written : ' If thou seest the
oppression of the poor and violent perverting of judgment and justice in a province, marvel not at the matter '
(Eccl. v. 1). Whoever is convinced of the duration of
the soul after the destruction of the body, as well as of

its incorporeal nature and of its being as far removed
from corporeality as the angels are, will pay no attention
to the idea that the activity of the soul is stopped during
sleep or illness which submerges the mental powers,
that it is subject to the vicissitudes of the body, and
similar disquieting ideas.

44. Al Khazari : Yet I am not satisfied as long as I
leave those details undiscussed, though I have admitted
those general principles.

45. The Rabbi : Say what thou wilt.

46. Al Khazari : Does not our Tōrāh teach retaliation, viz. ' eye for eye, tooth for tooth, as he hath caused
a blemish in man, so shall be done to him ' (Lev. xxiv.
20) ?

47. The Rabbi : And is it not said immediately afterwards : ' And he that killeth a beast shall make it good,
life for life ' ? (ver. 18, cf. 21).   Is this not the principle
of ransom ?   It is not said : ' If anyone kills thy horse,
kill his horse,' but ' take his horse, for what use is it to
thee to kill his horse ? '   Likewise : If anyone has cut
off thy hand, take the value of his hand ; for cutting off
his hand profits thee not.   The sentence : ' Wound for
wound and stripe for stripe ' (Exod. xxi. 25), embodies
ideas antagonistic to common sense.   How can we determine such a thing ?   One person may die from a wound,
whilst another person may recover from the same.   How
can we gauge whether it is the same ?   How can we
take away the eye of a one-eyed person in order to do
justice to a person with two eyes, when the former would
be totally blind, the latter still have one eye ?   The
Tōrāh teaches : As he hath caused a blemish in man, so
shall be done to him.   What further need is there to
discuss these details, when we have just set forth the

necessity of tradition, the truthfulness, loftiness, and religious zeal of traditionists ?

48. Al Khazari : For all that, I am surprised that you observe the regulations of religious purity.

49. The Rabbi : Impurity and holiness are contradictory ideas ; one cannot be thought of without the other. Without holiness we should not know the signification of impurity. Impurity means that the approach to holy objects, hallowed by God, is forbidden to the person so affected. Such would be priests, their food, clothing, offering, sacrifices, the holy House, etc. In the same way the ideas of holiness include something which forbids the person connected with it to approach many ordinary objects. This chiefly depends on the vicinity of the Shekhinah, which we now lack entirely. The prohibition which still holds good, of cohabiting with a woman in her period or after confinement has nothing to do with impurity, but is an independent divine law. The practice we observe to keep aloof from them as much as possible is but a restriction and hedge to prevent cohabitation. The regulations of impurity proper ceased to exist for us, because we live in ' an unclean land and in unclean air,' especially as we move about among graves, vermin, lepers, persons affected with issue, corpses, etc. To touch carrion is not forbidden on account of its impurity, but it forms a special law connected with the prohibition of eating the same to which impurity is accessory. If Ezra had not ordained a bath for certain contaminated persons, this would not be a regulation but simply a matter of cleanliness. If these persons would conceive this regulation in the sense of cleanliness, it would lose nothing, as long as it is not taken for a religious law.

Otherwise they might draw conclusions from their own folly, try to improve upon the law and cause heterodoxy, I mean the splitting of opinions, which is the beginning of the corruption of a religion. They would soon be outside the pale of ' one law and one regulation.' Whatever we might allow ourselves in matters of touching even repulsive things, is out of proportion to their (the Karaites) schismatic views, which might cause us to find in one house ten persons with as many different opinions. Were our laws not fixed and confined in unbreakable rules, they would not be secure from the intrusion of strange elements and the loss of some component parts, because argument and taste would become guiding principles. The Karaite would have no compunction in using the implements of idolatry, such as gold, silver, frankincense and wine. Indeed, death is better than this. On the other hand, he would abstain from using parts of the pig, even for purposes of medicine, although this is in reality one of the lighter transgressions, and only punished with ' forty stripes.' In the same way he would allow the Nazirite to eat raisins and grapes rather than be intoxicated with mead and cider. But the opposite is true. This prohibition only refers to the products of the vine, but there was no intention of prohibiting intoxication altogether, as one might surmise. This is one of the secrets known only to God, his prophets and the pious. One must not, however, charge traditionists or those who draw their own conclusions, with ignorance in this matter, because the word *shēkhār* is common property. They have a tradition that the ' wine and strong drink ' (Lev. x. 8), mentioned in connexion with the priests includes all kinds of intoxication, whilst the same words

in the case of the Nazirite only refer to the juice of
grapes. Every law has certain limits fixed with scientific accuracy, though in practice they may appear il-
logical. He who is zealous tries to avoid them, without,
however, making them unlawful, as e.g. the flesh of an
animal in peril of death, which is lawful. For it is
uncertain whether this animal will die, because some
one might assert that it will recover, and then be permitted. A diseased animal which externally looks in
good health is unlawful, if it suffers internally from an
incurable illness, with which it can neither live nor
recover. Those who judge according to their own
taste and reasoning may arrive in these matters at an
opposite conclusion. Follow not, therefore, thy own
taste and opinion in religious questions, lest they throw
thee into doubts, which lead to heresy. Nor wilt thou
be in harmony with one of thy friends on any point.
Every individual has his own taste and opinion. It is
only necessary to examine the roots of the traditional
and written laws with the inferences codified for practice,
in order to trace the branches back to the roots. Where
they lead thee, there put thy faith, though thy mind
and feeling shrink from it. Common view and assumption deny the non-existence of the vacuum, whilst
logical conclusion rejects its existence. Appearance
denies the infinite divisibility of a body, whilst logic
makes it an axiom. Appearance denies that the earth
is a globe and the one hundred and sixtieth [28a] part of
the sun disc. There are also other matters which astronomy establishes against mere appearances. Whatever
the Sages declared lawful they did neither in obedience
to their own taste or inclination, but to the results of
the inherited knowledge, handed down to them. The

same was the case with what they declared unlawful.
He who is unable to grasp their wisdom, but judges their
speech according to his own conception, will misinterpret
them in the same way as people do with the words of
natural philosophers and astronomers. Whenever they
settle the limits of the code, and explain what is lawful or unlawful in strictly juridical deduction, they
indicate apparently unseemly points. They consider it
revolting to eat the flesh of a dangerously sick animal,
or to gain money by means of legal trickery, or to travel
on the Sabbath with the assistance of the *Erūb*,[29] or to
render certain marriages lawful in a cunning manner, or
to undo oaths and vows by circumvention, which may
be permitted according to the paragraph of the law,
but is devoid of any religious feeling. Both, however,
are necessary together, for, if one is guided by the legal
deduction alone, more relaxation would crop up than
could be controlled. If, on the other hand, one would
neglect the legalized lines which form the fence round
the law, and would only rely on religious zeal, it
would become a source of schism, and destroy everything.

50. Al Khazari : If this be so, I willingly admit that
the Rabbanite who unites these two points of view is
superior to the Karaite both in theory and practice.
He would also perform his religious duties cheerfully,
because they are handed down to him by trustworthy
authorities who derived their knowledge from God.
However far a Karaite's zeal may lead him, his heart
will never be satisfied, because he knows that his zeal
is but based on speculation and reasoning. He will
never be sure whether his practice is God-pleasing.
He is also aware that there are among the gentiles

some who are even more zealous than he. Now I wish
to ask thee concerning the Erūb,[30] which is one of the
licences of the law of Sabbath. How can we make
lawful a thing which God has forbidden by means
so paltry and artificial ?

51. The Rabbi: Heaven forbid that all those pious men
and Sages should concur in untying one of the knots of
the divine law. Their intention was to make it tighter
and therefore they said : Build a fence round the law.
Part of this is the Rabbinic prohibition of carrying
things out of private to public ground or *vice versa*, a
prohibition not of Mosaic origin. In constructing
this fence they introduced this licence, to prevent their
religious zeal ranking with the Tōrāh, and at the same
time to give people some liberty in moving about.
This liberty was gained in a perfectly lawful way and
takes the form of the Erūb, which marks a line between
what is entirely legal, the fence itself, and the secluded
part inside the latter.

52. Al Khazari : This is enough for me. Yet I
cannot believe that an Erūb is strong enough to restore
a connexion between two areas.

53. The Rabbi : In this case the whole law is in-
efficient in thy opinion. Dost thou consider the release
of money, property, persons, and slaves valid by assuring
the right of property or last will ? Likewise the divorce
of a woman, or a second marriage, after having been
single, by means of the formula : ' Write, sign and hand
her the letter of divorce ; ' or her singleness after having
been married ? All these matters depend upon a
ceremony or a formula and are laid down in the Third
Book of Moses. The leprosy of a garment or house
[officially] depends upon the declaration of ' clean ' or

' unclean ' by a priest. The holy character of the Tabernacle was subject to its being erected by Moses and anointed with the anointing oil. The consecration of the priests depended upon the initiatory sacrifices and wave offerings ; that of the Levites upon purifying and wave offerings. Unclean persons were purified by means of ' water of separation ' (Num. xix.) to which were added ashes of the red heifer, hyssop, and scarlet. The redemption of a house required two birds (Lev. xiv. 49). All these ceremonies, the remission of sins on the Day of Atonement, the cleansing of the sanctuary from impurities by means of the he-goat of Azāzēl, with all accompanying ceremonies ; the blessing of Israel through Aaron's uplifted hands and the reciting of the verse : ' the Lord bless thee ' ; upon every one of these ceremonies the Divine Influence rested. Religious ceremonies are, like the work of nature, entirely determined by God, but beyond the power of man. Formations of nature, are, as thou canst see, composed of accurately measured proportions of the four elements. A trifle renders them perfect and gives them their proper animal or plant form. Every mixture receives the shape beseeming it, but can also lose it through a trifle. The egg may be spoiled by the slight accident of too much heat or cold, or a movement, and become unable to receive the form of a chicken which otherwise the hen achieves by sitting on it three weeks. Who, then, can weigh actions upon which the Divine Influence rest , save God alone ? This is the error committed by alchymists and necromancers. The former thought, indeed, that they could weigh the elementary fire on their scales, and produce what they wished, and thus alter the nature of materials, as is done in living beings

by natural heat which transforms food into blood, flesh,
bone and other organs. They toil to discover a fire of
the same kind, but are misled by accidental results of
their experiments, not based on calculation, just in the
same manner as the discovery was made that from the
planting of seed within the womb man arises. When
those necromancers heard that the appearance of the
Divinity from Adam down to the children of Israel
was gained by sacrifices, they thought it was the result
of meditation and research ; that the prophets were but
deeply learned persons who accomplished these wonders
by means of calculation. Then they, on their part,
were anxious to fix sacrifices to be offered up at
certain times and astrological opportunities, accompanied by ceremonies and burning of incense which
their calculations prescribed. They even composed
astrological books and other matters the mention of
which is forbidden. Beside these, the adepts of magic
formulas, having heard that a prophet had been spoken
to in this or that manner, or had experienced a miracle,
imagined that the words were the cause of the miracle.
They, therefore endeavoured to accomplish a similar
feat. The artificial is not like the natural. Religious
deeds are, however, like nature. Being ignorant of
their designs one thinks it but play till the results
becomes apparent. Then one praises their guide and
mover, and professes belief in him. Suppose thou hast
heard nothing of cohabitation and its consequences,
but thou feelest thyself attracted by the lowest of female
organs. If thou considerest the degradation of a woman's
surrender, or the ignominy of surrendering to a woman,
thou wouldst say wonderingly : this is as vain as it is
absurd. But when thou seest a being like thyself

born of a woman, then dost thou marvel and notice
that thou art one of the preservers of mankind created
by God to inhabit the earth. It is the same with religious actions fixed by God. Thou slaughterest a lamb
and smearest thyself with its blood, in skinning it,
cleaning its entrails, washing, dismembering it and
sprinking its blood. Then thou arrangest the wood,
kindlest the fire, placing the body on it. If this were
not done in consequence of a divine command, thou
wouldst think little of all these actions and believe that
they estrange thee from God rather than bring thee near
to Him. But as soon as the whole is properly accomplished, and thou seest the divine fire, or dost notice
in thyself a new spirit, unknown before, or seest true
visions and great apparitions, thou art aware that this is
the fruit of the preceding actions, as well as of the great
influence with which thou hast come in contact. When
arrived at this goal care not that thou must die. Thy
death is but the decay of thy body, whilst the soul
having reached this step, cannot descend from it nor
be removed. This will shew thee that the approach to
God is only possible through the medium of God's
command, and there is no road to the knowledge of the
commands of God except by way of prophesy, but not
by means of speculation and reasoning. There is, however, no other connexion between us and these commands except truthful tradition. Those who have
handed down these laws to us were not a few sporadic
individuals, but a multitude of learned and lofty men
nearly approaching the prophets. And if the
bearers of the Law had only been the priests, Levites and
the Seventy Elders, the chain beginning with Moses himself would never have been interrupted.

54. Al Khazari : I only know that the people of
the second Temple forgot the Tōrāh, and were ignorant
of the law of Succāh till they found it written. A
similar thing happened with the law that ' an Ammonite
shall not enter the congregation of God ' (Deut. xxiii. 3).
With regard to these two points it is said : ' They
found written.' (Neh. viii., 4 ; xiii. 1). This proves
that they had lost the knowledge of the law.

55. The Rabbi : If this be so we are to-day more
learned and erudite than they, since we think we know
the Tōrāh.

56. Al Khazari : That is what I say.

57. The Rabbi : Should we be commanded to bring
a sacrifice, would we know how and where to slaughter
it, catch its blood, skin and dismember it, and into
how many pieces, how to offer it up, how to sprinkle
the blood, what to do with its meal and wine offering ;
with what songs to accompany it ; what duties of holiness, purity, anointment, clothing, and demeanour the
priests had to observe ; how, when and where they
should eat the holy meat, and other matters which it
would lead us too far to commemorate ?

58. Al Khazari: We cannot know this without a
priest or prophet.

59. The Rabbi : See how the people of the second
Temple were engaged many years in the construction
of the altar, till God assisted them to build the Temple
and the walls. Dost thou think that they brought
offerings in a haphazard fashion ?

60. Al Khazari : ' A burnt offering ' cannot be ' an
offering made by fire a sweet savour ' (Lev. i. 9)—being
a law not dependent on reasoning—except if all its
details are arranged on the authority and command

of God. The people were also well acquainted with the regulations of the Day of Atonement, which are more important than the regulations of the Succāh. All these things required the detailed instruction of a teacher.

61. The Rabbi : Should a person versed in these minute regulations of the Tōrāh have been ignorant of the way how to construct a hut, or of the law concerning the Ammonites ?

62. Al Khazari : What can I say, then, about ' they found written ' ?

63. The Rabbi : The compiler of the Holy Writ did not pay so much attention to hidden matters as to those generally known. He, therefore, mentions nothing of the wisdom Joshua had received from God and from Moses, but only the days when he stood at the Jordan, the day when the sun stood still, and the day of the circumcision, since these matters concerned the whole people. The tales of Samson, Deborah, Gideon, Samuel, David and Solomon contain nothing about their own learning and religious practices. In the history of Solomon we find an account of his luxurious table, great wealth, but of his great wisdom nothing except the case of the two women (1 Kings iii. 16), because this took place in public. The wisdom he displayed in his intercourse with the Queen of Sheba [31] and elsewhere is not mentioned, because it was not the author's intention to relate anything that did not concern or interest the whole people. Special records referring to special individuals only, are lost with the exception of a few, besides the magnificent prophetic speeches which everyone took a delight in learning by heart on account of their lofty contents and noble

language. Even of the history of Ezra and Nehemiah
nothing is related except that which concerned the whole
people. The day of the building of the tabernacles was
a public affair, because on that day the people set out
to ascend the mountains and gather olive, myrtle and
palm branches. The words : 'they found written,'
mean that the whole people gave attention to them and
commenced to build their tabernacles. The erudite
were not unacquainted with the details of the law, and
still less with the general tenor of it. The author's
intention was to single out this day, as well as the other
one on which the Ammonite and Moabite wives were
divorced. This was a remarkable day, when men had
to divorce their wives and the mothers of their children,
a grave and painful matter. I do not believe that
any other people than the chosen would give a similar
proof of their obedience to their Lord. It is on account
of this public affair that the words : ' they found written,'
were said. It means that, when the public Reader read
the words : 'An Ammonite or Moabite shall not
enter . . .' the people was moved, and a great perturb-
ation arose on that day.

64. Al Khazari : Give me an example of the manner
of tradition which proves its verity.

65. The Rabbi : Prophecy lasted about forty years
during the second Temple among those elders [32] who
had the assistance of the Shekhināh from the first
Temple. Individually acquired prophecy had ceased
with the removal of the Shekhinah, and only appeared
in extraordinary times or on account of great force, as
that of Abraham, Moses, the expected Messiah, Elijah
and their equals. In them the Shekhinah found a
worthy abode, and their very existence helped their

contemporaries to gain the degree of prophecy. The people, after their return, still had Haggai, Zechariah, Ezra and others. Forty years later these prophets were succeeded by an assembly of Sages, called the Men of the Great Synode. They were too numerous to be counted. They had returned with Zerubbabel and inherited their tradition from the Prophets, as it is said : ' The prophets handed [the law] down to the Men of the Great Synode' (Aboth, I. i.). The next generation was that of the High Priest Simon the Just and his disciples and friends. He was followed by Antigonos of Sōchō of great fame. His disciples were Ṣādōk and Boethos who were the originators of the sects called after them Saddōcaeans and Boethosians. The next was Jōsē b. Jō'ēzer ' the most pious among the priests,' [33] and Josef b. Jōḥānān and their friends. With regard to the former it was said : ' At the death of Jōsē b. Jō'ezēr the grapes ceased' [34] as it is said : ' No grapes to eat ; ' (Mic. vii. 1), for no sin of his was know from his youth to his death. He was followed by Joshua b. Peraḥyāh whose history is known. Among his disciples was Jesus the Nazarene, and Nittāi of Arbela was his contemporary. After him came Judah b. Tabbāi and Simon b. Shētaḥ, with the friends of both. At this period arose the doctrine of the Karaites in consequence of an incident between the Sages and King Jannai who was a priest. His mother was under suspicion of being a ' profane ' woman. One of the Sages alluded to this, saying to him : ' Be satisfied, O king Jannai, with the royal crown, but leave the priestly crown to the seed of Aaron.' His friends prejudiced him against the Sages, advising him to browbeat, expel, and scatter or kill them. He replied : ' If I destroy the Sages what

will become of our Law ? ' 'There is the written law,'
they replied, whoever wishes to study it may come and
do so ; take no heed of the oral law.' He followed their
advice and expelled the Sages and among them Simon b.
Shetah, his son-in-law. [35] Rabbanism was laid low
for some time. The other party tried to establish a
law built on their own conception, but failed, till Simon b.
Shetah returned with his disciples from Alexandria,
and restored tradition to its former condition. Karaism
had, however, taken root among people who rejected
the oral law, and called all kinds of proofs to their aid,
as we see to-day. As regards the Sādōcaeans and
Boēthosians, they are the sectarians who are anathem-
ised in our prayer. [36] The followers of Jesus are the Bap-
tists who adopted the doctrine of baptism, being baptized
in the Jordan. The Karaites turned their attention
to the fundamental principles, deducing the special
laws from them by means of arguments. The damage
often extended to the roots, through their ignorance
rather than intention. The next generation was that
of Shemaʿyāh and Abtaliōn, whose disciples were Hillēl
and Shammāi. Hillēl was famous for his learning and
gentleness. He was a descendant of David and lived
a hundred and twenty years. [37] He had thousands of
pupils. The following was said about the most select
of these : [38] Hillēl the elder had eighty disciples. Thirty
were worthy of association with the Shekhinah ; thirty
were fit to declare embolismic years, and twenty stood
between the two former groups. The greatest of them
was Jōnāthān b. Uzziʿēl, the least of them was Johānān b.
Zakkāi, who left unstudied no verse in the Bible, nor
Mishnāh, Talmud, Halākhā, Agādā, explanatory rules
of the Sages and Scribes, nor any word of the law code.

It was said concerning him, that he never held a profane conversation, was always the last and first in the house of study, never slept there even for a few minutes, never walked four yards without a word of Tōrāh or phylacteries, never sat idle, but studied deeply. No one lectured to his pupils but he, said nothing but what he had heard from the mouth of his teacher, and never said that it was time to leave the house of study. This was also characteristic of his disciple R. Eliezer. R. Jōhānān b. Zakkāi lived a hundred and twenty years like his master, and saw the second Temple. [39] Among his disciples was R. Eliezer b. Hyrcanos, the author of the 'Chapters of R. Eliezer,'[40] a famous work on astronomy, calculation of the spheres and earth and other profound astronomical subjects. His pupil was R. Ishmael b. Elisha, the High Priest. He is the author of the works entitled ' Hēkhālōth '[41], ' Hakhārath Panim,' and the ' Ma'asē Merkābāh,' [42] because he was initiated in the secrets of this science, being worthy of a degree near prophecy. He is responsible for the following utterance : ' Once I entered [the Holy of Holiest] in order to burn the incense, and I saw Akhteriēl Yāh, the Lord of Hosts,' etc. [43] Another pupil of his was the famous R. Joshua between whom and Rabbān Gamaliēl occurred the well known affair ;[44] further R. Jōsē, and R. Elāzar b. Arākh. Of the last named it was said : 'If all Sages of Israel were placed on one scale and Elāzar b. Arākh on the other, he would outweigh them.[45]' Beside those famous men and many Sages, priests and Levites whose calling was the study of the law, there flourished undisturbed in the same period the seventy learned members of the Synhedrion [46] on whose authority officials were appointed or deposed. With

reference to this it is told : R. Simon b. Joḥai said : ' I
heard from the mouth of the seventy elders on the day
when R. Eliezer b. Azariāh was appointed President of
the Academy.[47] ' These seventy had a hundred followers,
the latter ·thousands ; for, seventy such accomplished
men can best be selected from hundreds standing beneath
them and so on by degrees. In the next generation
after the destruction of the Temple, there lived R.
Akībāh and R. Tarfōn and R. Jōsē of Galilee with their
friends. R. Akībāh reached a degree so near prophecy
that he held intercourse with the spiritual world, as it
is said : Four persons entered paradise ;[48] one of them
peeped in and died, the other did the same and was
hurt ; the third did likewise and cut the plants down,
and only one entered in peace and left in peace. This
was R. Akībāh. The one who died was unable to bear
the glance of the higher world, and his body collapsed.[49]
The second lost his mind and whispered divine frenzy
without benefiting mankind.[50] The third fell into bad
ways, because he ascended above human intelligence
and said : ' Human actions are but instruments which
lead up to spiritual heights. Having reached these I
care not for religious ceremonies. He was corrupt and
corrupted others, erred and caused others to err.[51] '
R. Akībāh conversed with both worlds without harm,
and it was said of him : He was as worthy of associating
with the Shekhinah as Moses, but the period was not
propitious.[52] He was one of the ten martyrs, and during
his torture enquired of his pupils, whether the time of
reading the Shema' had arrived. They answered : ' O
our master ; even now ? ' 'All my days,' he answered, ' I
endeavoured to practise the words: "with all thy heart and
all thy soul—even if it costs thee thy life " ; now, when

the opportunity has arisen, I will make them true.'
He protracted the *ēhād* till his soul fled.[53]

66. Al Khazari : In this way one may spend a happy
life, and die a happy death, and then live an eternal
life in never-ceasing bliss.[54]

67. The Rabbi : In the next generation lived R.
Meīr, R. Judah, R. Simon b. Azzāi, and R. Hananyāh
b. Teradiōn and their friends. They were followed by
Rabbi, viz. R. Judāh Hannāsi, ' our Teacher.' His
contemporaries were R. Nāthān, R. Joshua b. Korhāh,
and many others who were the last teachers of the
Mishnāh, also called Tannāim. They were followed
by the Amōrāim, who are the authorities of the Talmud.
The Mishnāh was compiled in the year 530, according
the era of the ' Documents,'[55] which corresponds to
the year 150 after the destruction of the Temple, and
530 years after the termination of prophecy. In the
Mishnāh were reproduced those sayings and doings
which—few out of many—we have quoted. They
treated the Mishnāh with the same care as the Tōrāh,
arranging it in sections, chapters and paragraphs. Its
traditions are so reliable that no suspicion of invention
could be upheld. Besides this the Mishnāh contains a
large amount of pure Hebrew which is not borrowed
from the Bible.[56] It is greatly distinguished by terse-
ness of language, beauty of style, excellence of composition, and the comprehensive employment of homo-
nyms, applied in a lucid way, leaving neither doubt
nor obscurity. This is so striking that every one
who looks at it with genuine scrutiny must be aware
that mortal man is incapable of composing such
a work without divine assistance. Only he who is
hostile to it, who does not know it, and never en-

deavoured to read and study it, hearing some general
and allegorical utterances of the Sages deems them
senseless and defective, just as one who judges a person
after meeting him, without having conversed with him
for any length of time. The following saying of R.
Nahum the Scribe will show how the Sages based
their learning on that of the prophets : [57] 'I have
heard from R. Mayyāshā, who learnt from the " pairs," [58]
who had it from the prophets as an ordination given
to Moses from Sinai.' [59] They were careful not to
hand down the teachings of single individuals, as is
shown by the following saying uttered on the death-
bed of one of them, to his son : ' My son, retract thy
opinion on four subjects which I have taught thee.'
' Wherefore,' asked the son, ' didst thou not retract
thine ? ' ' I learnt,' answered the father, ' from many
who, in their turn, had learnt from many. I kept to
my tradition, and they to theirs. Thou, however,
didst learn only from one person. It is better to
neglect the teachings of a single individual, and to
accept that of the majority.' [60] These are a few sayings, like a drop from the sea, showing the excellence
of the traditions of the Mishnāh. To give thee a sketch
of the traditions and traditionists of the Talmud, and
its methods, sentences and aphorisms, would lead us
too far. And if there is in it many a thing which is
considered less attractive to-day, it was yet held proper
in those days.

68. Al Khazari : Indeed, several details in their
sayings appear to me inferior to their general principles. They employ verses of the Tōrāh in a manner
without regard to common sense. One can only say
that the application of such verses once for legal de-

ductions, another time for homiletic purposes, does not
tally with their real meaning. Their Agadās and tales
are often against reason.

69. The Rabbi : Didst thou notice how strictly and
minutely the comments on the Mishnāh and Boraithā
are given ? They speak with a thoroughness and
lucidity which do equal justice both to the words and
meaning of them.

70. Al Khazari : I am well aware to what perfection
they brought the art of dialectics, but this is an argument [60a] which cannot be refuted.

71. The Rabbi : May we assume that he who pro-
ceeds with so much thoroughness should not know as
much of the contents of a verse as we know ?

72. Al Khazari : This is most unlikely. Two cases
are possible. Either we are ignorant of their method of
interpreting the Tōrāh, or the interpreters of the Rabbinic law are not identical with those of the Holy Writ.
The latter point of view is absurd. It is seldom that we
see them give a verse a rational and literal rendition,
but, on the other hand, we never find them interpret a
halākhā except on the lines of strict logic.

73. The Rabbi : Let us rather assume two other
possibilities. Either they employ secret methods of
interpretation which we are unable to discern, and
which were handed down to them, together with the
method of the ' Thirteen Rules of Interpretation,' or
they use Biblical verses as a kind of fulcrum of interpretation in a method called *Asmakhtā*,[61] and make
them a sort of hall mark of tradition. An instance is
given in the following verse : ' And the Lord God
commanded the man, saying, Of every tree of the
garden thou mayest freely eat ' (Gen. ii. 16 sq.). It

forms the basis of the ' seven Noaḥide laws ' in the following manner :

[' He] commanded ' refers to jurisdiction.
' The Lord ' ' refers to prohibition of blasphemy.
' God ' refers to prohibition of idolatry.
' The man ' refers to prohibition of murder.
' Saying ' refers to prohibition of incest.
' Of every tree of the garden,' prohibition of rape.
' Thou mayest surely eat,' a prohibition of flesh
    from the living animal.

There is a wide difference between these injunctions and the verse. The people, however, accepted these seven laws as tradition, connecting them with the verse as aid to memory. It is also possible that they applied both methods of interpreting verses, or others which are now lost to us. Considering the well-known wisdom, piety, zeal, and number of the Sages which excludes a common plan, it is our duty to follow them. If we feel any doubt, it is not due to their words, but to our own intelligence. This also applies to the Tōrāh and its contents. We must ascribe the defective understanding of it to ourselves. As to the Agādās, many serve as basis and introduction for explanations and injunctions. For instance : the saying, ' When the Lord descended to Egypt,' etc. is designed to confirm the belief that the delivery from Egypt was a deliberate act of God, and not an accident, nor achieved with the assistance of human plotting, spirits, stars, and angels, jinn, or any other fanciful creation of the mind. It was done by God's providence alone. Statements of this kind are introduced by the word *kibᵉjākhōl*, which

means : If this could be so and so, it would be so and
so. Although this is not to be found in the Talmud,
but only in a few other works, it is to be so understood
wherever it is found. This is also the meaning of the
words of Micaiah, when he said to Ahab : I saw the
Lord sitting on his throne . . . host of heaven. And
the Lord said, who shall persuade Ahab. . . . And
there came forth a spirit,' etc. (1 Kings. xxii. 19 sqq.)
As a matter of fact all that he intended conveying was :
Behold, the Lord has put a lying spirit in the mouth of
all these prophets. Verses of this kind serve as a
fulcrum and induction, rendering a subject eloquent,
apposite, and showing that it is based on truth. To
the same category belong tales of visions of spirits, a
matter which is not strange in such pious men. Some
of the visions they saw were the consequence of their
lofty thoughts and pure minds, others were really
apparent, as was the case with those seen by the prophets. Such is the nature of the *Bāth Qōl*, often heard
during the time of the second Temple, and regarded
as ranking next to prophecy and the Divine voice. Do
not consider strange what R. Ishmael said : ' I heard
a voice cooing like a dove, etc.' For the histories of
Moses and Elijah prove that such a thing is possible,
and when a true account is given, it must be accepted
as such. In a similar sense we must take the words :
' Woe unto me that I have destroyed my house ' [62]
(Gen. vi. 6), which is of the same character as : 'And it
repented the Lord, . . . and it grieved Him at His
heart.' Other Rabbinic sayings are parables employed to express mysterious teachings which were not
to be made public. For they are of no use to the
masses, and were only handed over to a few select persons

for research and investigation, if a proper person suitable—one in an age, or in several—could be found. Other
sayings appear senseless on the face of them, but that
they have their meaning, becomes apparent after but a
little reflection. The following is an instance : Seven
things were created prior to the world : Paradise, the
Tōrāh, the just, Israel, the throne of glory, Jerusalem,
and the Messiah, the son of David.'[63] This is similar
to the saying of some philosophers : ' The primary
thought includes the final deed.' It was the object of
divine wisdom in the creation of the world to create
the Tōrāh, which was the essence of wisdom, and whose
bearers are the just, among whom stands the throne of
glory and the truly righteous, who are the most select, viz.
Israel, and the proper place for them was Jerusalem,
and only the best of men, viz. the Messiah, son of David,
could be associated with them, and they all entered
Paradise. Figuratively speaking, one must assume
that they were created prior to the world. Seemingly
against common sense is also the saying : Ten things
were created in the twilight, viz. the opening of the
earth, the opening of the spring, the mouth of the she
ass, etc.,[64] as otherwise the Tōrāh were out of harmony with nature. Nature claims to pursue its regular
course, whilst the Tōrāh claims to alter this regular
course. The solution is that ordinary natural phenomena are altered within natural limits, since they
had been primarily fixed by the divine will, and clearly
laid down from the six days of creation. I will not
deny, O King of the Khazars, that there are matters
in the Talmud of which I am unable to give thee a
satisfactory explanation, nor even bring them in connexion with the whole. These things stand in the

Talmud through the conscientiousness of the disciples, who followed the principle that ' even the common-place talk of the Sages requires study.' [65] They took care to reproduce only that which they had heard from their teachers, striving at the same time to understand everything they had heard from their masters. In this they went so far as to render it in the same words,[66] although they may not have grasped its meaning. In this case they said : ' Thus have we been taught and have heard.' Occasionally the teacher concealed from his pupils the reasons which prompted him to make certain statements. But the matter came down to us in this form, and we think little of it, because we do not know its purport. For the whole of this relates to topics which do not touch on lawful or unlawful matters. Let us not therefore trouble about it, and the book will lose nothing if we consider the points discussed here.

74. Al Khazari : Thou hast pleased me greatly, and strengthened my belief in tradition. Now I should like to learn something of the scientific pursuits of the Sages. But previously give me a discourse on the names of God. On this subject thou canst speak at greater length.

END OF THE THIRD PART.

1. THE Rabbi: *ELŌHIM* is a term signifying the ruler or governor of the world, if I allude to the possession of the whole of it, and of a portion, if I refer to the powers either of nature or the spheres, or of a human judge. The word has a plural form, because it was so used by gentile idolators, who believed that every deity was invested with astral and other powers. Each of these was called *Elōah*; their united forces were therefore, called *Elōhim*. They swore by them, and behaved as if bound to abide by their judgments. These deities were as numerous as are the forces which sway the human body and the universe. ' Force ' is a name for any of the causes of motion. Every motion arises from a force of its own, to the exclusion of other forces. The spheres of the sun and moon are not subject to *one* force, but to different ones. These people did not take into account the prime power from which all these forces emanated, because they did not acknowledge its existence. They asserted that the sum total of these forces was styled *Elōah*, just as the sum total of the forces which control the human body was called ' soul.' Or they admitted the existence of God, but maintained that to serve Him was of no use. They considered Him too far removed and exalted to

have any knowledge of us, much less to care about us.[1]
Far from God are such notions. As a result of their
theories they worshipped, not one being, but many,
which they styled ' Elōhim.' This is a collective form
which comprises all causes equally. A more exact and
more lofty name is to be found in the form known as
the Tetragrammaton. This is a proper noun, which
can only be indicated by attributes, but has no location,
and was formerly unknown. If He was commonly
styled ' Elōhim,' the Tetragrammaton was used as
special name. This is as if one asked : Which God is
to be worshipped, the sun, the moon, the heaven, the
signs of the zodiac, any star, fire, a spirit, or celestial
angels, etc. ; each of these, taken singly, has an activity
and force, and causes growth and decay ? The answer
to this question is : ' The Lord,' just as if one would
say : A. B., or a proper name, as Ruben or Simeon,
supposing that these names indicate their personalities.

2. Al Khazari : How can I individualise a being, if
I am not able to point to it, and can only prove its existence by its actions ?

3. The Rabbi : It can be designated by prophetic
or visionary means. Demonstration can lead astray.
Demonstration was the mother of heresy and destruc-
tive ideas. What was it, if not the wish to demon-
strate, that led the dualists to assume two eternal
causes ? And what led materialists to teach that the
sphere was not only eternal, but its own primary cause,
as well as that of other matter ? The worshippers of
fire and sun are but the result of the desire to demon-
strate. There are differences in the ways of demonstration, of which some are more extended than others.
Those who go to the utmost length are the philosophers,

and the ways of their arguments led them to teach of
a Supreme Being which neither benefits nor injures,
and knows nothing of our prayers, offerings, obedience,
or disobedience, and that the world is as eternal as He
Himself. None of them applies a distinct proper name
to God, except he who hears His address, command, or
prohibition, approval for obedience, and reproof for
disobedience. He bestows on Him some name as a
designation for Him who spoke to him, and he is convinced that He is the Creator of the world from nought.
The first man would never have known Him if He had
not addressed, rewarded and punished him, and had
not created Eve from one of his ribs. This gave him
the conviction that this was the Creator of the world,
whom he designated by words and attributes, and
styled 'Lord.' Without this he would have been
satisfied with the name Elōhim, neither perceiving
what He was, nor whether He was a unity or many,
whether He was cognizant of individuals or not. Cain
and Abel were made acquainted with the nature of His
being by the communications of their father as well
as by prophetic intuition. Then Noah, Abraham,
Isaac and Jacob, Moses and the prophets called Him
intuitively 'Lord,' as also did the people, having been
taught by tradition that His influence and guidance
were with men. His influence also being with the
pious, they comprehended Him by means of intermediaries called : glory, Shekhinah, dominion, fire, cloud,
likeness, form, ' the appearance of the bow,' etc. (Ezek.
i. 28). For they proved to them that He had spoken
to them, and they styled it : Glory of God. Occasionally they addressed the holy ark by the name of
God, as it is written : 'Rise up, O Lord,', (Numb. x.

35, 36), when they made a start, and ' Return, O Lord '
when they halted, or ' God is gone up with a shout,
the Lord with the sound of the trumpet' (Ps. xlvii. 6),
With all this only the ark of the Lord is meant.
Sometimes the name ' Lord ' was applied to the connecting link between God and Israel, as it is written : ' Do
not I hate them, O Lord, that hate thee ? ' (Ps.
cxxxix, 21). By ' haters of the Lord ' are meant those
who hate the name, or covenant, or the law of God. For
there exists no connexion between God and any other
nation, as He pours out His light only on the select
people. They are accepted by Him, and He by them.
He is called ' the God of Israel,' whilst they are ' the
people of the Lord,' and ' the people of the God of
Abraham.' Even supposing some nations had followed Him and worshipped Him, their conversion
being the result of hearsay and tradition, yet where do
we find His acceptance of them and His connexion with
them, His pleasure in their obedience, His anger for
their disobedience ? We see them left to nature and
chance by which their prosperity or misfortune are
determined, but not by an influence which proves to
be of divine origin alone. Thus also we alone are meant
in the words : ' So the Lord alone did lead him, and
there was no strange god with him (Deut. xxxii. 12).
The Tetragrammaton is a name exclusively employ-
able by us, as no other people knows its true meaning.
It is a proper name which takes no article, as is the
case with Elohim in the form *hāelōhim*. It belongs,
therefore, to the prerogatives by which we are distinguished. Although its meaning is hidden, the letters
of which it is composed speak. For it is the letters
alef, hē, wāv and *yōd* which cause all consonants to be

sounded, as no letter can be pronounced as long as it
is not supported by one of these four, viz. *a* by *alef* and
hē, *u* by *wāv*, and *i* by *yōd*. They form, so to speak, the
spirit in the bodies of the consonants. The name *yāh*
is like the Tetragrammaton (Exod. iii. 14). As to
EH'YEH, it can be derived from the latter name, or from
the root *hāyāh*, and its tendency is to prevent the
human mind from pondering over an incomprehensible
but real entity. When Moses asked : ' And they shall
say to me, What is His name ? ' the answer was :
Why should they ask concerning things they are unable
to grasp ? In a like manner the angel answered :
' Why askest thou thus after my name, seeing it is
secret ? ' (Judg. xiii. 18). Say to them *eh'yēh*, which
means : ' I am that I am,' the existing one, existing
for you whenever you seek me. Let them search for
no stronger proof than My presence among them, and
name Me accordingly. Moses therefore answered :
' *Eh'yēh* has sent me to you.' God had previously
given a similar proof to Moses in the words : ' Certainly I will be with thee, and this shall be a token
unto thee,' etc. (Exod. iii. 12), viz. that I have sent
thee, and am with thee everywhere. This is followed
by a similar phrase, viz. ' The God of your fathers, the
God of Abraham, the God of Isaac and the God of
Jacob,' persons known to have been favoured by the
Divine Influence perpetually. As regards the terms :
Elōhē hāelōhim, it is a designation for the fact that all
creative forces are depending upon God, who arranges
and guides them. ' *Lord of lords* ' has the same meaning. EL is derived from *ayālūth*, being the source of
the forces [of nature], but exalted above them. The
expression : ' Who is like unto thee among the *ēlim*,'

is, therefore, permissible, placing *ēl* into the plural form. Holy expresses the notion that He is high above any attribute of created beings, although many of these are applied to him metaphorically. For this reason Isaiah heard an endless : 'Holy, holy, holy,' which meant that God is too high, too exalted, too holy, and too pure for any impurity of the people in whose midst His light dwells to touch Him. For the same reason Isaiah saw him 'sitting upon a throne, high and lifted up.' *Holy* is, further, a description of the spiritual, which never assumes a corporeal form, and which nothing concrete can possibly resemble. God is called : *the Holy One of Israel*, which is another expression for the Divine Influence connected with Israel himself and the whole of his posterity, to rule and guide them, but not to be merely in external contact with them. Not everyone who wishes is permitted to say, 'My God and Holy One !' except in a meta-phorical and traditional way. In reality only a prophet or a pious person with whom the Divine Influence is connected may say so. For this reason they said to the prophet : 'Pray to the Lord, thy God' (1 Kings xiii. 6). The relation of this nation to others was to have been like that of a king to ordinary people, as it is written : 'Holy shall ye be, for holy am I the Lord, your God' (Lev. xix. 2). Adonai, spelt *alef*, *dalēth*, *nūn*, *yōd* points to something which stands at such an immeasurable altitude that a real designation is impos-sible. Indication is possible in one direction only. We can point to things created by Him, and which form His immediate tools. Thus we allude to the intellect, and say that its seat is in the heart or brain. We also say ' this ' or ' that intellect.' In reality we can only point

to a thing enclosed by a space. Although all organs
obey the intellect, they do so through the medium of
the heart or brain, which are its primary tools, which
are considered as the abode of the intellect.

In a like manner we point to heaven, because it is
employed to carry out the divine will directly, and without the assistance of intermediary factors. On the other
hand we cannot point to compound objects, because
they can only operate with the assistance of intermediary causes, and are connected with God in a chainlike manner. For He is the cause of causes.[2] He is
also called ' He who dwelleth in heaven ' (Ps. cxxiii. 1),
and " For God is in heaven,' (Eccl. v. 1). One often
says, ' Fear of heaven,' and ' fearing heaven in secret,'
' mercy shall come for them from heaven.' In a similar
way we speak of the ' pillar of fire,' or the ' pillar of
cloud,' worship them, and say that God is therein,
because this pillar carried out His will exclusively,
unlike other clouds and fires which arise in the air from
different causes. Thus we also speak of the ' devouring
fire on the top of the mount' (Exod. xxiv. 17), which
the common people saw, as well as of the spiritual form
which was visible only to the higher classes : ' under His
feet as it were a paved work of a sapphire stone '(ver. 10).
He is further styled : *Living God*. The holy ark is
alluded to as ' The Lord of the whole earth,' because
miracles happened as long as it existed, and disappeared
with it. We say that it is the eye which sees, whilst in
reality it is the soul that sees. Prophets and pious Sages
are spoken of in similar terms, because they, too, are
original instruments of the divine will which employs
them without meeting with unwillingness, and performs
miracles through them. In illustration of this the

Rabbis said : ' The words : Thou shalt fear the Lord
thy God,' include the learned disciples. He who
occupies such a degree has a right to be styled ' a man
of God,' a description comprising human and divine
qualities, and as if one would say : godly man. Now
in speaking of a divine being we use the appellation,
Adōnāi—*alef, dalēth, nūn, yōd*—as if we wished to say :
' O Lord.' Metaphorically speaking, we point to a
thing encompassed by a place as : ' He who dwells
between the cherubim,' or ' He who dwells in Zion,' or,
' He who abides in Jerusalem.' The attributes of this kind
are many, although His essence is only one. The variety
arises from the variety of places where God's essence
dwells, just as the rays of the sun are many whilst the
sun is everywhere the same. This simile is not quite
complete. Were only the rays of the sun visible, but
not the sun itself, their origin would have to be demonstrated. I must enlarge on this subject a little more,
because there are debatable points about it, viz. firstly,
how it is possible to speak of space in connexion with
a being that has no place ; secondly, how can one
believe that a subject to which one can point could be
the Prime Cause ?   In reply to these objections we say
in the first instance, that the senses can only perceive the
attributes of things, not the substrata themselves. In
a prince e.g., thou perceivest his external and visible
form and proportions. It is not these to which thou
must render homage. Thou seest him in war in one
habit, in his city in another, in his house in a third.
Following thy judgment rather than thy perception,
thou sayest that he is the king. He may appear first
as a boy, then as a youth, then in his prime, and
finally as an old man ; or as a healthy or sick man, his

appearance, manner, disposition and qualities being
changed. Still thou considerest him to be the same and
the king, because he has spoken to thee and given thee
his commands. The royal side of him is but the
intellectual and rational one, but this is essence, not
limited to space and not to be pointed to, although thou
dost so and sayest that he is the king. But if he is
dead, and thou seest the same old form, thou wilt conclude that this is not the king, but a body which can
be moved by whoso wishes, which depends upon
chance and other peoples' humour, like a cloud in the
air which one wind brings hither and another drives
away, one wind gathers, another disperses. Previously
he was a body which was subject to the royal will alone,
resembling the divine pillar of cloud which no wind
was able to disperse. Another instance is offered by the
sun, which we see as a round, flat body, resembling a
shield and giving forth light and heat, being in repose.
Reason considers it to be a globe a hundred and sixty-six
times larger than the globe of the earth,[3] neither hot nor
immovable, but moving in two opposite directions, from
west to east, and from east to west, under conditions it
would lead us too far to discuss. The senses have not
the faculty of perceiving the essence of things. They
only have the special power of perceiving the accidental
peculiarities belonging to them which furnish reason
with the arguments for their essence and causes. Why
and wherefore are accessible to pure reason only. Everything that shares active intellect, like the angels, grasps
the subjects in their true essence without requiring the
medium of accessories. But our intellect which *a priori*
is only theoretical, being sunk in matter, cannot pene-
trate to the true knowledge of things, except by the

grace of God, by special faculties which He has placed
in the senses, and which resemble those perceptible
accessories, but are always found with the whole species.
There is no difference between my perception and thine
that this circumscribed disc, giving forth light and heat,
is the sun.   Should even these characteristics be denied
by reason, this does no harm, because we can derive from
it arguments for our purposes.   Thus also a sharp-eyed
person, looking for a camel, can be assisted by a weak-
eyed and squinting one who tells him that he has seen
two cranes at a certain place.   The sharp-eyed person
then knows that the other has only seen a camel, and
that the weakness of his eyes made him believe that it
was a crane, and his squint that there were two cranes.
In this way the sharp-eyed person can make use of the
evidence of the weak-eyed one, whilst he excuses his
faulty description by his defective sight.   A similar
relation prevails between senses and imagination on
one side, and reason on the other.   The Creator was
as wise in arranging this relation between the exterior
senses and the things perceived, as He was in fixing the
relation between the abstract sense and the uncorpor-
eal substratum.   To the chosen among His creatures He
has given an inner eye which sees things as they really
are, without any alteration.   Reason is thus in a position
to come to a conclusion regarding the true spirit of these
things.   He to whom this eye has been given is clear-
sighted indeed.   Other people who appear to him as
blind, he guides on their way.   It is possible that this
eye is the power of imagination as long as it is under
the control of the intellect.   It beholds, then, a grand and
and awful sight which reveals unmistakeable truths.
The best proof of its truth is the harmony prevailing

among the whole of this species and those sights. By
this I mean all the prophets. For they witnessed things
which one described to the other in the same manner as
we do with things we have seen. We testify to the
sweetness of honey and the bitterness of the coloquinth.
and if anyone contradicts us, we say that he has failed
to grasp a fact of natural history. Those prophets
without doubt saw the divine world with the inner eye ;
they beheld a sight which harmonized with their
natural imagination. Whatever they wrote down, they
endowed with attributes as if they had seen them in
corporeal form. These attributes are *true* as far as
regards what is sought by inspiration, imagination, and
feeling ; they are *untrue* as regards the reality which is
sought by reason, as we have seen in the parable of the
king. For anyone who says that he is a tall, white
figure clothed in silk, and wearing the royal insignia on
his head has spoken no untruth. Whilst he who says
that this is none other than the intelligent, sagacious
person, who issues commands and prohibitions, in this
city, in this age, and rules this people, has not spoken an
untruth either. If a prophet sees with his mind's eye the
most perfect figure ever beheld in the shape of a king
or judge, seated on his throne, issuing commands
and prohibitions, appointing and deposing officials,
then he knows that this figure resembles a powerful
prince. But if he sees a figure bearing arms or writing
utensils, or ready to undertake work, then he knows
that this figure resembles an obedient servant. Do
not find it out of place that man should be compared
to God. Upon deeper consideration reason might
compare him to light, because this is the noblest and
finest of all material things, and which has the greatest

power of encompassing the component parts of the world.
If we reflect on the attributes (which are essential
whether they be taken in metaphorical or real sense)
such as : living, omniscient, almighty, omnipotent,
guiding, arranging, giving everything its due, wise and
just, we shall find nothing resembling God more
closely than the rational soul—in other words, the perfect
human being. But here we must lay stress on his
human character, not on his corporeality (which he has
in common with the plant), or on his being endowed
with life (which he has in common with the animals).
Philosophers compared the world to a great man, and
man to a small world.[4] If this be so, God being the spirit,
soul, intellect and life of the world—as He is called : the
eternally Living, then rational comparison is plausible.
Nay, a prophet's eye is more penetrating than speculation. His sight reaches up to the heavenly host
direct, he sees the dwellers in heaven, and the spiritual
beings which are near God, and others in human form.
They are alluded to in the verse : ' Let us make man in
our image after our likeness ' (Gen. i. 26). The meaning
is : I have displayed wisdom in arranging the creation in
the following order : elements, metals, animals which
live in the water as well as in the air, and those with
fully developed senses and wonderful instincts. Next
to this class there is only one which approaches
the divine and celestial. God created man in the form of
His angels and servants which are near Him, not in
place but in rank, as we cannot speak of place in connexion with God. Even after these two comparisons,
imagination can give him no other form than that of the
noblest human being, who arranges order and harmony
for the rest of mankind, in the same systematic way as

God has done for the universe. At times the prophet
sees princes deposed and others raised to the throne,
and kingdoms judged, ' till the thrones were placed, and
the Ancient of Days did sit' (Dan. vii. 9); at other
times he sees wrath poured out and the people in
mourning on account of their threatened abandonment
by Him, ' Who is sitting upon a throne high and lifted
up . . . above it stood the seraphim.' (Is. vi. 1 sq.). At
other times, even outside the confines of prophecy, he sees
the departure of the chariot as Ezechiel saw it, and
retained it in his memory. For when the geographical
limits of the land of prophecy were fixed, ' from the
Red Sea, till the sea of the Philistines,' the desert of
Sinai, Paran, Seir and Egypt were included. This
area was also privileged. Whenever a person was found in
it who fulfilled all the necessary conditions, these sights
became distinctly visible to him, ' apparently, and not
in dark speeches,' just as Moses saw the Tabernacle,
the sacrificial worship, and the land of Canaan in all
its parts; or in the scene when, ' the Lord passed by
before him.' Elijah had a vision also within this area.
These things, which cannot be approached by speculation, have been rejected by Greek philosophers,
because speculation negatives everything the like of
which it has not seen. Prophets, however, confirm it,
because they cannot deny what they were privileged to
behold with their mind's eye. Such a number of them,
living as they did in various epochs, could not have acted
upon some common understanding. These statements
were borne out by contemporary sages who had witnessed
their prophetic afflatus. Had the Greek philosophers seen
them when they prophesied and performed miracles,
they would have acknowledged them, and sought by

speculative means to discover how to achieve such
things. Some of them did, so especially gentile philosophers. The name Adonāi, (spelt alef, dalēth, nūn,
yōd) must be understood in a similar way, because
of the idea of divine sovereignty which it conveys.
We say : ' O my Lord,' or, ' Messengership of the Lord,'
which is another name for divine ordination. Some
angels are only created for the time being from fine
elementary corpuscles, others are lasting, and are
perhaps those spiritual beings of which the prophets
speak. We have neither to refute nor to adopt their
views. Concerning the visions seen by Isaiah, Ezechiel,
and Daniel, there is some doubt whether their objects
were newly created, or of the number of those lasting
spiritual beings. ' Glory of God ' is that fine substance
which follows the will of God, assuming any form God
wishes to show to the prophet. This is one view.
According to another view the Glory of God means the
whole of the angels and spiritual beings, as well as the
throne, chariot, firmament, wheels, spheres, and other
imperishable beings. All this is styled ' Glory,' just
as a king's retinue is called his splendour. Perhaps
that was what Moses desired, when he said : ' I beseech
Thee, shew me Thy glory.' God fulfilled his wish on
the condition that he should not see His face which no
mortal could endure, as He said : ' And thou shalt see
My back parts, but My face shall not be seen.' This
includes the glory which the prophet's eye could bear,
and there are things in its wake which even our eye can
behold, as the ' cloud,' and ' the devouring fire,' because we are accustomed to see them. The higher
degrees of these are so transcendental that even prophets cannot perceive them. He, however, who

boldly endeavours to do so impairs his constitution, even
as the power of sight is impaired. People with weak
eyes only see by subdued light after sunset, like the bat.
Weak-eyed people can only see in the shadow, but people
with strong eyes can see in sunlight. No eye, however,
can look into the bright sun, and he who attempts to do
so is stricken with blindness. Such is the explanation
of the 'Glory of God,' 'the Angels of the Lord,' and the
'Shekhinah of the Lord,' as they are called in the Bible.
Occasionally they are applied to objects of nature, e.g.,
'Full is the whole earth of His glory,' (Is. vi. 6), or,
'His kingdom ruleth over all' (Ps. ciii. 19). In truth,
glory and kingdom do not become visible except to the
pious, and the pure, and to the prophets who impart
the conviction to the heretic that judgment and rule
on earth belong to God, who knows every action
of man. If this be so, it can truly be said, 'The Lord is
King,' and 'the Glory of God shall be revealed.' 'The
Lord shall reign for ever, thy God O Zion, unto all
generations,' 'Say ye to Zion, thy God reigneth,' 'the
Glory of the Lord is risen upon thee.' Now thou wilt
not reject everything that has been said concerning such
verses as : 'The similitude of the Lord shall he behold'
(Num. xii. 8), 'they saw the Lord of Israel,' nor *ma'aseh
merkābāh* and *Sheur Kōmàh*, because in the opinion
of some interpreters the reverence of God is implanted
in the human mind, as it is written : 'That His fear
may be before your faces.'

4. Al Khazari : If there be conviction in the mind
that God's is the kingdom, the unity, omnipotence, and
omniscience, and that everything is dependent upon
Him, He being dependent upon no one, then is not
reverence and love for Him a necessary consequence,
without such anthropomorphisms ?

5. The Rabbi : This is a doctrine of philosophers. We
see that the human soul shows fear whenever it meets
with anything terrible, but not at the mere report of
such a thing. It is likewise attracted by a beautiful
form which strikes the eye, but not so much by one
that is only spoken of. Do not believe him who considers himself wise in thinking that he is so far advanced
that he is able to grasp all metaphysical problems with
the abstract intellect alone, without the support of
anything that can be conceived or seen, such as words,
writing, or any visible or imaginary forms. Seest thou
not that thou art not able even to collect the burden
of thy prayer in thought alone, without reciting it ?
Neither canst thou reckon up to a hundred without
speaking, still less if this hundred be composed of
different numbers. Were it not for the sensible perception which encompasses the organization of the intellect
by means of similar sayings, that organization could
not be maintained. In this way, prophets' images
picture God's greatness, power, loving kindness, omniscience, life, eternity, government, and independence,
the dependence of everything on Him, His unity,
and holiness, and in one sudden flash stands revealed
this grand and majestic figure with its splendour, its
characteristics, the instruments which typify power,
etc., the up-lifted hand, the unsheathed sword, fire, wind,
thunder and lightning which obey his behest, the word
which goes forth to warn, to announce what has happened, and to predict. Many angels stand humbly
before Him, and He gives them according to their
requirements without stint. He raises the lowly,
humbles the mighty, and holds out His hand to the
repentant, saying to them : ' Who is conscious [of

a sin] shall repent ' (Jonah iii. 9). He is wroth with the
wicked, deposes and appoints, whilst before Him
' thousand thousands minister unto Him ' (Dan. vii. 10).
Such are the visions which the prophet sees in one second.
Thus fear and love come to him naturally, and remain
in his heart for the whole of his life. He even yearns
and longs to behold the vision again and again. Such a
repetition was considered a great event for Solomon, in
the words : ' The Lord who has appeared to him
twice ' (1 Kings xi. 9). Will a philosopher ever achieve
the same result ?

6. Al Khazari : That is impossible. Thinking is like
narrating, but one cannot recount two things at the
same time. Should this even be possible, no one
who hears them, can absorb them simultaneously.
The details of a country and of its inhabitants which it is
possible to see in one hour would not find room in a large
volume, whilst in one moment love or hatred of
a country could enter my heart. If all this were
read to me from a book it would not impress me
so greatly, but would, on the contrary, confuse my
mind, being mixed up with errors, fancies and previous impressions. And nothing would be completely
clear.

7. The Rabbi : We are like those weak-eyed persons
who cannot bear the brightness of the light. We,
therefore, imitate the sharp-eyed who lived before us
and were able to see. Now just as a person with sound
eyes can only look at the sun, shew it to others and
observe it from certain elevated spots, and at a certain
hour of the day when it rises, so also he who may gaze
at the divine light, has his times and places in which he
can behold it. These times are the hours of prayer,

especially on days of repentance, and the places are
those of prophecy.

8. Al Khazari : I see, then, that thou dost admit
the dominion of hours, days, and places, as the astrologers do.

9. The Rabbi : We cannot deny that the heavenly
spheres exercise influence on terrestrial matters. We
must admit that the material components of growth
and decay are dependent on the sphere, whilst the forms
take their origin from Him who arranges and guides
them, and makes them the instruments for the preservation of all the things which He wishes should
exist. The particulars are unknown to us. The astrologer boasts of knowing them, but we repudiate it,
and assert that no mortal can fathom them. If we
find that any element of this science is based on the
divine law, we accept it. But even then we must
rest satisfied with such astronomical proficiency as
was possessed by the Sages, since we desire that it be
supported by divine power, and correct withal. If
this be wanting, it is but fiction, and there is more
truth in our earthly lot than in the celestial one. He
who is capable of gauging these matters is the real
prophet ; the place where they are visible is the true
place of worship. For it is a divine place, and the law
coming forth from it is the true religion.

10. Al Khazari : Certainly, if later religions admit
the truth, and do not dispute it, then they all respect
the place, and call it the stepping stone of the prophets,
the gate of heaven, the place of gathering of the souls
[on the day of judgment].[5] They, further, admit the
existence of prophecy among Israel, whose forefathers
were distinguished in a like manner. Finally they

believe in the work of creation, the flood, and nearly all that is contained in the Tōrāh. They also perform pilgrimages to this hallowed place.

11. The Rabbi : I would compare them to proselytes who did not accept the whole law in all its branches, but only the fundamental principles, if their actions did not belie their words. Their veneration of the land of prophecy consists chiefly in words, and at the same time they also revere places sacred to idols. Such is the case in places in which an assembly happened to meet, but in which no sign of God became visible. Retaining the relics of ancient idolatry and feast days, they changed nothing but the forms. These were, indeed, demolished, but the relics were not removed. I might almost say that the verse in the Bible, occurring repeatedly : ' Thou shalt not serve strange gods, wood and stone ' (Deut. xxviii. 36, 64), contains an allusion to those who worship the wood, and those who worship the stone.[6] We, through our sins, incline daily more towards them. It is true that they, like the people of Abimelech and Nineveh, believe in God, but they philosophize concerning God's ways. The leader of each of these parties maintained that he had found the divine light at its source, viz., in the Holy Land, and that there he ascended to heaven, and commanded that all the inhabitants of the globe should be guided in the right path. They turned their faces towards the land in prayer, but before long they changed and turned towards the place where the greatest number of their people lived.[7] This is as if a person wished to guide all men to the place of the sun, because they are blind and do not know its course. He, however, leads them to the south or north pole, and tells them : " the sun

is there, if you turn towards it, you will see it."
But they see nothing. The first leader, Moses, made
the people stand by Mount Sinai, that they might see
the light which he himself had seen, should they be
able to see it in the same way. He, then, invited the
Seventy Elders to see it, as it is written : ' They saw
the God of Israel (Exod. xxiv. 10). Then he assembled
the second convocation of Seventy Elders to whom he
transferred so much of his prophetic spirit, that they
equalled him, as is written : ' And he took of the spirit
that was upon him and gave it unto the seventy elders '
(Num. xi. 25). One related to the other concerning
what they saw and heard. By these means all evil suspicion was removed from the people, lest they opined
that prophecy was only the privilege of the few
who claimed to possess it. For no common compact
is possible among so many people, especially where
large hosts of them are concerned, and equally well-in-
formed as Elisha, who knew the day on which God
would remove Elijah, as it is written : ' Knowest thou,
that the Lord will take away thy master . . . to-day ? '
(2 Kings ii. 5) Each elder served as a witness for
Moses, and admonished the people to keep the law.

12. Al Khazari : But the followers of other religions
approach you more nearly than the philosophers ?

13. The Rabbi : They are as far removed from us as the
followers of a religion from a philosopher. The former
seek God not only for the sake of knowing Him, but also
for other great benefits which they derive therefrom.
The philosopher, however, only seeks Him that he may
be able to describe Him accurately in detail, as he would
describe the earth, explaining that it is in the centre of
the great sphere, but not in that of the zodiac, etc. Ig-

norance of God would be no more injurious than would
ignorance concerning the earth be injurious to those
who consider it flat. The real benefit is to be found
only in the cognizance of the true nature of things, in
order to resemble the Active Intellect. Be he believer
or free-thinker, it does not concern him, if he is a
philosopher. His axiom is that : ' God will do no good,
neither will He do evil ' (Zeph. i. 12). If he believes
in the eternity of matter, he cannot assume that there
was a time when it did not exist prior to its creation.
He opines that it was never non-existing, that it will
never cease to exist, that God can only be called its
creator in a metaphorical sense. [8]   The term ' Creator,'
and ' Maker ' he explains as cause and prime mover of
the world. Effect lasts as long as the cause does. If the
latter is only potential, the former is potential ; if real,
real. God is cause in reality ; that which is caused by Him
remains, therefore, so long in existence as He remains its
cause.   We cannot blame philosophers for missing the
mark, since they only arrived at this knowledge by way of
speculation, and the result could not have been different,
The most sincere among them speak to the followers
of a revealed religion in the words of Socrates : ' My
friends, I will not contest your theology, I say, however, that I cannot grasp it ; I only understand human
wisdom.' [9]   These [speculative] religions are as far
removed now as they were formerly near.   If this
were not so, Jeroboam and his party would be nearer
to us, although they worshipped idols, as they were
Israelites, inasmuch as they practised circumcision,
observed the Sabbath, and other regulations, with
few exceptions, which administrative emergencies had
forced them to neglect. They acknowledged the God

of Israel who delivered them from Egypt, in the same
way as did the worshippers of the golden calf in the
desert. The former class is at best superior to the
latter inasmuch as they prohibited images. Since,
however, they altered the *Kibla*, and sought Divine
Influence where it is not to be found,[10] altering at the
same time the majority of ceremonial laws, they wandered far from the straight path.

14. Al Khazari : A wide difference should be made
between the party of Jeroboam and that of Ahab.
Those who worship Baal are idolators in every respect.
In reference to this Elijah said : ' If the Lord be God,
follow Him ; but if Baal, follow him ' (1 Kings xviii. 21).
For this reason the Sages are in a dilemma as to how Josa-
phat could partake of Ahab's food.[11]   They have no such
doubts concerning Jeroboam.   Elijah's protest had no
reference to the worship of the calves, since he said :
' I have been very jealous for the Lord, the God of
Israel ' (1 Kings xix. 10).   The party of Jeroboam considered itself belonging to the Lord, the God of Israel,'
also all their actions, their prophets were the prophets
of God, whilst the prophets of Ahab were Baal's
prophets.   God appointed Jehu to destroy the works
of Ahab.   He proceeded with much zeal and cunning,
saying : ' Ahab served Baal a little, Jehu will serve
him much ' (2 Kings x. 18).   He destroyed all vestiges
of Baal, indeed, but did not touch the calves.   The worshippers of the first calf, the party of Jeroboam, and
the worshippers of the heights and the image of Micah
had no other idea than that they were serving the God of
Israel, though in the way they did it they were disobedient
and deserved death.   This is as if a man marries his sister
either under compulsion or from lust, and yet observes

the marriage regulations as commanded by God. Or
if one would eat swine's flesh, but carefully observe the
rules concerning slaughtering, blood and ritual.

15. The Rabbi : Thou hast called attention to a
debatable point, although there is no doubt about it for
me. But we have wandered from our subject, viz. the
attributes. To return to it, let me explain the matter to
thee by a simile taken from the sun. The sun is only a
single body, whilst those receiving their light from it
are in many ways dependent on each other. The most
fitted to annex its lustre are the ruby, crystal, pure
air and water, and their light is therefore called transparent. On glittering stones and polished surfaces it is
called luminous ; on wood, earth, etc., visible light, and
on all other things it is simply designated light without
any specific qualification. This general term, light,
corresponds to what we call *Elōhim*, as is now clear.
Transparent light corresponds to ' Eternal,' a proper
name which describes especially the relation between
Him and His earthly creatures, I mean, the prophets,
whose souls are refined and susceptible to His light,
which penetrates them, just as the sunlight penetrates
the crystal and ruby. Their souls take their origin and
development (as has been explained before) from
Adam. Essence and heart [of Adam] reappear in
every generation and age, whilst the large mass of
mankind are set aside as husks, leaves, mud, etc. The
God of this essence is only and solely Adōnāi, and
because He established a connexion with man, the name
Elōhim was altered after the creation into *Adonāi
Elōhim*. This the Sages express in the words : A ' full
name over a full universe ' (Ber. Rabbāh chap. xi.). The
world was but completed with the creation of man who

forms the heart of all that was created before him.
No intelligent person will misunderstand the meaning
conveyed by ' Elōhim,' although this is possible with
regard to ' Adōnāi,' because prophecy is strange and
rare in single individuals, and much more so in a multitude. For this reason, Pharaoh disbelieved and said :
' I know not the Lord ' (Exod. v. 2), as if he interpreted
the Tetragrammaton in the way penetrating light is
understood, and was reminded by it of God whose light
is intimately attached to man. Moses supplemented
his words by adding : ' the God of the Hebrews,' in
order to call to mind the patriarchs who testified by
means of prophecy and marvels. Elōhim was a name
well known in Egypt. The first Pharaoh said to Joseph :
' Forasmuch as *Elōhim* has shewn thee all this,' (Gen.
xli. 39), and ' A man in whom the spirit of *Elōhim* is '
(ver. 38). This is as if one man alone sees the sun, knows
the points of its rising and course, whilst we others
never behold it and live in shadow and mist. We find,
then, that his house has much more light than ours,
because he is acquainted with the course of the sun and
can arrange his windows according to his desire. We
also see his crops and plantations thriving, which, as
he says, is the consequence of his knowing the course of
the sun. We however, would deny this, and ask : ' What
is the sun ? We know the light and its manifold
advantages, but it comes to us merely by accident.'
' To me,' he would answer, 'it comes as much and as
frequently as I desire,because I know its cause and course.
If I am prepared for it and arrange all my plans and
works for their proper seasons, I reap the full benefit
of it.—A substitute for *Adonāi* is *Presence*, as in the
verse : ' My Presence shall go with thee ' (Exod. xxxiii.

14, sq.), or ' If thy Presence go not with me.' The same
is meant in the verse : ' Let my Lord, I pray Thee, go
among us ' (ibid. xxxiv. 9). The meaning of *Elōhim* can
be grasped by way of speculation, because a Guide and
Manager of the world is a postulate of Reason. Opinions
differ on the basis of different speculations, but that of
the philosophers is the best on the subject. The
meaning of *Adonāi*, however, cannot be grasped by
speculation, but only by that intuition and prophetic
vision which separates man, so to speak, from his kind,
and brings him in contact with angelic beings, imbuing
him with a new spirit, as it is written : ' Thou shalt be
turned into another man,' ' God gave him another
heart ' (1 Sam. x. 6. 9), 'A spirit came over Amasai '
(1 Chron. xii. 18). ' The hand of the Lord was upon me '
(Ezek. xxxvii. 11). ' Uphold me with Thy free spirit '
(Ps. li. 14) All these circumscribe the Holy Spirit
which enwraps the prophet in the hour of his ministry,
the Nazirite, and the Messiah, when they are anointed
for priesthood, or for the royal dignity by a prophet ;
or when God aids and strengthens him in any matter ;
or when the priest makes prophetic utterances by
means of the mystic power derived from the use of the
Urim and Tummim. Then all previous doubts concerning *Elōhim* are removed, and man deprecates those
speculations by means of which he had endeavoured to
derive the knowledge of God's dominion and unity.
It is thus that man becomes a servant, loving the object
of his worship, and ready to perish for His sake, because
he finds the sweetness of this attachment as great as the
distress in the absence thereof. This forms a contrast
to the philosophers, who see in the worship of God
nothing but extreme refinement, extolling Him in

truth above all other beings, (just as the sun is placed on a higher level than the other visible things), and that the denial of God's existence is the mark of a low standard of the soul which delights in untruth.

16. Al Khazari : Now I understand the difference between *Elōhim* and *Adonāi*, and I see how far the God of Abraham is different from that of Aristotle. Man yearns for *Adonāi* as a matter of love, taste, and conviction ; whilst attachment to *Elōhim* is the result of speculation. A feeling of the former kind invites its votaries to give their life for His sake, and to prefer death to His absence. Speculation, however, makes veneration only a necessity as long as it entails no harm, but bears no pain for its sake. I would, therefore, excuse Aristotle for thinking lightly about the observation of the law, since he doubts whether God has any cognizance of it.

17. The Rabbi : Abraham bore his burden honestly, viz. the life in Ur Kasdim, emigration, circumcision, the removal of Ishmael, and the distress of the sacrifice of Isaac, because his share of the Divine Influence had come to him through love, but not through speculation. He observed that not the smallest detail could escape God, that he was quickly rewarded for his piety and guided on the right path to such an extent that he did everything in the order dictated by God. How could he do otherwise than deprecate his former speculation ? [12] The Sages explain the verse : ' And He brought him forth abroad, ' as meaning : ' give up thy horoscopy ! ' [13] That is to say, He commanded him to leave off his speculative researches into the stars and other matters, and to follow faithfully the object of his inclination, as it is written : ' Taste and see that the Lord is good ' (Ps.

xxxiv. 9). *Adonāi* is, therefore, called rightly the God of
Israel, because this view is not found among Gentiles.
He is also called God of the land, because this possesses a
special power in its air, soil and climate, which in connexion with the tilling of the ground, assists in improv-
ing the species. He who follows the divine law, follows
the representatives of this view. His soul finds satis-
faction in their teachings, in spite of the simplicity of
their speech and ruggedness of their similes. This is
not the case with the instructions of philosophers, with
their eloquence and fine teachings, however great the
impressiveness of their arguments. The masses do not
follow them, because the human soul has a presenti-
ment of the truth, as it is said : ' The words of truth will
be recognised.'

18. Al Khazari : I see thee turning against the philosophers, attributing to them things of which just the
opposite is known. Of a person who lives in seclusion and acts rightly, it is said, he is a philosopher,
and shares the views of philosophers. Thou deprivest
them of every good action.

19. The Rabbi : Nay, what I told thee is the foundation of their belief, viz. that the highest human happiness consists in speculative science and in the conception
by reason and thought of all intelligible matters. This
is transformed into the active intellect, then, into emanating intellect, which is near the creative intellect without
fear of decay.[14] This cannot, however, be obtained except by devoting one's life to research and continual reflection, which is incompatible with worldly occupations.
For this reason they renounced wealth, rank, and the
pleasure of children, in order not to be distracted from
study. As soon as man has become acquainted with

the final object of the knowledge sought for, he need not
care what he does. They do not fear God for the sake
of reward, nor do they think that if they steal or murder
they will be punished. They recommend good and dis-
suade from evil in the most admirable manner. And
in order to resemble the Creator who arranged everything
so perfectly, they have contrived laws, or rather regulations without binding force, and which may be over-
ridden in times of need. The religious law, however,
is not so except in its social parts, and the law itself sets
down those which permit exceptions and those which
do not.[15]

20. Al Khazari : The light of which thou speakest
has not gone out without hope of its being re-kindled.
It has completely disappeared, and no one is able to
trace it.

21. The Rabbi : It is only extinguished for him who
does not see us with an open eye, who infers the extinc-
tion of our light from our degradation, poverty and
dispersion, and concludes from the greatness of others,
their conquests on earth and their power over us, that
their light is still burning.

22. Al Khazari : I will not use this as an argument,
as I see two antagonistic religions prevailing, although
it is impossible that the truth should be on two opposite
sides. It can only be on one or on neither. I have explained to thee in connexion with the verse : ' Behold
My servant shall prosper ' (Is. lii. 13), that humility
and meekness are evidently nearer to the Divine Influence than glory and eminence. The same is visible in
these two religions. Christians do not glory in kings,
heroes and rich people, but in those who followed Jesus
all the time, before His faith had taken firm root

among them. They wandered away, or hid themselves, or were killed wherever one of them was found, suffered disgrace and slaughter for the sake of their belief. These are the people in whom they glory, whose ministers they revere, and in whose names they build churches. In the same way did the ' Helpers,' [16] and friends of Islām bear much poverty, until they found assistance. In these, their humility and martyrdom do they glory; not in the princes who boasted of their wealth and power, but rather in those clad in rags and fed scantily on barley bread. Yet, O Jewish Rabbi, they did so in the utmost equanimity and devotion to God. Had I ever seen the Jews act in a like manner for the sake of God, I would place them above the kings of David's house. For I am well aware of what thou didst teach me concerning the words : ' with him also that is of a contrite and humble spirit ' (Is. lvii. 15), as well as that the light of God only rests upon the souls of the humble.

23. The Rabbi : Thou art right to blame us for bearing degradation without benefit. But if I think of prominent men amongst us who could escape this degradation by a word spoken lightly, become free men, and turn against their oppressors, but do not do so out of devotion to their faith : [17] is not this the way to obtain intercession and remission of many sins ? Should that which thou demandest of me really ever take place we should not remain in this condition. Besides this, God has a secret and wise design concerning us, which should be compared to the wisdom hidden in the seed which falls into the ground, where it undergoes an external transformation into earth, water and dirt, without leaving a trace for him who looks down upon it. It is, however, the seed itself which transforms earth and

water into its own substance, carries it from one stage to another, until it refines the elements and transfers them into something like itself, casting off husks, leaves, etc., and allowing the pure core to appear, capable of bearing the Divine Influence. The original seed produced the tree bearing fruit resembling that from which it had been produced. In the same manner the law of Moses transforms each one who honestly follows it, though it may externally repel him. The nations merely serve to introduce and pave the way for the expected Messiah, who is the fruition, and they will all become His fruit. Then, if they acknowledge Him, they will become one tree. Then they will revere the origin which they formerly dispersed, as we have observed concerning the words : " Behold My servant prospers." Consider not their abstention from idolatry, and energetic declaration of the unity of God, as a reason to praise ; nor cast a reproving glance at the Israelites because their history tells of idol worship. On the other hand consider that many of the former incline towards heresy and endeavour to spread it, that they praise it in popular songs which are in everybody's mouth, and which are loud in asserting that there is no king who rules over the actions of man, none who rewards or punishes them,[18] a doctrine never mentioned in connexion with Israel. The people only sought to derive advantages from talismans and spirits, in addition to the practice of their faith of which they observed the laws, because the adoption of magic practices was universally prevalent at their time. Had this not been so, they should not have become converted to the belief of the peoples amongst whom they lived as exiles. Even Manasseh and Zedekiah and the greatest apostates in Israel had no particular wish to forsake the

religion of Israel. They did it chiefly for victory and
worldly gain which they hoped to obtain by means which
they considered effective in spite of divine prohibition.
If these things were so lightly considered to-day, thou
wouldst see us and them deceived by them, as we are
deceived by other vanities, such as astrology, conjuring,
magic practices, and other tricks which are rejected as
completely by nature as by the Law.

24. Al Khazari : I ask thee now to give me an explanation of the relics of the natural science which thou
hast stated existed among you.

25. The Rabbi : To this belongs the 'Book of Creation' by the Patriarch Abraham.[19] Its contents are
very profound, and require thorough explanation. It
teaches the unity and omnipotence of God by means of
various examples, which are multiform on one side and
uniform on the other. They are in harmony with regard
to the One, their Director. This results in the three
factors: *S'fār, Sēfer,* and *Sippūr* (Jesīrāh i. 1). As to *S'fār*
it means the calculation and weighing of the created
bodies. The calculation which is required for the harmonious and advantageous arrangement of a body is
based on a numerical figure. Expansion, measure,
weight, relation of movements, and musical harmony,
all these are based on the number expressed by the word
S'fār. No building emerges from the hand of the archi-
tect unless its image had first existed in his soul. *Sippūr*
signifies the language, or rather the divine language, ' the
voice of the words of the living God.' This produced
the existence of the form which this language assumed
in the words : ' Let there be light,' ' let there be a
firmament.' The word was hardly spoken, when the
thing came into existence. This is also *Sēfer,* by which

writing is meant, the writing of God means His creatures, the speech of God is His writing, the will of God is His speech. In the nature of God, therefore, *S'fār*, *Sippūr*, and *Sēfer* are a unity, whilst they are three in human reckoning. For man wills with his reason, speaks with his mouth, and writes such speech with his hand. These three factors characterize one of God's creatures. Man's will, writing, and word are marks of the thing, but not the nature of the same. The will, however, expressed in the word of God signifies the essence of the thing, and is at the same time His script. Imagine a silk weaver considering his work The silk obeys him, accepts the colours and patterns which he has contrived. The garment therefore comes into existence by his will and design. If we were able when speaking of, or drawing a human figure, to produce a human form, then we should have the word of God in our power and could create, just as we are able to do partially in forming objects in the mind. Spoken or written words have certain advantages over each other. In some cases the name fits the object exactly ; in others less so. The language created by God, which He taught Adam and placed on his tongue and in his heart, is without any doubt the most perfect and most fitted to express the things specified, as it is written : ' And whatsoever Adam called every living creature, that was the name thereof ' (Gen. ii. 19). This means that it deserved such name which fitted and characterized it. This shows the excellence of the ' holy tongue ' as well as the reason why the angels employed it in preference to any other. Writing is judged from a similar point of view. The shapes of the letters are not the result of accident, but of a device which is in harmony with the character of each letter. Thou shouldst

not, now, deem it impossible that names and combinations of letters, whether spoken or written, have certain
effects. In either case, calculation, viz. the thought of
the pure, angelic soul precedes the act. Thus the three
factors : *S'făr, Sippūr,* and *Sefer* become a unity, and
the calculation appears as if a being, endowed with a
pure soul, had made, spoken, and written it. The book
further states with regard to God : He created His world
with three *Sefīrāh* factors : *S'făr, Sippūr,* and *Sefer.* In
God's nature they are all *one,* but this one forms the
beginning of the ' thirty-two miraculous and mysterious
ways of the divine wisdom,' composed of the ten Sefi-
rōth and the twenty-two letters [of the Hebrew alpha-
bet]. This points to the actuality of existing things and
their differences with regard to quantity and quality.
Quantity means a number. The mystery of the number is in the number *ten,* as is expressed in the passage :
' Ten Sefīrōth without anything else ; ten and not nine,
ten and not eleven ' (ibid. i. 4–5). A deep secret lies in
the fact that the counting stops at ten, neither more nor
less. The next sentence, therefore, runs : ' Understand
judiciously and judge intelligently, examine and search
them, mind, weigh, and consider, render everything
lucid, and place the Creator in His sphere ; their measure is *ten* in endless progression ' (ibid. 4–5). This is
followed by a division as to quality. The twenty-two
letters are divided into three groups, viz. three *mothers,*
seven double, twelve single [consonants]. The three
mothers are *alef, mem, shin.* They cover a great and
profound secret ; for from them emanate air, water,
and fire by means of which the universe was created.
The grouping of these consonants united with the order
of the macrocosm and the microcosm, viz. man, and the

order of time into *one* line, called ' true witnesses,' viz.
universe, soul, year. This also demonstrates that the
one order is the work of a one-Master, who is God. And
although things are multifarious and different from each
other, their difference is the result of the difference of
their material, which is partly of higher and partly lower
order, and of impure or pure character. The giver of
forms, designs and order, however, has placed in them
all a unique wisdom, and a providence which is in complete harmony with this uniform order, and is visible in
the macrocosm, in man, and in the arrangement of the
spheres. It is this that is called the ' true witnesses ' of
His Oneness, viz. universe, soul, year. This yields
approximately the following table—

THREE MOTHERS

In the Universe : Air, Water, Fire.
In the Soul :   Chest, Belly, Head.
In the Year :   Moisture, Cold, Heat.

SEVEN DOUBLE [CONSONANTS].
Beth, Gimel, Daleth, Kaf, Pe, Resh, Tāv.

In the Universe : Saturnus, Jupiter, Mars, Sun, Venus, Mercury,
    Moon.[20]
In the Soul :   Wisdom, Wealth, Government, Life, Grace,
    Progeny, Peace.
In the Year :   Sabbath, Thursday, Tuesday, Sunday, Friday,
    Wednesday, Monday.
In the Universe : Aries, Taurus, Gemini, Cancer, Leo, Virgo.
In the Soul :   Organs of Sight, Hearing, Smelling, Speaking,
    Tasting, Feeling.
In the Year :   Nisān, Iyyār, Sivān, Tammuz, Ab, Ellul.

TWELVE SIMPLE [CONSONANTS].
In the Universe : Libra, Scorpio, Arcitenens, Caper, Amphora,
    Pisces.
In the Soul :   Organs of Working, Walking, Thinking, Being
    Angry, of Laughing, and Sleeping.
In the Year :   Tishri, Marheshwān, Kislēv, Tēbēth, Shebat
    Adār.

'One upon three, three upon seven, and seven upon
twelve' (ibid. vi. 3). All these organs have one spot in
common, e.g. counselling kidneys, laughing spleen
[angry liver], sleeping stomach. It cannot be denied
that the kidneys have the faculty of giving good advice,
as we know a similar circumstance to be connected with
other organs. A eunuch is of weaker intelligence than a
woman ; both lack the beard and sound judgment.
The spleen is called 'laughing' because it is its nature
to cleanse both blood and spirit from unclean and ob-
scuring matter. If they are pure, cheerfulness and
laughing arise. The 'angry liver' is so termed on
account of the gall which takes its origin from it.
'Stomach' is the name for the digestive organs. The
heart is not mentioned because it is the principal organ,
neither are the diaphragm and the lung, because they
serve the heart especially, but the rest of the body
only incidentally, and were not originally so intended.
The brain's task is to collect the different senses connected with it. The organs which are situated below
the diaphragm have another secret, because they represent primary nature. The diaphragm separates the
physical world from the animal one, just as the neck
separates the animal world from the rational one, as
Plato points out in the *Timaeus*.[21] Primary matter
originates in the physical world, and here is to be
found the origin of existence. From here the seed
is sent forth and the embryo produced out of the four
elements. Here also God selected the parts which are
used as offerings, viz. fat, blood, the caul above the
liver, and the two kidneys. He selected neither the
heart, nor the brain, nor the lung, nor the diaphragm.
This is a most profound secret, the lifting of which is

prohibited. It is therefore taught : ' One should not
examine the work of creation '[22] except under
rare circumstances. The book says further : ' Seven
double [consonants], six plains for the six sides, and the
holy Temple placed in the middle. Blessed be He from
His place ; He is the Place of the universe, but the universe is not His place ' (ibid. iv. 2). This is an allusion to
the Divine Influence which unites the contrasts. The
book compares Him to the central point of a body, with
six sides and three dimensions. As long as the centre
is not fixed, the sides cannot be fixed. Attention is
further called to the relation between these and the
power which bears the universe, and through which
contrasts are united by eliciting comparisons between
Universe, Soul, and Year. To each of these a something is given which comprehends and arranges its component parts. ' The dragon in the universe is as a king
on his throne ; the sphere in the year is as a king in the
country ; the heart in the soul is as a king in war ' (ibid.
vi. 2). ' Dragon '[23] is the name of the moon sphere,
and is employed as an appellation for the world of reason,
because things hidden and imperceptible by the senses
are called dragon. The ' sphere ' relates to the ecliptic
of the sun sphere, because it regulates the seasons of the
year. The ' heart ' regulates the animal life, and directs
its divisions. The meaning of the whole is that the
wisdom visible in all three is one, and the Divine Influence is *one*, whilst the difference existing between
them is based on the difference of matter. The authority
ruling the spiritual world is compared to a king on his
throne, whose commands, or even smallest hints, are
obeyed by his servants, high and low, who know him,
without any movement on his part or on theirs. When

directing the spheres he is compared to the king in the country. For he must show himself at the borders in order that all parts should see him as a redoubtable and benevolent ruler. When controlling the animal world, he is compared to 'a king in war,' who is swayed by contradictory feelings ; he wishes success to his friends and defeat to his enemies. Wisdom, however, is one only. But the wisdom displayed in the spheres is not greater than in the smallest animals. The former, it is true, is of a higher class, because it consists of pure and lasting matter which cannot be destroyed except by its Creator, whilst animals are made from a matter which is susceptible to contradictory influences, such as heat, cold, and others which affect its nature. Time would have destroyed them, had not Providence instituted the masculine and feminine principles in order to preserve the species, in spite of the decay of the individual. This is a consequence of the revolution of the sphere as well as of the rising and setting [of the heavenly bodies]. The book calls attention to this circumstance, and says that there is no physical difference between woman and man except certain external and internal organs. Anatomy teaches that the female genitals are but the inverted male ones. The book expresses this thus : 'Man is alef, mēm, shin ; woman is alef, shin, mēm; (ibid. iii. 5) the wheel turns forwards and backwards ; nothing better above than pleasure, nothing worse below than injury.' [23a] This means that the letter groups alef, mēm, shin, and alef, shin, mēm; ʿaynh, nūn, gimel, and nūn, gimel, ʿayn (ibid. ii. 2) are always the same, only differently grouped, just as the rising and setting of the sphere remain stationary, only appearing to us to move forwards and backwards. Then the book allegorises the

human organs in the following manner: ' Two mumbling,
two rejoicing, two counselling, two jubilant. He put
them in contrast, placed them in opposition, one part
of one side being allied to one of the other, standing up
for each other, or against one another ; some are nothing
without others, but all are linked to each other ' (ibid.
v. 2). The allusion is clear when considered in its
entirety, however difficult it may be to explain it in
detail,—to explain that the animal needs contrasts, that
its preservation is the result of this strife, and that it
could not exist without the latter. Counting up the
creatures which are headed by the noblest, viz. ' spirit
of the living God,' the book goes on to say : ' Firstly,
the spirit of the living God ; secondly, air emanating
from the spirit ; thirdly, water from the wind ; fourthly,
fire from water ' (ibid. i. 9, 10). The earth element is
not mentioned, because it forms the gross material of
the creatures which are all made of earth. One says
rather : ' This is a fiery body, or an atmospheric one,
or an aqueous one.' For this reason the three mothers,
fire, water, and air, are placed in front, but they are preceded by the spirit of God, which is the Holy Ghost, of
which were created the angels and with which the soul
is connected. After this comes the perceptible atmosphere, then the water which is above the firmament,
and neither grasped nor acknowledged by philosophic
speculation. A solution might be found in the circumstance that this is the zone of intense cold which forms
the limit of the clouds. Above this is the ether, which
is the place of the elementary fire, as the book hath it :
' Fire from water,' or as the Bible says : ' And the spirit
of God moved upon the face of the water ' (Gen. i. 2).
This water is the primary matter, not qualified, but

tōhū wabōhū, which, by the encompassing will of God,
assumed a certain character and the name 'Spirit of
God.' The comparison of the primary matter with
water is most suitable, because no compact substance
can arise from a material which is finer than water.
But a substance which is of greater density than water
does not, on account of this density, admit the influences of nature. Earthly matter alone can be wrought,
because in handling it only the surfaces of the material are concerned, but not all its particles. Nature
however, penetrates the atoms. There is consequently
no product of nature which did not, at one time, exist in
a liquid condition. If this had not been so, it could not
have been called a natural, but only an artificial compound, or accidental formation. Nature can only exercise her influence on liquid matters, which she can
form at her will, but leave alone as soon as it is
necessary for them to become hard. Concerning this
the book says : ' He made substance from chaos, and
the non-existent existing. He carved great pillars from
intangible air.' Further : ' Water from air ; he has
carved and hewn *tōhū* and *bōhū*, mud and clay ; he
made them into a kind of flower bed, raised them like a
wall, covered them like a floor, poured water over them,
and they became dust' (ibid. i. 9 sq. ; ii. 4). *Tōhū* is the
green line which surrounds the whole universe.[24] *Bōhū*
are the mud-covered stones which are submerged in the
ocean, and from between which water comes forth.' In
the following portions light is shed on the secret of the
holy name, viz. the Tetragrammaton, which corresponds
to the nature of the One God, which is without quiddity.
For the quiddity of a thing is outside its essence, whilst
the existence of God is identical with His quiddity. The

quiddity of a thing is its definition, and the latter is composed of the species and divisibility of the thing defined. The primary cause, however, has neither species nor divisibility. He therefore can be nothing but He. The book, then, shows that the revolution of the sphere is the cause of the variety of things, in the following words : ' The wheel turns forward and backward ' (ibid. ii. 4). This is compared to the combination of single letters, viz. *alef* placed in combination with all the others, all the others with *alef* ; *bēth* with all the others, all the others with *bēth* (ibid. 5). This continued through the whole alphabet results in two hundred and thirty-one combinations.[25] The variety would be greater in groups of three and four letters [which is expressed in the following formula] : ' Three stones build six houses, four stones build four-and-twenty houses [26] ; go and calculate that which the human mouth cannot express nor the ear hear.' An inquiry is also necessary into how things multiplied prior to the revolution of the sphere, the Creator being One, whilst the sphere, so to speak, has six sides. The book, then, in spiritual language, finds a name for the Creator, choosing, in order to express it in physical speech, the slenderest consonants which are as a breath in comparison to the other letters, viz. *hē, wāw, yōd*. The book says that the divine will, when going forth under this great name, carries out everything God wishes. There is no doubt that He and the angels speak that spiritual language, and knew, even before the world was created, everything that was to happen in the physical world, as well as how speech and intelligence would emanate from Him on mankind, which was to be created in the world. From this it follows that the physical world

was created in a manner congruous to the tangible
element of the holy and spiritual name, which, in its
turn, is congruous to the tangible name, JHW, JWH,
HWJ, HJW, WJH, WHJ.   Each of these groups
was responsible for one direction of the universe, and
thus arose the sphere.   This, however, is not satisfactory, because the object of research is either too profound to be fathomed, or our minds are inadequate, or
for both reasons simultaneously.   Philosophers speculating on these things arrive at the conclusion that
from *one* only one can issue.   They conjectured an
angel, standing near to God, and having emanated from
the Prime Cause.   To this angel they attributed two
characteristics ; firstly, his consciousness of his own
existence by his very essence ; secondly, his consciousness of having a cause.   Two things resulted from this,
viz. an angel and the sphere of fixed stars.   From his
recognition of the Prime Cause a second angel emanated, and from his consciousness of his existence emanated the sphere of Saturnus, and so forth to the moon,
and the Creative Intellect.[26a]   People accepted this
theory, and were deceived by it to such an extent, that
they looked upon it as conclusive, because it was attributed to Greek philosophers.   It is, however, a mere
assertion without convincing power, and open to various
objections.   Firstly, for what reason did this emanation
cease; did the Prime Cause become impotent ?   Secondly,
it might be asked : Why, from Saturnus' recognition of
what was above, did not one thing arise, and from his
recognition of the first angel another thing, so that the
Saturnine emanations counted four ?   Whence do we
know altogether that if a being became conscious of its
essence a sphere must arise, and from the recognition of

the Prime [Cause], an angel must arise ?   When Aristotle
asserts that he was conscious of his existence, one may
consistently expect that a sphere should emanate from
him, and when he asserts that he recognised the Prime
Cause, an angel should emanate.   I communicated these
rudiments to thee lest philosophers confuse thee and
thou think that by following it thou might satisfy thy
soul with a clear demonstration.   These rudiments are
as unacceptable to reason as they are extravagant in the
face of logic.   Neither do two philosophers agree on
this point, unless they be disciples of the same teacher.
But Empedocles, Pythagoras. Aristotle, Plato, and many
others entirely disagree with each other.

26. Al Khazari : Why should the letters H W J or an
angel or a sphere or other things be required if we
believe in the Divine will and creation, and if we believe
that God created the immense variety of things and
species in one moment, as is related in the Book of
Genesis—that He placed in everything the faculty of
preservation and propagation, and sustains them every
moment by His divine power ?   Do we not say : ' His
bounty renews every day for ever, the work of
creation ? ' [27]

27. The Rabbi : Just so, O King of the Khazars, by
God ! This is the truth, the real faith, and everything
else may be abandoned.   Perhaps this was Abraham's
point of view when divine power and unity dawned
upon him prior to the revelation accorded to him.   As
soon as this took place, he gave up all his speculations
and only strove to gain favour of God, having ascertained
what this was and how and where it could be obtained.
The Sages explain the words : 'And he brought him forth
abroad' (Gen.xv.), thus : Give up thy horoscopy ! [28] This

means : Forsake astrology as well as any other doubtful
study of nature. Plato relates that a prophet, who
lived at the time of the king Morinus,[29] said prophetically
to a philosopher who was zealously devoted to his art :
Thou canst not reach me on this road, but only those
whom I have placed as intermediaries between me and
mankind, viz. the prophets and the true law. The
Book Jeṣīrāh is constructed on the mystery of *ten units*
equally acknowledged in east and west, but neither from
natural causes, nor rational conviction. The following
sentences are a Divine mystery : ' Ten Sefīrōth without
anything else ; close thy mouth from speaking, close thy
heart from thinking. If thy heart runs away, return to
God ' [30] (Jez. i. 8) ; for with reference to this [the pro-
phet] says : ' Running and returning ' (Ezek. i. 15). On
this basis the covenant was made. — Their measure
is ten in endless progression, (ibid. i. 7) the end
being linked to the beginning, and the beginning
to the end just as a flame which is attached to the coal.
Know thou, think and reflect that the Creator is one,
without another, and there is no number which thou
canst count before ' one.' (vi. 4). The book concludes
as follows : As soon as Abraham had understood,
meditated, discerned and clearly grasped, the Lord
of the universe revealed Himself to him, called him His
friend and made a covenant with him between the
ten fingers of his hand, which is the covenant of the
tongue ; and between the ten toes of his feet, which is
the covenant of circumcision, and He pronounced upon
him the word : ' Before I formed thee in the belly I knew
thee ' (Jer. i. 5).

28. Al Khazari : Give me now an idea of the Sages'
accomplishments in natural science.

29. The Rabbi : I have already [31] called thy attention to the fact that they were so skilled in real astronomical observations that they knew the revolution of the moon which, according to Davidian tradition, amounts to twenty-nine days, twelve hours and seven hundred and ninety-three fractions.[32]   No flaw has been found in it hitherto. They also calculated the solar year, taking care that Passover should not fall till after the *Tekūfāh* [33] of Nīsān, as some of them explained : ' If you see that the equinox of Nisān would be on the sixteenth of Nisān, make the year an embolismic one,' [34] lest Passover fell in the winter season. God's command fixed the feast in the words : ' Observe the month of Abīb.' (Deut. xvi. 1). The *Tekūfāh*, as accepted by the people, is not the true one, but only approximate, on account of the division of the year into four seasons, viz. ninety-one days, seven and a half hours. According to this calculation Passover would fall in the winter. This induced the Christians to attack the Jews and to think that the latter had lost the basis of their belief. They themselves are without a basis, since their Easter would, according to their calculation of the commonly known equinox, take place before the beginning of spring. They did not, however, pay attention to the true equinox, which was kept secret and not given up to common knowledge. According to their calculation Passover never falls otherwise than when the sun has reached the head of Aries, though only by one day. For the last thousand years no mistake has occurred, and this agrees with the calculation of Al Battāni,[35] being most correct and accurate. Can the revolutions of sun and moon be calculated otherwise than by a most intimate knowledge of astronomy ? The problem of the

sentence : ' If the new moon appears before noon, etc. . .'
has been discussed before.[36]   There exists a book on this
special subject, styled 'Chapters of R. Eliezer,' [37] in which
we find dissertations on the extent of the globe and every
sphere, the nature of the stars, the signs of the zodiac,
constellations, houses, happy omens, good and evil influences, ascensions and descensions, elevations and the
extent of their movements. He was one of the best
known doctors of the Mishnāh. Samuel, one of the
doctors of the Talmud said : ' The roads of heaven are as
familiar to me as the streets of Nehardaea '.[38]   They
devoted themselves to this study only in the service
of the Law, because the calculation of the revolution of
the moon with the disturbances of her course did not
completely tally with the calculation of the time of her
conjunction with the sun, viz., the $M\bar{o}l\bar{a}d$.[39] The time
when the moon is not visible prior to the $M\bar{o}l\bar{a}d$ and immediately after it also, can only be calculated with the
help of sound astronomical knowledge. Similarly, the
knowledge of the changes of the four seasons can only
be properly obtained with the aid of a knowledge of the
lowest and highest points and the various ascensions
of stars as well as their variations. He who occupies
himself with this study must bring to bear on it also the
knowledge of spheres. The remarkable knowledge of
natural history displayed in the sayings of the Sages,
without any intention on their part of teaching this
science, is quite astonishing. What books, in thy
opinion, must have been at the disposal even of the
students among them ?

30. Al Khazari : I wonder how it is that the books
written for the purpose were lost whilst these incidental
sayings were saved.

31. The Rabbi : Because their contents were retained in the minds of a few people, only one of whom was an astronomer, another a physician or an anatomist. If a nation perishes it is first the higher classes which disappear, and literature with them.   There only remain the law books which the people require, know by heart, copy and preserve.   Whatever element of those sciences was embodied in the Talmudical law codes was thus protected and preserved by the zeal of many students. To these belong everything appertaining to the rules for slaughtering cattle, or making them unlawful to be eaten.   A large amount of this remained unknown to Galen.[40]   If this were not so, why does he not mention easily recognisable diseases to which the Law calls attention.   Among these are diseases of the lungs and heart, growths on the latter and on its sides, the growing together of the lobes of the lung, deficiency or redundance of the same, or if they are dried up or lacerated.[41] Their acquaintance with the vital and vegetative organs is shown in the following sentence : The brain has two skins to which correspond two on the testicles.[42]   Two bean-shaped growths are situated at the lower end of the skull ; inside them is the brain, outside is the spine.[43] Further : There are three arteries ; one leads to the heart, the second to the lung, and the third to the liver.[43] They distinguished between fatal diseases and less dangerous ones in the following words : If the skin of the spine is preserved, the marrow remains intact. He whose marrow becomes soft cannot beget children.[43] Further : a skin formed in consequence of a wound on the lung is no real skin.[43a]   The regulation concerning the ' sinew that shrinks ' does not apply to birds, because they have no hollow of the hip.[44]   Worth mentioning

are the following regulations : The contents of the
stomach of a lawful animal suckled by an unlawful
one is unlawful, but the contents of the stomach of
an unlawful animal suckled by a lawful one are
lawful, because the milk becomes compact in the entrails.[45] Very profound, though beyond our grasp, is
the following prohibition : Five cuticles are unlawful,
viz. that of the brain, testicles, spleen, kidneys and lower
end of the spine, all these it is unlawful to eat.[46] They
have also very skilfully determined the height from
which a fall would make an animal unlawful on
account of 'shattering of limbs,' which means the tearing of limbs which endangers its life. They say as
follows : ' If one has left an animal above [a structure],
and finds it below, shattering of limbs is not to be feared,
because the animal ' measures itself,' which means that
the animal measures and prepares for the leap, without
damage. This would not be the case if it were pushed.
Leaping is assisted by presence of mind, whilst a push
produces fear.[47] The following regulation is also interesting : The naturally reduced lung is lawful, the
artificially reduced one is unlawful on account of ' shrink-
ing.' This can be examined by keeping it in tepid
water for four and twenty hours. If it re-assumes a
healthy appearance, it is lawful, but not otherwise.[48]
If the lung has the colour of antimony it is lawful, if it
is like ink it is unlawful, because this blackness is a
morbid transformation of red.[49] The yellow lung is
lawful. If a lung is partially red, it is lawful, but unlawful if it is completely red. A child of a yellowish
tint was brought before R. Nathan of Babylon who
decided : ' Wait until the blood has gone down.' He
meant to say that the circumcision should not take

place till the blood had spread through the whole body.
This was done and the life of the child was saved, although other children of the same mother had died
soon after the circumcision. Subsequently a child
was brought before of a reddish hue, and he said :
' Wait till the blood has been absorbed.' The child
was saved in consequence and was called after him :
Nathan Habbabli.[50] They further said : Lawful fat
can close up an internal wound, but not unlawful
fat.[51] A very acute decision is the following : If a
needle is found in the thick wall of the stomach together
with a drop of blood, [it must have entered before
the animal was killed] if no blood is visible, it must have
entered afterwards. The issue of this effects the validity
of the sale, because after the killing no blood could
approach the needle, as the blood does not flow in a
dead animal. The buyer cannot, therefore, return
the animal to the seller. If, however, blood is found,
he can return it with the plea : ' Thou hast sold me an
animal liable to die.' [52] A scab on a wound shows that
the latter was three days old before the animal was
killed, if no scab is to be seen the plaintiff must bring
other evidence. The characteristics of a clean bird are
the following : Place the bird on a stretched rope; if it
divides its claws two by two, it is an unclean bird, if it
divides them three by one, it is a clean one. Further :
Every bird that catches its food in the air is unclean,
a bird that lives with notoriously unclean ones, as the
starling among ravens, is of the same character.[53] A
symptom of birth among small cattle is a flow of blood ;
among big cattle after-birth ; in a woman : placenta and
after-birth.[54] Very strange are the sayings concerning
the poison contained in the claws of certain animals : a

cat, a sparrow-hawk, and martin strike poison into kids
and lambs ; the weasel wounds birds.   The fox and
the dog convey no poison.   This poisoning is conveyed
by the claw, but not by the teeth ; only by the forefoot,
but not by the hindfoot ; only when the animal does it
purposely, and is alive.   All this means that an animal
can only poison any other by striking it purposely, but
not accidentally, or if the claw remains sticking in the
flesh without any tearing intention.   The addition
' living animal ' is therefore most remarkable.[55]   For
it the striking foot were cut off and the claw remained
in the flesh of the wound of the other animal, no poisoning takes place, because the poison is not conveyed till
the claw is withdrawn For this reason the words
' while living ' are placed intentionally after ' on purpose.'   They say further : If the liver is missing excepting the size of an olive near the gall, its natural place,
the animal is lawful.[56]   Matter is harmless on the lung,
but not on the kidneys.   Clear water and a hole are
harmless on the kidney but fatal for the lungs.[57]   If an
animal has been skinned, a piece as large as a coin remaining on the spine suffices to make the animal lawful.[58]
The Mishnāh also contains regulations concerning unlawful food, defects of first-born animals, defects of
priests,[59] too many to enumerate, not to speak of com-
menting on them.   Apart from this the anatomy of the
skeleton is given in very concise, yet clear description.[60]
An admirable saying is : If the intestines protrude,
but show no hole, the animal is lawful.   This, however,
the Mishnāh adds, is only the case if they have not been
inverted. If this has taken place, the animal is unlawful ;
for it is written : ' He has made thee and established
thee ' (Deut. xxxii. 6), which means that God has

created man as a well established being. If one of
his organs were inverted, he could not live. The
Sages further distinguish the various appearances of
blood of issue or wounds and haemorrhoids, the rules
of menstruation and male issue, symptoms of leprosy,
and other matters too deep for our capacity.

Finished is Part Four, and we begin—

PART FIVE

1. AL KHAZARI : I must trouble thee to give me a clear and concise discourse on religious principles and axioms according to the method of the Mutakallims. Let me hear them exactly as thou didst study them, that I may accept or refute them. Since I have not been granted a perfect faith free from doubts, and I was formerly sceptical, had my own opinions, and exchanged ideas with philosophers and followers of other religions, I consider it most advantageous to learn and to instruct myself how to refute dangerous and foolish views. Tradition in itself is a good thing if it satisfies the soul, but a perturbed soul prefers research, especially if examination leads to the verification of tradition. Then knowledge and tradition become united.

2. The Rabbi : Where is the soul which is strong enough not to be deceived by the views of philosophers, scientists, astrologers, adepts, magicians, materialists, and others, and can adopt a belief without having first passed through many stages of heresy ? Life is short, but labour long. Only few there are to whom belief comes naturally, who avoid all these views, and whose soul always detects the points of error in them. I hope that thou art one of those few. Since I cannot resist, I will not lead thee the way of the Karaites, who ascended the heights of metaphysics without inter-

mediate steps. I will give thee a clear standpoint, which will assist thee to acquire clear notions of matter and form, elements, nature, soul, intellect, and metaphysics in general. After this I will prove to thee, as briefly as possible, that the rational soul can exist without a body ; further, the existence of reward hereafter, providence and omnipotence. As regards tangible objects, we can perceive their quantity and quality by means of our senses, whilst reason maintains that they are borne by a fulcrum which is difficult to imagine. How can we imagine a thing that has neither quantity nor quality ? [Imagination denies its existence, but reason answers that quantity and quality][1] are accidents which have no independent existence, but must necessarily have an object to support them. Philosophers call this object *matter*, adding that our intelligence grasps its meaning only imperfectly, since imperfection is its nature ; that it does not really exist, and therefore cannot claim any predicate, and although it only exists virtually, its predicate is corporeal. Aristotle says that it is, so to speak, ashamed to appear naked, and therefore only shows itself clothed in a form. Some people believe that the ' water ' spoken of in the biblical account of the creation is an appellation for this matter, and that ' the spirit of the Lord hovering over the surface of the water ' only expresses the divine will which penetrates all atoms of matter, with which He does what, how, and when He desires, as the potter with the shapeless clay. The absence of form and order is called darkness and *tōhū wabōhū*. After this the wise, divine will ordained the revolution of the uppermost sphere, which completes one revolution in four and twenty hours, carrying all

other spheres with it. Through this the matter which
fills the sphere of the moon underwent a change, which
was in accordance with the movements of the spheres.
The first process was that the air near the moon sphere
became hot, because it was nearest to the periphery.
It thus became an aetherial fire, called *elementary fire*
by natural philosophers, having neither colour nor com-
bustion, and being a fine, delicate, and light substance.
It is called the fire sphere. Then comes the water
sphere, and then the terrestrial globe, which forms a
heavy and compact centre, being removed farthest
from the periphery. These are the four elements,
from the intermixture of which all things arise.

3. Al Khazari: In the opinion of philosophers, as
I see, things arise by accident, since they say that that
which happened to be nearest to the sphere became
fire, and what was remotest became earth, whilst the
middle part, according to proximity either to the periphery or to the centre, became air or water.

4. The Rabbi: Yet necessity forces them to acknowledge a divine wisdom in the distinction of one
element from the other. The fire element is not distinguished from the atmospheric element, the latter
from that of water, and the aqueous one from the
terrestrial one by quantity or strength, but by the form
specific to each; one is made into fire, another into air, the
third into water, and the last into earth, otherwise one
might say that the whole sphere is filled up with earthy
matter, but that one portion was finer than another.
Another may assert that it is all fire, only the lower
parts are denser and cooler. We see that the [spheres
of the] elements touch one another, but each preserves
its form and speciality. We see how air, water and

earth are in contact in one place without absorbing each other, till they are transformed one into another by other causes. Water assumes the form of air, air the form of fire, and then the element justly takes the other's name. Since substances, apart from their accidences, are distinguished by their forms, philosophers found it correct to assert the activity of a divine creative intellect which bestows these forms, just as it bestowed them to plants and animals, which are all composed of the four elements. The vine and palm are not distinguished by accidental qualities, but by forms which made the substance of one different from the substance of the other. Accidental qualities would only distinguish one vine from another, and one palm from another, one, e.g. being black, the other one white, one sweeter, one longer or shorter, one thicker or thinner than the other. The forms of substances have no quantity ; one horse cannot be less equine than another, nor one man more human than another, because the definitions ' equine ' and ' human ' are common to each individual horse and man. Philosophers involuntarily acknowledged that these forms could only be given by the Divine Influence, which they call form-giving Intelligence.

5. Al Khazari : This, as thou livest ! is belief, considering that reason forces us to acknowledge such a thing. How can we now speak of accidents, or why do we not say that he who made this being a horse, and the other a man, by wisdom incomprehensible in detail, is the same who made fire fire, and earth earth through a wisdom beheld by God, but not by accidental proximity to or distance from the sphere ?

6. The Rabbi : This is the religious argument. Evi-

dence of it is to be found in the Children of Israel,
for whose sake changes in nature were wrought, as well
as new things created. If this evidence be removed,
thy opponent and thou might agree that a vine, e.g.
grew in this place because a seed happened to have
fallen there. The seed assumed its form only by
accident, because the revolution of the sphere resulted
in a constellation which caused a mixture of elements
productive of what thou now seest.

[7.[2] Al Khazari: I should refer my opponent to
the uppermost sphere and its mover, and ask him
whether or not, this is the result of accident. I should
further refer him to the spherical constellations, which
are unlimited. We see, however, that the number of
forms of animal and plant life is not unlimited, allowing neither increase nor diminution. One might think
that new constellations would produce new formations,
and that others would perish.]

8. The Rabbi: This is all the more correct, as with
regard to many we understand their inherent wisdom
as well as purpose, just as Aristotle explained in his
discourse on ' The utility of the species of animals,'[3]
or Galen in ' The utility of the organs,' not to speak
of other wonderful achievements of the divine wisdom.
In the instance of domestic animals, such as sheep,
cattle, horses and asses, it is clear that they were
created for the benefit of man. For in a wild state
they are imperfect, but useful when domesticated.
David's allusion in the words: ' How great are Thy
works, O Lord ' (Ps. civ. 24), serves to refute Epicurus'
view that the universe arose by accident.

9. Al Khazari: Although it may be a digression,
explain the meaning of this psalm to me.

10. The Rabbi: It runs parallel with the history of creation. The words: ' He who covereth Himself with light ' (ver. 2), correspond to ' Let there be light, and there was light ' (Gen. i. 3). The words: ' He stretcheth out the heavens like a carpet ' run parallel to ' Let there be a firmament ' ; the words : ' He who layeth the beams ' to ' the water above the firmament ' (ver. 3). He then describes the atmospheric phenomena, clouds, winds, fires, lightnings, and thunder, which all stand under God's guidance, as it is written : ' For by them judgeth He the people ' (Job xxxvi. 31). In the psalm this is described in the words : ' He who maketh the clouds His chariot, who walketh upon the wings of the winds, who maketh the winds His messengers, and His ministers a flaming fire ' (ver. 3–4). This means that He dispatches them whither and on what errand He desires. Thus far the phenomena of the atmosphere. The psalm, then, passes on to ' let the waters . . . be gathered . . . and the dry land appear ' (ver. 9), which is parallel to : ' He founded the earth on its bases.' According to its nature water would close up above the earth, covering it completely, hills and dales, like a garment, as the psalm hath it : ' With the flood, as with a robe, Thou coveredst it ; waters stand above the mountains.' Divine Providence, however, obviated its natural inclination, and sent it down to the ocean's deep, to let animals arise and God's wisdom appear. The words : ' At Thy rebuke they flee,' describe the retirement of the water in the seas and underneath the earth. The same condition is alluded to in the words : ' To Him that spread out the earth above the water ' (Ps. cxxxvi. 6), a sentence which seemingly contradicts the other : ' With the flood as

with a robe Thou coveredst it,' the latter corresponding
to the nature of the water, whilst the former describes
God's wisdom and omnipotence. Then the psalm
continues : ' Thou didst appoint a bound, that they
might not pass over, nor turn again to cover the earth '
(Ps. civ. 9). All this is intended for the benefit of
mankind. By means of certain clever works and
dykes man keeps off the floods of rivers, utilising only
so much water as is required for mills and irrigation.
The psalm now says : ' He sends forth springs into the
valleys ' (ver. 10), that they should ' give drink to every
beast of the plain ' (ver. 11), as soon as the wild beasts
were created. The words : ' Upon them dwell the
birds of the heaven ' (ver. 12) refer to the creation of the
birds. The psalm, then, passes on to ' Let the earth
bring forth ' (Gen. i. 11) in the words : ' To the mountains He gives drink from His upper chambers ' (ver. 13).
This is only another expression for : ' But there went
up a mist from the earth ' (Gen. ii. 16) likewise for the
benefit of Adam and his posterity. The psalm
says : ' He causes grass to spring up for the cattle '
(ver. 14), lest the grass be despised, since it is of service
for the domestic animals, oxen, sheep, and horses.
This is described in the words : ' Service of man,' (ibid.),
viz. agriculture, by means of which he produces corn
for himself, as is expressed in the words : ' To bring
forth bread from the earth.' This is parallel to the
verse : ' Behold, I have given you every herb bearing
seed, viz. the corn for man, and the chaff for the rest
of creatures ' (Gen. i. 29), as it is said : ' And to every
beast of the earth, and to every fowl of the heaven
. . . every green herb for meat '(ibid. 30). The psalm
then mentions the three foods gained from the soil,

viz. corn, wine and oil, which are comprised in the
term *leḥem*, and their usages as follows : ' Wine which
gladdens man's heart, to make his face shine more than
oil,' ' and bread,'—viz. the loaf—sustains man's heart '
(ver. 15). Then he mentions the importance of rain for the
trees in the words : ' The trees of the Lord have their
fill ' (ver. 16). These high trees have a use for some
animals, as is expressed in the words : ' Wherein the
birds make their nests ' (ver. 17), just as the high mountains serve other animals, viz. ' The high mountains
are for the wild goats, the crags a refuge for the coneys.'
Thus far the description of the dry land. The psalm
then discusses the Biblical words : ' Let there be lights '
as follows : ' The moon He made to measure time,'
(ver. 19). After this is mentioned the utility of the night
which is not the work of accident, but of intention.
There is no trifling in His work, nor even in the accidental consequences of the same. The night is but the
time of the absence of sunlight, yet instituted for a
purpose. This is expressed in the words : ' Thou
makest darkness, and it is night ' (ver. 20). This is followed by the description of beasts dangerous to man,
which go forth at night and hide by day, whilst man
and domestic animals sleep at night and walk abroad
during the day. ' Man goes forth to his work and to
his labour until the evening ' (ver. 23). Having thus
included all terrestrial animals in the discussion of the
rivers and heavenly lights, and having also mentioned
man, there only remain the animals which live
in water, the life of which is very little known to us,
because Divine Wisdom lavished on them is not so
manifest to us as in the former. Speaking of the
wisdom which is visible, the psalmist breaks out in

praise and says : ' How manifold are Thy works, O
Lord ! ' (ver. 24). He then resumes the subject of the
ocean and what is therein, concluding with the words :
' Let the glory of the Lord endure for ever ; let the
Lord rejoice in His works' (ver. 31). This is a rendering
of the words : ' And God saw everything that He had
made, and behold it was very good ' (Gen. i. 31). At
the same time it is an allusion to the seventh day in the
words : ' He rested,' ' He blessed,' ' He sanctified,'
because it marked the completion of the works of
nature, which had a time limit, and placed man on a
par with angels, which, being spirits, are above natural
impulses, and not bound by time in their works. Intellect can, as we see, picture heaven and earth in one
moment. This is the world of celestial life and bliss
where the soul finds ease at the moment when it reaches
it. The Sabbath is, therefore, called ' a taste of the
world to come.'—Let us now resume the discussion on
the opinion held by philosophers that the elements
having entered various combinations relative to the
variety of climes, atmosphere, and constellations,
received a variety of forms from the Giver of forms.
All minerals are, therefore, but the sum total of the
specific powers and faculties. Others assert that the
powers and qualities of minerals are the product of
combination only, and consequently do not require
forms of divine origin. The latter are only necessary
for plants and animals to which a soul is attributed.
The finer this mixture is, the nobler is the form proper
for it in which the divine wisdom manifests itself in a
higher degree. It becomes a plant which is possessed
of some feeling and perception, penetrates the earth,
and derives nourishment from good, moist soil and

sweet water, avoiding the contrast. Thus it grows, until it comes to a stand-still, having given life to another like it and produced seed. This seed, then, according to a wisdom implanted in it, pursues a similar course. Philosophers call this nature,[4] or rather powers which guard the preservation of the species, since the essence of the individual cannot be preserved, it being composed of various component parts. A thing which possesses these powers of growth, propagation and nourishment, is devoid of the power of motion, and is, in the opinion of philosophers, guided by nature. As a matter of fact, it is God who controls it in a certain condition. Call this condition what thou wilt, nature, soul, power, or angel. If the mixture is still finer, and fit to be impressed by the divine wisdom, it is favoured with a higher form than the bare physical power. It is able to bring its food from a distance, and is possessed of organs subject to it, which cannot move except by its desire. It has more control over its parts than the plant with which the wind plays, which cannot ward off damage, nor obtain what is useful to it. The animal has limbs to move about from place to place. The form allotted to it above its physical life is called *soul*. The souls vary greatly according to the preponderance of one or the other of the four elements. The wisdom of Providence has also constituted each living being for the benefit of the whole world. We may not be aware of the use of most of them, any more than we know of the use of ships' implements, and consider them therefore useless, whilst the master and builder of the ship knows it. We would not know the purpose of many of our bones and other organs if they lay de-

tached before us, and so we are in ignorance of the
purpose of every bone and limb, although we use it,
and are convinced that if we lacked one, our actions
would be impaired, and we could not do without it.
All atoms of the world are known to, and mustered by,
their Creator, and nothing can be added to it, nor anything taken away from it. It is necessary that souls
should differ from each other, and that the organs of
each soul should be suitable to it. For this reason He
endowed the lion with organs for seizing its prey, such
as teeth and claws, in addition to courage ; but to the
hart He gave the means of flight as compensation for
its timidity.[5] Every soul instinctively uses its faculties
according to their nature, but nature does not reach
perfection in any part of animal life, and consequently
has no desire to obtain a form higher than the living
soul. This, however, is possible in man, in whom it
strives for a higher form. The Divine Influence
grudges nothing. It bestows on him a higher form,
called material or passive intellect. Men differ from each
other, because most of them are physically of different
constitutions, and the intellect follows the latter. If
his gall be yellowish, he is quick and alert ; if blackish,
he is quiet and sedate. The temperament follows the
mixture of humours. If an individual is found of
evenly balanced humour, which controls his contrasting
dispositions (like the two scales of a balance in the
hand of the person who weighs and regulates them
by adding or subtracting at his will), such a person
possesses without doubt a heart which is free from
strong passions. He covets a degree of divine character above his own. He is perplexed, not knowing
which inclination should have preponderance. He

does not give way either to anger, or to lust, or to any
other passion, but controls himself, and seeks divine
inspiration to walk the right path. This is the person
on whom the divine and prophetic spirit is poured out,
if he is fit for prophecy, but if he stands below that
degree, he is only endowed with inspiration. In the
latter case he is a pious man, but no prophet. There
is no niggardliness with God, who allows every one his
due. Philosophers call the giver of this degree Active
Intellect, and regard it as an angel below God.
If a man's intellect is in conjunction with the former,
this is called his paradise and lasting life.

11. Al Khazari : Give me a brief discourse on all
this.

12. The Rabbi : The existence of the human soul
is shown in living beings by motion and perception, in
contradistinction to the movements of the elements.
The cause of the former is called *soul*, or *animal power*.
This is divided into three divisions. The first is that
which is common to animal and plant-life, and is called
vegetative power ; the second, which is common to man
and the rest of living beings, is called *vital power* ; the
third specific of man is called *rational power*. The
nature of the soul in the comprehensive and generic
sense is defined by the examination of its actions as
issuing from the forms adhering to matter, but not from
matter, inasmuch as it is matter only [without form].
The knife, for instance, does not cut inasmuch as it is
a substance, but inasmuch as it has the form of a knife.
In the same way the animal does not feel and move
inasmuch as it is a substance, but inasmuch as it has
the form of a living being. This is what is called *soul*.
These forms are called perfections (*entelechies*), be-

cause through them the structures of things become perfect. *The soul is therefore a perfection.* We distinguish a primary and a secondary perfection. The former is the principle of actions, the latter the nature of the actions which arise out of the principle. *The soul is a primary perfection,* because it is a principle from which something else [i.e. a secondary entelechy] may issue forth. The entelechy is either entelechy to a corporate object, or entelechy to amorphous matter. *The soul is entelechy to a corporate object.* Corporate objects are either natural or artificial. The soul is *first entelechy to a natural corporate object.* A natural corporate object is either organic or inorganic, which means that it performs its actions either by means of organs or without them. *The soul is entelechy to a natural corporate object, endowed with organs, and potentially with life,* viz. a mainspring of potentially vivified actions, or susceptible to such. The next consequence is that the soul is not the result of a combination of elements of substance. If a thing arises from a combination of component parts, one or more of these component parts preponderate, its form shapes itself accordingly. Or the component parts struggle with one another, so that not one of them retains its form, but their medium yields a new form. The soul which is not composed of corporeal ingredients is therefore nothing but external form, like the impression made by the seal in the clay which is composed of water and earth. The seal is not the result of the forms of water and earth. The first of the [vegetative] powers is that of nutrition, which forms, so to speak, the beginning, whilst that of propagation forms the end. The faculty of growth is in the middle, linking the beginning to the end. The faculty of propagation occupies the first place, and although it appears to be placed at the end, it rules supreme over the substance which is fitted to receive life. Assisted by growth and nutrition, it clothes it with the intended form. It then leaves the further management to the latter two till the moment of propagation. Propagation is aided, nutrition aids, growth aids and is aided. Nutrition has those four well-known powers at its disposal. Everything that moves does so by the will of a perception; otherwise perception were useless. Providence, however, produces nothing that is either useless or injurious. Neither does it withhold anything that is necessary or useful. Even mollusks, though apparently lying quietly, can contract and stretch themselves, and if placed on their backs, move till they turn over on their bellies, in order to reach their food. The exterior senses are thus known. As to the interior ones, the first is the general sense,[6] because that which is useful or injurious can only be learnt by experience. God therefore gave man the faculty of conception, that he may grasp by its means the forms of objects perceived. This is what is meant under the term *general sense*. Then He gave him the faculty of remembering, to retain the notions of things perceived; further, the power of imagination, in order to restore what had been lost to memory; the faculty of judgment, in order to pause again and again at the new products of imagination, correct or false, till it is restored to memory. Lastly, He endowed him with the power of motion, in order to procure what is required from near and far, and to remove what is injurious. All the powers of a living being are either perceptive or motive. The

motive power is of optative character, and is divided
into two classes, viz. firstly moving to obtain what is
desired, i.e. avidity; secondly, moving to repel what
is undesirable, i.e. dislike. Perception is also divided
into two classes, viz. external faculties, as the external
senses; and internal faculties, as the internal senses.
The motive power acts on the judgment of conception
and with the assistance of imagination. It forms the
extreme limit of animal life; for the motive power fails
it in restoring the causes of perception and imagination.
It is only endowed with the sense of instinct to regulate
the causes of motion. Rational beings, on the other
hand, are endowed with motion in order to obtain the
rational soul, which has action and memory. The five
senses, as is known, offer the means of perceiving form,
number, size, motion, and rest. The existence of the common sense is explained if we, for instance, judge when we
find honey that it is sweet. This is only possible
because we possess a faculty common to the five senses,
viz., the perceptive power, which is active both in
waking and sleeping. To this is added a faculty which
either combines all that which is united in the common
sense, or separates, and fixes their differences without,
however, depriving forms of the common sense. This
is the faculty of imagination which is sometimes correct,
sometimes incorrect, whilst the faculty of perception
is always correct. The next is the faculty of judgment,
which is of a deciding character, and judges whether an
object is desirable or undesirable. The faculties of
perception and imagination can neither judge nor
decide, but can only picture an object. The faculty
of recollection retains the objects it has perceived, e.g.
that the wolf is an enemy, and the child beloved. Love

and hatred, belief and unbelief belong to the realm of judgment. Memory retains that which the faculty of judgment declares to be true. The faculty of imagination is so called when in the service of judgment, but if employed by reason, it is called cogitation. The seat of the faculty of perception is in the fore part of the brain, that of imagination in the middle, that of memory at the back. The seat of judgment is in the whole brain, principally at the border line of the faculty of imagination. All these faculties perish with their organs, and no duration is granted to reasonable beings, although it claims the nucleus, so to speak, of these faculties as its own, and renders their real character manifest. This is the result of the philosopher's discourses on that which is beneath the rational soul. They call the soul *hylic intellect*, i.e. potential intellect, because it resembles matter which forms the connecting link between nothingness and actuality; in other words, all potential objects. They obtain rational forms either by way of divine inspiration or by application. Those obtained by inspiration are the result of original conception shared by all human beings guided by nature. Those acquired by application are gained by speculation and dialectic corollary. The result is the formation of logical conclusions, as species, classes, divisions, specialities, words simple and composed in various ways; compound conclusions true or untrue; propositions from which arise either apodictic, dialectic, rhetoric, sophistic, or poetic conclusions. [There arise further] the establishment of physical notions, as matter, form, nothingness, nature, place, time, motion, spherical and elementary substances, growth and decay in general ; the

origin of meteorological, mineral and terrestrial phenomena, as plants and animals ; the essence of man ;
the nature of the soul according to its own conception ;
further, things mathematical, such as arithmetic,
geometry, music, astronomy ; further, things metaphysical, such as the knowledge of beginning and existence
as such in general, and the accessories thereof either
potential or actual, principle, cause, substance, accident,
species and class, contrast and connaturality, congru-
ence and difference, unity and plurality ; the establishment of the principles of speculative subjects, as mathe-
matics, natural history, from logic, [all of] which can only
be gained by a knowledge of the last-named ; further, the
establishment of the existence of the Prime Creator, of
the universal soul, the nature of species, the relation of the
intellect to the Creator, the relation of the soul to the
intellect, the relation of nature to the soul, the relation
of matter and form to nature, the relation of the spheres,
stars and other phenomena to matter and form.   Then
we must consider why they are constructed with such
differences of sequence,* the knowledge of divine
guidance, of universal nature, of divine providence.
The rational soul sometimes derives certain forms from
the senses by applying to its own needs perception and
memory, and making use of imagination and judgment.
We shall then find that these forms have some attributes in common, but that they differ in others ; some
of these attributes are essential, others accidental.
The soul divides or combines, and produces species,
categories, divisions, specialities, and accidences.   It

---

* Lit. earlier and later.

then combines them by means of syllogisms, and produces satisfactory conclusions with the assistance of
the universal intellect. Although, at first, it reposed
on the faculties of perception, it does not require them
for the formation of the ideas themselves, nor in the
composition of the syllogisms, be it to verify them, or
to form a conception. Just as the faculties of perception only acquire something relative to the object
perceived, thus the intellectual faculties only conceive something relative to the conceived object, by
abstracting the form from the matter, and remaining
attached to the former. The faculty of perception,
however, does not act spontaneously as does the
rational soul, but it requires the motive power as well
as the assistance of intermediaries which establish a
connexion between the forms and itself. The power
of intellect conceives spontaneously and conceives
itself as often as it desires. The faculty of perception
is therefore called *passive*, but the power of intellect is
called *active*. Actual reason is nothing but the abstract
of objects conceived, potentially existing in reason
itself [and rendered actual by the same]. It is therefore also said that actual reason comprehends and is
comprehended simultaneously. It is one of the special
characteristics of reason that, by means of synthesis
and analysis it transforms plurality into unity and
unity into plurality. Although the activity of reason
in combining proportions by means of careful consideration appears to require a certain time, the deduction
of the conclusion is not dependent on time, reason
itself being above time. When the rational soul turns
its attention towards science, its activity is called
theoretical reason. If, however, it undertakes to subdue

animal instincts, its activity is called guidance, and it
assumes the name of *practical reason*. Some people's
reasoning power succeeds in establishing so intimate
a connexion with the universal reason, that it is lifted
above logical conclusions and meditation, escaping such
necessity by inspiration and revelation. This special
distinction is styled sanctity, or holy spirit. A proof
that the soul is real, though incorporeal and no accessory, is to be found in the circumstance that it is the
form of a corporeal object. According to its nature it
cannot be divided like a corporeal object, or like an
accessory when the substratum of the same is divided.
Colour, smell, taste, heat and cold are divided as soon
as their substrata are divided, though their nature is
indivisible. The form of the intellect consists in the
object conceived. A human being's conception cannot
be divided, because half, or a piece of a human being
cannot be styled man, although part of a corporeal
object, or a colour can retain their names. Colour and
corporeal object, if only existing in conception, allow
no division even in thought. One cannot say : Half
of a conceived colour, or half of a conceived corporeal
object, as one can say : ' Half of this object is perceived,' or ' Half of the colour borne by it and referring
to it.' One cannot speak of half of Zeid's soul, as one
can speak of half of his body ; for the former can neither
be limited locally, nor defined in any way, nor pointed
to. Now if it cannot be either a corporeal object nor
an accessory borne by a corporeal object, its existence
is manifested by its activity. There remains nothing
but to see in it a substance with an existence of its own,
endowed with angelic attributes and divine substan-
tiality. Its primary tools are those spiritual forms

which shape themselves in the centre of the brain from the psychical spirit by means of the power of imagination. The latter gives the faculty of reflecting, as soon as it becomes predominant enough to produce synthetical and analytical knowledge. It had been imaginative prior to this, when judgment was predominant in it, as is the case with children, animals, and with people whose constitution has been tried by illness. As a consequence the human soul is deprived of those formations on account of the synthetical and analytical processes which are required for the unimpaired consideration of an opinion. In such a case the opinion becomes a defective judgment, wholly or partially. A proof that the soul is distinct from the body, and does not require it, is to be found in the circumstance that the physical powers are weakened by strong influences. The organ of the eye is damaged by the sun, and the ear by too strong a sound. The rational soul, however, retains whatever stronger knowledge it has obtained. Moreover, old age attacks the body, but not the soul. The latter is stronger after the fiftieth year, whilst the body is on the decline. The activity of the body is limited, which is not the case with that of the soul, for geometrical, arithmetical, and logical forms are unlimited. There now remains to be shown that there exists a spiritual substance, distinct from the body, which stands in the same relation to the soul as the light to the eye, and as soon as the soul is separated from the body, it is united to that substance. The soul does not gain its knowledge empirically. For the results of experience cannot be judged apodictically. No one can assert apodictically that no man can move his ears, just as we may judge that every human being

feels ; that every one who feels, lives ; that every one
who lives is a substance ; that the whole is larger than
a part, and other fundamental truths. For our belief
in the correctness of opinions is not regulated by instruction, otherwise we should come to an endless
chain of conclusions. But then the rational soul comes
into connexion with the divine emanation. As long
as this divine emanation is not defined by the general
spiritual form, it cannot impregnate the soul with it.
Every being possessed of an essentially spiritual form
is an incorporeal substance. If this be so, this emanation is a spiritual, incorporeal substance, with an
existence of its own. The conception which the soul
has of the form is a perception (entelechy) for it. It
would succeed in coming into contact with the spiritual
substance, if its intimacy with the body did not interfere. A complete connexion is, however, impossible,
unless all physical powers are subdued. For it is the
body alone which prevents this connexion. As soon
as the soul is separated from it, it becomes perfect,
connected with what renders it immune to injury, and
united with the noble substance which is styled the
higher knowledge.[7] All other powers only act for the
body, and perish together with organs. The rational
soul, however, having fashioned them, appropriated
their kernel, as has been explained before.

13. Al Khazari : This philosophical discourse appears
to be more accurate and true than others.

14. The Rabbi : I feared that thou wouldst be
deceived, and acquiesce in their views. Because they
furnish mathematical and logical proofs, people accept
everything they say concerning physics and metaphysics, taking every word as evidence. Didst thou not,

from the very beginning, doubt their theories of the four elements, their search of the fire world, in which they place the aetherial fire, which is colourless, and therefore prevent the colour of the sky and stars from being seen. When did *we* ever accept an elementary fire ? The highest degree of heat, if found in the earth, appears as coal ; in the air as flame ; in the water at boiling point. When did we ever witness an igneous or atmospheric substance entering into the substance of the plant or animal, and asserted that it was composed of all four elements, viz. fire, air, water, and earth ? Supposing we did perceive water and earth enter the substance of a plant in altered form ; but air and heat only assisted the process through their quality, but not as igneous and atmospheric bodies. Or when did we ever see them dissolved into the four real elements ? If a part is reduced to a kind of dust, it is not real dust, but ashes, which can be used for healing purposes. Another part which is reduced to a kind of water is not real water, but an expressed liquid, a juice either poisonous or nourishing, but not drinkable water. The portion which is dissolved into a kind of air is vapour or fume, but no air fit to be breathed. Sometimes they alter their condition when absorbed by an animal or a plant, or enter a combination with earthly particles, move from alteration to alteration, but only in rare cases are they reduced to the pure element. Science, it is true, forces us to accept the theory that heat, cold, moisture, and dryness are primary qualities, the influences of which nobody can escape ; that reason reduces compound things to them, or declares them to be composed of them ; and places substances at their disposal which bear them,

calling them fire, air, water, and earth. This is, however, but a conception and nomenclature, but it does
not mean that they can emerge from mere theory into
reality, and produce, by combination, all existing
things. How can philosophers make such an assertion,
whilst teaching the eternity of matter, and that man
never arose otherwise than from issue and blood, blood
from food, food from vegetables, and vegetables, as
we have said, from seeds and water transformed with
the assistance of sunlight, air, and earth. All stars
and spherical constellations also exercise their influence. This is the objection to the view of philosophers concerning the elements. According to the
Tōrāh, it was God who created the world, together
with animals and plants. There is no need to pre-
suppose intermediaries or combinations [of elements].
If we make creation a postulate, all that is difficult
becomes easy, and all that is crooked straight, as soon
as one assumes that this world once did not exist, but
came into existence by the will of God at the time He
desired. Why dost thou trouble to examine the way
in which bodies arose and were equipped with souls ?
Why art thou reluctant to accept the ' firmament ' and
' the water above the heavens,' and the evil spirits
mentioned by the Sages, the description of the events
to be expected during the days of the Messiah, the
resurrection of the dead and the world to come ? Why
should we need such artificial theories in order to prove
the life of the soul after the dissolution of the body,
considering that we have reliable information with
regard to the return of the soul, be it spiritual or corporeal. If thou wouldst endeavour to confirm or
refute these views logically, life would be spent in vain.

Who vouchsafes the truth of the theory quoted above, that the soul is a spiritual substance which cannot be encompassed by space, and which is not subject to growth and decay ?   In what way differs my soul from thine, or from the Active Intellect, from other causes and the Prime Cause ?   Why, also, did not Aristotle's soul become united to that of Plato, either of them knowing the other's belief and innermost thought ? Why do not all philosophers conceive their notions simultaneously, as is the case with God and the Active Intellect ?   How can they be subject to forgetfulness, and require reflection for every single one of their notions ?   Why is not a philosopher conscious of himself when he is asleep or intoxicated, or is prostrate with pleurisy, or has brain fever, or is old and decrepit ?   How should we judge a person who, having arrived at the extreme limit of philosophic speculation, is stricken by melancholy or depression, which makes him forget all his knowledge ?   Is he not himself in his eyes, or shall we say that he is some one else ?   Suppose he recovers gradually from his complaint, and begins to learn over again, but becomes old without having reached the former extent of his knowledge, has he two souls, the one different from the other ?[8]   Suppose, further, that his temperament undergoes a change in the direction of love, ambition, or desire, shall I say that he has one soul in paradise and another in hell ? Which are the limits of metaphysical knowledge by means of which the human soul is separated from the body without perishing ?   If this is the complete knowledge of existing things, much remains of which philosophers are ignorant concerning heaven, earth, and ocean.   If one, however, must be satisfied with

partial knowledge, then every rational soul exists
separate, because primary notions are implanted in it.
But if the isolated existence of the soul is based on the
conception of the Ten Categories, or higher still, on the
principles of intuition, in which all existing things are
included ready to be grasped logically without following up all details, so is this a knowledge easily acquir-
able in one day. It would be strange if man could
become an angel in one day. If it is incumbent to go
the whole length and comprehend all these things in
logical and scientific study, then the matter is unattain-
able and ends, in their opinion, infallibly in the death
of the one who pursues it. Now thou didst allow thyself to be deceived by injurious fancies, didst seek that
which thy Creator did not grant thee, and to obtain
which no facilities have been granted to human nature.
Only a few privileged individuals are allowed to grasp
such things on the conditions mentioned before.[8a] These
are the souls which comprehend the whole universe,
know their Lord and His angels ; who see one another,
and know each other's secrets, as the prophet says :
' I, too, know it ; be ye silent ' (2 Kings ii. 3). We
others, however, would not know how and by what
means this came to pass, unless by way of prophecy.
If what philosophers know of the matter were true,
they would surely acquire it, since they discourse on the
souls and prophecy. They are, however, like ordinary mortals. As regards human wisdom, they indeed
occupy a high rank, as Socrates said : ' O my people, I
do not deny your knowledge of the gods, but I confess
that I do not understand it. As for me, I am only
wise in human matters.' Philosophers justify their
recourse to speculation by the absence of prophecy

and divine light. They established the demonstrative sciences on a broad and unlimited basis, and on that account separated without either agreeing or disagreeing with each other concerning that on which they held such widely diverging views later on in metaphysics, and occasionally in physics. If there exists a class representing one and the same view, this is not the result of research and investigation, but because they belong to the same philosophic school in which this was taught, as the schools of Pythagoras, Empedocles, Aristotle, Plato, or others, as the Academy and Peripatetics, who belong to the school of Aristotle. They start with views which deprecate reason, but are deprecated by the latter. An example of this is their explanation of the cause of the revolution of the sphere, and the endeavour of the latter to remedy its imperfection, so as to be absolutely exact on all sides. As, however, this is not always possible and in all points, it tries to revolve the opposite way. They contrived similar theories with regard to the emanations from the Prime Cause, viz., that from the intuition of the first cause an angel arose ; and from its knowledge of itself a sphere arose, and thence downward in eleven degrees, until the emanation arrived at the Active Intellect, from which neither an angel nor a sphere developed. All these things are still less satisfactory than the " Book of Creation." They are full of doubts, and there is no consensus of opinion between one philosopher and another. Yet they cannot be blamed, nay, deserve thanks for all they have produced in abstract speculations. For their intentions were good ; they observed the laws of reason, and led virtuous lives. At all events, they have earned this praise, because the same duties were not imposed on them as they were on us when we were given revelation, and a tradition which is tantamount to revelation.

15. Al Khazari : Give me a brief abstract of the views rife among the doctors of theology, whom the Karaites style : The Masters of the Kalām.[9]

16. The Rabbi : This would be of no use ; it would merely be an exercise in the dialectics of the Kalām, and a lesson on the Rabbinic sentence : ' Be careful to learn what answer to give to an Epicurean' (Aboth ii. 14). The consummate philosopher, like the prophet, can only impart little to another person in the way of instruction, and cannot refute his objections dialectically. As to the master of Kalām, learning sheds its lustre on him, thereby inducing his hearers to place him above the pious and immaculate whose learning consists in prin-ciples of a creed which allow of no refutation. The final aim of the Mutakallim in everything he learns and teaches is that these principles of creed enter his soul as well as that of his disciples in the same natural form as they exist in the soul of the pious person. In some cases the art of the Kalām does him greater harm than the principles of truth, because it teaches doubts and traditional prejudices. We experience a similar thing with people who apply themselves to prosody and practice scanning metres. There we can hear braying and a babel of words in an art which offers no diffi-culties to those naturally gifted. The latter enjoy making verses in which no fault can be found. The aim of the former class is to be like the latter who appear ignorant of the art of verse-making, because they cannot learn what the others are able to teach. The naturally gifted person, however, can teach one

similarly endowed with the slightest hint. In the same manner sparks are kindled in the souls of people naturally open to religion and approachment to God, by the words of the pious, sparks which become luminaries in their hearts, whilst those who are not so gifted must have recourse to the Kalām. He often derives no benefit from it, nay, he comes to grief over it.

17. Al Khazari : I do not expect an exhaustive discourse on this subject, but I ask thee for some abstracts like those given to me before. For thou didst strike my ear, and my soul yearns for it.

18. The Rabbi : The FIRST AXIOM deals with the creation of the world, with the object of making it an established fact, and it denies the theory that it is without beginning. If time had no beginning, the number of individuals existing in the past down to our own age would be endless. That which is endless cannot be actual. How could those individuals have become actual, being so many as to be without number ? There is no doubt, however, that the past had a beginning, and that the existing individuals are limited by a number. It is within the power of the human mind to count thousands or millions multiplied without end, at least in theory, but this cannot be done in reality. For that which becomes actual and can be counted as *one*, is like the number which is both actual and finite without doubt. How can the infinite become actual ? The world has, therefore, a beginning, and the revolutions of the spheres are subject to a finite number. Further, that which is infinite can neither be halved nor doubled, nor subjected to any arithmetical calculation. We are aware that the revolutions of the sun are one-twelfth of those of the

moon, and that the other movements of spheres stand
in similar relation to each other, one being the divisor
of the other. The infinite, however, has no divisor.
How could the one be like the other, which is infinite,
being either below or above it, I mean larger or smaller
in number ? How could the infinite come to us ? If
an infinite number of things existed before us, how
could the [idea of] number come to us ? If a thing
has an end, it must also have had a beginning, otherwise each individual object must have waited for the
[prior] existence of an infinite number of others ; so
none would ever come into existence.

SECOND AXIOM : The world is created, because it
is a corporeal object. A corporeal object cannot be
conceived without movement and rest, which are both
attributes of accessory but not simultaneous character.
That which is accessory must be newly made in accordance with its very nature. That which preceded has
also been created. For had it been eternal, it could not
have been non-existent. Consequently both [motion
and rest] are created. A thing that cannot exist without newly created accessories is created itself, because it
could not have been preceded by its accessories. If
the latter are created, the former must be so likewise.

THIRD AXIOM : Every created object must have a
cause which created it. For the created object is connected with a certain time, irrespective of an earlier
or later epoch. The circumstance that it is encompassed by a specific time, irrespective of the period,
renders a specificator necessary.

FOURTH AXIOM : God is eternal, without beginning
and without end. For had He been created, He would
require a Creator. This would result in a chain of

conclusions without end, until we came to the first Creator, whom we look for.

FIFTH AXIOM : God is everlasting, and will never cease to exist. For a being proved to be without beginning cannot have had a non-existence. Non-existence must have a cause, just as the disappearance of a thing from existence must also have a cause. Nothing vanishes from existence on its own account, but on account of its contrast. God, however, has neither a contrast nor His equal. For if anything were like Him in every respect, it would be Himself, but He cannot be described as twofold. The thing which causes non-existence cannot be without beginning, as has been explained before in connexion with the eternity of God's existence. He cannot, therefore, be a created Being, because everything newly arising must have its cause in the eternal Being. But how can the thing caused make its cause disappear ?

SIXTH AXIOM : God is not corporeal. A corporeal object cannot be free from new accessories. A thing that is not free from new accessories is created. God cannot be called accidence, because the accidence cannot exist except on a substratum. The accidence is caused by the corporeal object by which it is attracted and borne. God, however, cannot be defined by a particular outline or place, since this is the characteristic of a corporeal object.

SEVENTH AXIOM : God knows all that is great or small, and nothing escapes His omniscience. For it has been shown that He created, arranged, and instituted everything, as it is written : ' He that planted the ear, shall He not hear ; He that formed the eye, shall He not see ? ' (Ps. xciv. 9). Further, ' Yea, darkness hideth not from Thee,' etc., and ' For Thou hast created my reins ' (ib. cxxxix. 12–13).[10]

EIGHTH AXIOM : God lives. His omniscience and omnipotence having been demonstrated, He must be living. His life, however, is not like ours, created with senses and movement, but a life of pure reason. His life and He are identical.

NINTH AXIOM : God has will. For it is in His power to issue forth the opposite of all He caused to exist, or its non-existence, or anticipation, or postponement. His omnipotence is the same in any case. There must exist a will which fixes His omnipotence on one of these issues to the exclusion of the other. One might also say that His omniscience can spare both His omnipotence and will. In this case His omniscience would be identical with one particular time and issue, and His eternal omniscience would be the cause of every existing being just as it is. This agrees with the view of philosophers.

TENTH AXIOM : The divine will is without beginning, and corresponds to His omniscience. Nothing in it can be renewed or altered. He is living through the very life of His nature, but not by means of an acquired life. He is omnipotent through His own power, has will through His own will. For the coexistence of a thing and that which negatives it is impossible. One cannot therefore say in a general way : Omnipotent without power.

19. Al Khazari : This is sufficient to refresh my memory. There is no doubt that thy discourse on the soul and reason, as well as these axioms, was quoted from other authorities. Now I desire to hear thy own opinion and principles of faith. Thou didst

declare thy willingness to examine this and similar
points. It seems to me that it will not be possible to
omit the questions of predestination and human free
will, since they are of actual importance. Now tell
me thy mind.

20. The Rabbi: Only a perverse, heretical person would
deny the nature of what is possible, making asser-
tions of opinions in which he does not believe. Yet
from the preparations he makes for events he hopes
for or fears, one can see that he believes in their possibility, and that his preparations may be useful. If he
believed in absolute necessity, he would simply submit,
and not equip himself with weapons against his enemy,
or with food against his hunger. If he, on the other
hand, thinks that either preparation or the omission
of the same is necessary in accordance with the nature
of the case, he admits intermediary causes, as well as
their consequences. He will encounter his desire in
every intermediary cause, and if he is just and not perverse, he will find himself placed between himself and
his desire to obtain achievable objects, which he can
pursue or abandon as he likes. Such a belief is not
incompatible with a belief in Divine Providence, but
everything is led back to him in various ways, as I am
going to explain. My opinion is that everything of
which we are conscious is referred to the Prime Cause
in two ways, either as an immediate expression of the
divine will, or through intermediaries. An instance
of the first kind is found in the synthetic arrangement
visible in animals, plants and spheres, objects which
no intelligent observer would trace back to accident,
but to a creative and wise will, which gives everything
its place and portion. An instance of the second kind

is to be found in the burning of a beam. Fire is a fine,
hot, and active substance, whilst wood is a porous and
passive one. It is the nature of the fine and active
substance to affect its object, whilst heat and dryness
warm and volatilize the moisture of the object till it is
completely dissolved. If thou seekest the causes of
these processes, active as well as passive, thou wilt not
fail to discover them. Thou mayest even discover the
causes of their causes till thou arrivest at the spheres,
then at their causes, and finally at the Prime Cause.
One might justly say that everything is ordained by
God, and another is equally right in making man's free
will or accident responsible for it, without, however,
bringing it outside the divine providence. If thou
likest thou mayest render the matter more intelligible
by means of the following classification. Effects are
either of divine or of natural origin, either accidental
or arbitrary. The *divine* ones issue forth actively,
having no other causes except God's will. The *natural*
ones are derived from intermediate, preparatory causes
which bring them to the desired end, as long as no
obstacle arises from one of the other three classes.
The *accidental* ones are likewise the result of intermediary causes, but accidentally, not by nature or
arrangement, or by will power. They are not prepared to be brought to completion and standstill, and
they stand apart from the other three classes. As
regards the arbitrary actions, they have their roots in
the free will of man, when he is in a position to exercise
it. Free will belongs to the class of intermediary
causes, and possesses causes which reduce it, chainlike,
to the Prime Cause. This course is not compulsory,
because the whole thing is potential, and the mind

wavers between an opinion and its opposite, being
permitted to turn where it chooses. The result is
praise or blame for the choice, which is not the case in
the other classes. An accidental or natural cause
cannot be blamed, although some of them admit a
possibility. But one cannot blame a child or a sleeping person for harm done. The opposite was possible
just the same, and they cannot be blamed, because
they lack judgment. Dost thou think that those who
deny the potential are not wroth with those who injure
them purposely. Or do they acquiesce in being robbed
of their garments, and consequently also in suffering from
cold, just as they would expose themselves to the north
wind on a cold day ? Or do they believe that the anger
about it is but a fallacious exertion, instituted for no
purpose, that man may feel anger about one particular
thing, or give praise and blame, show hatred etc. ?
In these cases free will, as such, has no forcing cause,
because it is itself reduced to compulsion. Man's
language, then, would be as little free as the beating
of his pulse. This would be against evident appearances. Thou perceivest that speaking or being silent
is in thy power as long as thou art in possession of thy
reason, and not controlled by other casualties. If all
incidents would be the result of the original will of the
Prime Cause, they would, each in its turn, be created
anew in every moment. We might then say that the
Creator created anew the whole world this very moment.
The servant of God would be no better than the wicked,
as both would be obedient, and only do that for which
they are fated. A conviction of this kind has many
objections, whilst the refutation of appearances is
most difficult, as we said before. The objection made

against those who assert that some matters are removed from the bounds of Providence by human free
will is to be refuted by what was said before, viz. that
they are completely outside the control of Providence,
but are indirectly linked to it. There is still another
objection, viz. that these matters are outside the divine
omniscience, because the absolutely potential is naturally an unknown quantity. The Mutakallims considered this matter in detail, with the result that the
divine knowledge of the potential is but casual, and that
the knowledge of a thing is neither the cause of its
coming into existence, nor of its disappearance therefrom. There is, withal, a possibility of existence and
non-existence. For the knowledge of events to come
is not the cause of their existence, just as is the case
with the knowledge of things which have been. This
is but a proof that the knowledge belongs to God, or
to the angels, or the prophets, or the priests. If this
knowledge were the cause of the existence of a thing,
many people would be placed in paradise solely for the
sake of the divine knowledge that they are pious, even
if they have done no pious act. Others would be in
Gehenna, because God knows them to be wicked, without their having committed a sin. Man should also
be satisfied without having eaten, because he knows
that he is accustomed to be satisfied at certain times.
Another consequence would be that intermediary
causes would cease to exist, and their disappearance
would be shared by that of the intermediary factors.
This renders the following verse intelligible : 'And
God did prove Abraham ' (Gen. xxii. 1), in order to
render his theoretical obedience practical, and let it
be the cause of his prosperity. He says subsequently :

" Because thou hast done this thing . . . I will bless thee ' (ver. 10). Now since events must be either of divine origin, or arise out of one of the other classes, and the possibility exists that they are all providential, the people preferred to refer them all to God, because this encourages belief most effectually. He, however, who knows how to distinguish one people from another, one person from another, one time from another, one place from another, and certain circumstances from others, will perceive that heavenly dictated events mostly came to pass in the chosen and holy land, and among the privileged Israelitish people, and in that time and under circumstances which were accompanied by laws and customs the observation of which was beneficial, whilst their neglect wrought harm. Matters natural or accidental were of no avail against the undesired effect, nor could they do harm at the time of pious conduct. For this reason Israelites serve every religion as evidence against the heretics who followed the view of the Grecian Epicurus, viz. that all things are the outcome of accidents, since no settled purpose is ever discernible in them. His school is called that of the Hedonists, because they held the opinion that pleasure is the desired aim and goodness absolute. The endeavour of him who observes a law-giver's regulations is to find favour in his eyes, and to place his desires before him. He seeks inspirations if he is pious, or miracles if he is a prophet, or if his people enjoys the divine pleasure on the basis of the conditions of time, place and action, as put down in the Tōrāh. He need not be concerned about natural or accidental causes, since he knows that he is protected from their evil consequences, either through preceding

instruction which drives the evil away, or through
some wonderful incident which is collateral with that
evil. The good issuing from accidental causes is not
denied to the sinner, much less to the virtuous. Happy
events occurring to the wicked have their origin only in
those accidental and natural causes, but no one can ward
off threatening calamities. The good, on the contrary,
prosper through the same causes, whilst being
protected from misfortune. But I have diverged
a little from my subject. Returning to the same, I say
that David laid down three causes of death, viz. ' God
may slay him,' i.e. divine cause ; ' Or his day shall
come to die,' i.e. natural cause ; ' Or he shall descend
into battle and perish,' i.e. accidental cause (1 Sam.
xxvi. 10). He omits the fourth possibility, viz. suicide,
because no rational being seeks death voluntarily. If
Saul killed himself, it was not to seek death, but to
escape torture and derision. A similar classification
can be made with regard to speech. The speech of a
prophet at the time when he is enwrapped by the Holy
Spirit is in every part directed by the Divine Influence,
the prophet himself being powerless to alter one word.
Natural speech consists in communications and hints
which conform to the subject to be discussed, and the
mind follows without previous convention. Conventional
languages are composed of natural and arbitrary elements. Accidental speech is that of a madman, and is
neither in harmony with a subject, nor to the purpose.
Free speech is that of a prophet when not inspired, or the
words of an intelligent, thinking person who connects
his words, and chooses his expressions in accordance
with the subject under consideration. If he wished
he could replace each word by another, could even drop

the whole subject and take up another. All these cases, however, can be reduced indirectly to God, but not as immediate issues of the Prime Will, otherwise the words of a child, and mad people, the speech of an orator, and the song of a poet were the words of God. Far be this from Him. The excuse of a slothful person who tells the energetic one that that which is to be, exists previously in the knowledge of God, is inconclusive. For should he even assert that that which shall be must be, he is told : ' Quite so ; but this argument should not prevent thee to take the best counsel, to prepare weapons against thy enemy, and food for hunger, as soon as thou art aware that that both thy safety and destruction depend upon intermediary causes.' One of them, which is the most frequent, is the application of energy and industry, or of lassitude and indolence. Do not try to refute me with those rare and accidental cases, viz. that a circumspect person perishes, whilst the careless and unprotected one is saved. For the word safety means something quite different from the word risk. A sensible person will not flee from a place of safety to one of risk, just as one flees from a dangerous place to a safe one. If safety accrues in the place of danger this is considered rare, but if a person perishes in a safe place, it is called an extraordinary occurrence. One should, therefore, employ circumspection. One of the causes of carelessness is the view opposite to this advice. Everything, however, is indirectly related to God. Whatever happens through direct ordination belongs to the class of strange and miraculous events, and can dispense with intermediary causes. In some cases they are, however, necessary, as in the preservation of Moses during his

fast of forty days, when he was without food, or in the
destruction of Sanherib's army without a visible cause—
unless through a divine one—which we cannot consider as
such, as we do not know what it is.   Of such we say that
preparation avails them not, viz. preparation in the concrete sense.   Moral preparation, however, based on the
secret of the law, benefits him who knows and understands
it, because it brings what is good, and repels what is bad.
If man aids intermediary causes with energy, having left
to God the objects of his fear with a pure mind, he fares
well, and suffers no loss.   He, however, who courts danger
[transgresses the warning : ' You shall not tempt the
Lord' (Deut. vi. 16), in spite of his confidence in God.
But if one considers it absurd][11] to give commands to
a person who, as he knows beforehand, may either
disobey or obey him, this is not absurd.   We have
shown previously that disobedience and obedience
depend upon intermediary causes.   The cause of
obedience is the command for it.   [The obeying person
knew beforehand that he would do so and that the
cause of it was that he had heard reproof.][12]   He also
keeps in mind that disobedience depends on intermediary causes, which are to be found either in the
companionship of wicked people, or in the preponderance
of evil temperament, or inclination for comfort and rest.
Finally, he knew that his disobedience was lessened
through reproof.   Reproof, as is known, impresses the
mind in any case, and even the soul of an insubordinate
person is in some small way influenced by reproof.   In
a higher degree this takes place in a multitude, because
there is at any rate one person to be found who accepts
it.   Far from being useless, reproof is, therefore, useful.

THE FIRST PRINCIPLE, containing the confirmation

of the above-mentioned advice, establishes the existence of the Prime Cause. God is the wise Creator, in whose works nothing is useless. They are all founded upon His wisdom and an order which suffers no deterioration. Whoever contemplates this must find the conviction of the greatness of His creation deeply rooted in his mind. This results in the belief that no flaw can be found in His works. If in some minor matter a fault seems apparent, his belief is not shaken, but he ascribes it to his own ignorance and defective intelligence.

THE SECOND PRINCIPLE admits the existence of intermediary causes, which, however, are not active, but causes, either in the way of substance matter or instruments. Issue and blood are the materials of which man is formed, connected by the organs of propagation. The spirit and faculties are tools which employ them under the will of God, in order to produce a formation perfect in proportion, form and nurture. Intermediary causes are necessary for every created thing, as the dust which was required for the creation of Adam. It is therefore not superfluous to assume the existence of intermediary causes.

THE THIRD PRINCIPLE.—God gives every substance the best and most appropriate form. He is the All-benevolent, who does not withhold His goodness, wisdom, and guidance from anything. His wisdom visible in the flea and gnat is not less than in the order of the spheres.[13] The difference of things is the outcome of their substances. One cannot, therefore, ask : ' Why did He not create me an angel ? ' Just as little as the worm can ask : ' Why didst Thou not create me a human being ? '

THE FOURTH PRINCIPLE expresses the conviction that existing beings are of higher or lower degree. Everything that is possessed of feeling and perception is higher than those creatures which lack the same, since the former are nearer the degree of the Prime Cause which is Reason itself. The lowest plant occupies a higher rank than the noblest mineral, the lowest animal is higher than the noblest plant, and the lowest human being is higher than the noblest animal. Thus the lowest follower of the divine law occupies a higher place than the noblest heathen. For the divine law confers something of the nature of angels on the human mind, a thing which cannot be acquired otherwise. The proof is that prolonged practice of this law leads up to the degree of prophetic inspiration, than which there is no nearer degree to God for man. A froward monotheist is, therefore, preferable to the pagan, because the divine law empowered him to lead an angelic life and to reach the degree of angels, though it has become sullied and defaced by his frowardness. Some traces will always remain, and the fire of his longing for it is not quite extinguished. If he had his own choice, he would prefer to remain untutored, just as a sick and pain-plagued person would not prefer to be a horse, or fish, or bird, which, though happy and free from pain, is far removed from reason which brings near to the divine degree.

THE FIFTH PRINCIPLE.—The mind of him who listens to the reproof of an adviser is impressed by it, if it is acceptable. True reproof is useful in any case, and although the evil doer may not be brought back from his bad ways, a spark is kindled in his soul by this reproof, and he sees that his deed is bad. This is part and beginning of repentance.

THE SIXTH PRINCIPLE.—Man finds in himself this power of doing evil or avoiding it in matters which are in his hand. Any failure in this respect is accounted for by the absence of intermediary causes, or his ignorance of them. If, for instance, a strange beggar, unacquainted with the art of governing, desires to become the ruler of a nation, one could not comply with his wish. Were he, however, possessed of the intermediary causes, and were he to know how to employ them, his desire would be justified, just as it would for an object the causes of which are at his disposal, and which he knows and controls when ruling his house, children, and servants or, in a higher degree, his limbs, which latter he can move as he chooses, whilst speaking as he likes ; or, in a still higher degree, controlling his thoughts and imagining objects far and near in any way he likes. He is master over his intermediary causes. For a similar reason it is unlikely that the weak chess player should beat the strong one. One cannot speak of good or bad fortune in a game of chess, as in a war between two princes. For the causes of the game are open completely to study, and the expert will always be the conqueror. He need fear nothing in the ordinary way which can cause him great difficulty, neither need he fear anything accidental, except perhaps anything unusual arising from inattention. The last-named, however, comes under the name of ignorance, which was discussed before. This being so, everything can be traced back to the Prime Cause in the way intimated before. The Prime Will is visible in the history of the Israelites during the time when the Shekhināh dwelt among them. Afterwards it became doubtful, except in the hearts of the faithful, whether these even, were primarily caused by God or by spherical, or accidental causes.   No decisive proof of this exists.   It is, however, best to refer everything to God, particularly important events, such as death, victory, good and bad fortune, etc.

CONCLUSION OF THE BOOK

21. This and similar subjects afford proper points for research, comprising as they do the character of the divine decrees concerning man, as intimated in the prophetic words : ' He visits the sin of the fathers on the children . . . of his enemies . . . and showing mercy unto thousands of them that love Him and keep His commandments ' (Exod. xx. 5 sq.). This means that every iniquity is remembered till the time of punishment comes, as laid down in the Tōrāh and the teachings of the Sages ; that some punishments can be warded off by repentance, and some not.   It further includes the conditions of repentance, the trials, tribulations, and punishments for past transgressions which visit man as retaliation in this world, or the next, or for paternal transgressions, and, finally, the good fortune which we enjoy as a reward for former pious actions, or the ' merit of the fathers,' or which are sent to try us.   These points of view are complicated by others and deeper ones, and there remains some doubt whether an examination will disclose the majority of causes of the misfortune of the just and the prosperity of the wicked.[14] That which we cannot discover may be confidently left to God's omniscience and justice, and man must admit that he does not know the reasons, although they may

lie on the surface, and still less can be known those
which are really hidden. If man's contemplations lead
him to the Prime Being and to the necessary attributes,
he withdraws from it, because he sees a curtain of light
which blinds the eye. We are debarred from perceiving
it on account of our defective sight and narrow minds,
but not because it is hidden or faulty. To those endowed with prophetic vision it appears too bright and
resplendent to require any other proof. The culminating point of our appreciation of His nature is that we
are able to distinguish supernatural causes in natural
occurrences. This we ascribe to a non-corporeal and
divine power, just as Galen, speaking of the forming
power, places it above all other forces. In his opinion
it did not arise out of certain combinations, but miracu-
lously, by command of God, and we see substances
changed, the course of nature altered, and new things
produced without craft. This is the difference between
the work of Moses and that of the magicians whose
secret art was open to discovery, just as Jeremiah says :
' They are vanity, the work of errors ' (chap. x. 15). He
means to say that when they are closely examined they
appear vain as any contemptible thing. The Divine
Influence, however, if investigated, appears as pure
gold. If we have reached this degree, we say, that there
is surely an incorporeal being which guides all corporeal
substances, but which our mind is inadequate to examine. We therefore dwell on His works, but refrain
from describing His nature. For if we were able to
grasp it, this were a defect in Him. We take, however,
no heed of the words of philosophers who divide the
divine world into various degrees. As soon as we are
free from our bodies there is for us only one divine

degree. It is God alone who controls everything corporeal. The reason why philosophers adopted many
gods is to be found in their investigations of the movements of the spheres, of which they counted more than
forty. They found for every movement a separate
cause, from which they concluded that these movements
were independent rather than necessary or natural.
Each movement, therefore, originated with a soul.
Every soul has intellect, and this intellect is an angel
severed from material substance. They called these
intellects, or angels, or secondary causes and other
names. The nethermost degree, nearest to us, is the
Active Intelligence, of which they taught that it guided
the nether world. The next is the Hylic Intellect, then
comes the soul, nature, the natural and animal forces,
and the faculties of each [human] organ. All these,
however, are subtleties, and pleasant for investigation.[15]
He who is deceived by them is in any case a heretic.
Leave also alone the argument of the Karaites, taken
from David's last will to his son : ' And thou, Solomon,
my son, know thou the God of thy father, and serve
Him ' (1 Chron. xxviii. 9). They conclude from this
verse that a complete knowledge of God must precede
His worship. As a matter of fact, David reminded his
son to imitate his father and ancestors in their belief in
the God of Abraham, Isaac and Jacob, whose solicitude
was with them, and who fulfilled His promises in multi-
plying their descendants, gave them Palestine, and
caused His Shekhināh to dwell among them. It is also
written : ' Gods which ye did not know,' but this does
not allude to the real truth, but those objects from
which neither good nor evil can issue, and deserve
neither confidence nor fear.—

22. The Rabbi was then concerned to leave the land of the Khazari and to betake himself to Jerusalem. The king was loth to let him go, and spoke to him in this sense as follows : What can be sought in Palestine nowadays, since the divine reflex is absent from it, whilst, with a pure mind and desire, one can approach God in any place. Why wilt thou run into danger on land and water and among various peoples ?

23. The Rabbi answered : The visible Shekhināh has, indeed, disappeared, because it does not reveal itself except to a prophet or a favoured community, and in a distinguished place. This is what we look for in the passage : ' Let our eyes behold when Thou returnest to Zion.' As regards the invisible and spiritual Shekhināh, it is with every born Israelite of virtuous life, pure heart, and upright mind before the Lord of Israel. Palestine is especially distinguished by the Lord of Israel, and no function can be perfect except there. Many of the Israelitish laws do not concern those who do not live there ; heart and soul are only perfectly pure and im-maculate in the place which is believed to be specially selected by God. If this is true in a figurative sense, how much more true in reality, as we have shown.[16] Thus the longing for it is awakened with disinterested motives, especially for him who wishes to live there, and to atone for past transgressions, since there is no opportunity of bringing the sacrifices ordained by God for intentional and unintentional sins. He is supported by the saying of the Sages : ' Exile atones for sins,'[17] especially if his exile brings him into the place of God's choice. The danger he runs on land and sea does not come under the category of : ' You shall not tempt the Lord '[18] (Deut. vi. 16) ; but the verse refers to risks

which one takes when travelling with merchandise in
the hope of gain. He who incurs even greater danger
on account of his ardent desire to obtain forgiveness is
free from reproach if he has closed the balance of his
life, expressed his gratitude for his past life, and is
satisfied to spend the rest of his days in seeking the
favour of his Lord. He braves danger, and if he escapes
he praises God gratefully. But should he perish through
his sins, he has obtained the divine favour, and may be
confident that he has atoned for most of his sins by his
death. In my opinion this is better than to seek the
dangers of war in order to gain fame and spoil by courage
and bravery. This kind of danger is even inferior to
that of those who march into war for hire.

24. Al Khazari : I thought that thou didst love freedom,[19] but now I see thee finding new religious duties
which thou wilt be obliged to fulfil in Palestine, which
are, however, in abeyance here.

25. The Rabbi : I only seek freedom from the service
of those numerous people whose favour I do not
care for, and shall never obtain, though I worked for it
all my life. Even if I could obtain it, it would not profit
me—I mean serving men and courting their favour. I
would rather seek the service of the One whose favour
is obtained with the smallest effort, yet it profits in this
world andthe next. This is the favour of God, His service
spells freedom, and humility before Him is true honour.

26. Al Khazari : If thou believest in all that thou
sayest, God knows thy mind. The mind is free before
God, who knows the hearts and discloses what is hidden.

27. The Rabbi : This is true when action is impossible.
Man is free in his endeavours and work. But he de-
serves blame who does not look for visible reward for

visible work. For this reason it is written : ' Ye shall blow an alarm with the trumpets, and ye shall be remembered before the Lord your God (Num. x. 9) . . . They shall be to you for a memorial (ver. 10) . . . A memorial of blowing of trumpets ' (Lev. xxiii. 24). God need not be reminded, but actions must be perfect to claim reward. Likewise must the ideas of the prayers be pronounced in the most perfect way to be considered as prayer and supplication. Now if thou bringest intention and action to perfection thou mayest expect reward. This is popularly expressed by *reminding*, and ' the Tōrāh speaks in the manner of human beings.' [20] If the action is minus the intention, or the intention minus the action, the expectation [for reward] is lost, except in impossible things. It is, however, rather useful to show the good intention if the deed is impossible, as we express this in our prayer : ' On account of our sins have we been driven out of our land.' This sacred place serves to remind men and to stimulate them to love God, being a reward and promise, as it is written : ' Thou shalt arise and have mercy upon Zion, for the time to favour her, yea, the set time is come. For thy servants take pleasure in her stones and embrace the dust thereof ' (Ps. cii. 14 sq.). This means that Jerusalem can only be rebuilt when Israel yearns for it to such an extent that they embrace her stones and dust.[21]

28. Al Khazari : If this be so, it would be a sin to hinder thee. It is, on the contrary, a merit to assist thee. May God grant thee His help, and be thy protector and friend. May He favour thee in His mercy.[22]

Completed is the book with the help of God and His assistance. Praise without end be to the Giver of Help.

NOTES AND BIBLIOGRAPHY

ANNOTATIONS

INTRODUCTION

[1] Ch. iii. *v.* 21–22. Cf. Peters, *Der hebräische Text des Ecclesiasticus*, pp. 5 and 322.

[2] Ḥagīgāh II. i.

[3] Talmud Ḥagīgāh, fol. 13 vo ; Jerushalmi, ch. ii. hal. i.

[4] Berēshith rabbā, ch. viii.

[5] See Steinschneider, *Die arab. Literatur der Juden*, pp. 13–44.

[6] *Al Amānāt*, ed. S. Landauer, p. 3

[7] *Ibid.* p. 11. l. 4.

[8] On the Hebrew translations of these works see Steinschneider, *Die hebräischen Uebersetzungen*, etc. p. 298 sqq. and 326 sqq.

[9] See Kaufmann, *Geschichte der Attributenlehre*, p. 123 sqq.

[10] Through Judah b. Tabbon's Hebrew version the name *Kosari* (or *Kusari*) has become popular. Isaac b. Cardinal, however, retained the original name אלכזרי. See also my *Arabic Chrestomathy*, etc. p. 72. The pronunciations *Cosri* and *Kuzri* are incorrect.

[11] Only the preface and a short fragment (printed in D. Cassel's edition, pp. 16 and 338–357) have been preserved. See also Steinschneider, *Die arabische Literatur*, etc., p. 153.

[12] The name of Isaac Sangari (Sinjari) attributed to the Rabbi is not found either in the MSS. or in the earliest editions. This spurious name occurs first in Moses Naḥmāni's *Dissertation* (ed. Jellinek), p. 11. Facsimiles of the forged epitaphs of Isaac Sangari and his wife are given by Harkawy, *Altjüdische Denkmäler aus der Krim*.

[13] An English version of Ḥisdāi b. Shafrūt's letter to the king of the Khazars, as well as of the reply of the latter, is to be found in *Miscellany of Hebrew Literature*, vol. i. p. 92–112.

[14] Found in the colophon of the Bodleian MS. of the Arabic original.

[15] First mentioned in the speech of the Christian Scholar. In several places, e.g. iii. 17, it assumes quite a personal character.

The Arabic term *amr* for Logos appears already in the Korān, see my *New Researches into the Composition and Exegesis of the Qorān*, p. 15 sqq.

[16] See S. Landauer, *Die Psychologie des Ibn Sīnā*, ZDMG, vol. xxix. p. 335–418. Landauer offers many corrections of the (Hebrew) text of the Khazari. In one case, however, the Arabic text has the better reading, viz. לצאדר for לאצדאר (Land. p. 364, l. 4). In another case (p. 417, rem. 4) Landauer blames Judah Hallēvi for senseless copying. The fault, lies, however, with the editors of the Hebrew text of the Khazari. The Arabic original agrees entirely with Ibn Sīnā's text.

[17] Aristotle, *De Anima*, ii. 1, ἐντελέχεια ἡ πρώτη σώματος φυσικοῦ ὀργανικοῦ.

[18] See *Steinschneider = Jubelschrift*, p. 136, אמר הפילסוף הנפש היא עצם המשלים לגוף הטבעי אל החיים בכח

[19] See Book i. par. 13 ; iv. par. 25.

[20] According to Al Ghazāli ; see Schreiner in ZDMG, vol. xlii. p. 622.

[21] Mishnāh Sōtāh, i. 7.

[22] Talmud Jōmā, fol. 38 vo. This doctrine is seemingly opposed to the other (Berakhōth, fol. 58 vo), that even the distributor of water is appointed by heaven. The former, however, refers to man's actions, but the latter to his fate.

[23] See Albo's *Ikkārim*, IV. i.

[24] See p. 157.

[25] Divān ed. Luzatto, fol. 41 sq.

[26] Morning service, beginning יה שמך

[27] Attributenlehre, p. 270.

[27a] See *Monasschrift für Geschichte und Wissenschaft des Judenthums*, vol. xlii.

[28] *Ibidem*, p. 241 sqq.

[29] ZDMG, vol. xli. p. 541.

[30] *Emūnāh Rāmāh*, ed. Weil, p. 2.

[31] *Ibidem*, Principle v.

[32] Al Shahrastāni, *Creeds and Sects*, ed. Cureton, p. 165 sq. ; see also my article *Mohammedan Criticism of the Bible*, JQR, 1901, p. 222 sqq.

[33] *Em. R.* p. 78.

[34] See Guttmann, *Die Religionsphilosophie des Abraham b. Daud*, p. 209, and Saadyāh, *Amānāt*, Book IV. ; *Ikkārim*, IV. i.

[35] See Renan-Neubauer, *Ecrivains juifs français du 14 ème*, siècle, p. 401.

[36] MS. of the Montefiore Library, see my *Catalogue*, No. 305, 1.

[37] p. 27.

[38] אגרת אל תהי כאבותיך beginning and end.

[39] Printed Ferrara, 1555, and Vienna, 1859 (ed. Stern).

[40] מקור עינים, ch. xxxvi.

[41] Book IV, ch. i.

[42] Published in JQR, 1903.

[43] See my edition of the Arabic text, p. v.

[44] See Schreiner's articles in *Monatsschrift*, etc. vol. xlii.

[45] See Steinschneider, *Verzeichniss der hebr. MSS. (der Königl. Bibliothek zu Berlin)*, p. 76. The author admits that no one adopts Islām except from fear or other external reasons.

[46] *Polemische u. apologetische Literatur*, etc. p. 37 sqq.

[47] *Sa'd b. Manṣūr Ibn Kammūna und seine polemische Schrift* etc. Leipzig, 1893, p. 9 sq.

[48] See my *Chrestomathy*, pp. 69–103.

[49] *Arabische Literatur*, p. 240.

[50] See *Chrestomathy*, p. 76.

[51] Basle, 1660. A complete bibliography of the editions of the Hebrew version of the book, as well as the commentaries and older translations, is given by the late Dr. David Cassel in his two editions (Leipzig, 1853 and 1869), which are accompanied by a German translation. Since then the Arabic original, together with Judah b. Tabbon's Hebrew version revised on the basis of the former and the various MSS. of the latter, was edited by the present translator (1887). who also published a German translation direct from the Arabic in 1885.

[52] . . . . מטה דן וכוזרי חלק שני; second edition, Metz, 1780. An English translation of parts i. and ii. by the late Dr. L. Loewe was published London, 1853. A translation of the remaining parts by E. H. Lindo in MS. is preserved in the Montefiore Library, No. 527 (*Catalogue*, No. 307).

[53] Preface.

PART I

[1] Thus far wanting in the Arabic original, and supplemented from the Hebrew version.

[2] The anthromorphism of the Old Testament which Islām considers incompatible with true monotheism.

[3] Mohammed stamped every verse of the Korān a miracle.

[4] Koran ii. 21 and other places.

[5] *Ibidem.* xxxiii. 40. See my *New Researches*, etc. p. 23.

[6] *Ibid.* p. 5.

[7] "Arabic Korān" is a term intentionally employed by Mohammed.

[8] A. 1140, being the date of the composition of this work.

[9] The author's remark on the week of seven days should be restricted to Europe and Western Asia, as a seven days' week is unknown both in the ancient Persian as well as central and eastern Asiatic nations.

[10] This notion also requires certain modifications.

[11] The Nabataeans were an Aramaic tribe living in the northwest of the Arabian peninsula, whose many inscriptions give testimony of an ancient and highly developed civilization. The Nabataeans were credited with a work on agriculture which a certain Ibn Wahshiyya is said to have translated into Arabic. See Munk, *Le Guide*, iii. p. 231, and Steinschneider, *Zur Pseudepigraph. Literatur*, p. 4.

[12] See p. 18 and *Monatschrift* vol. xxxiii. pp. 374–8.

[13] Physics, II. i.

[14] The king here alludes to himself ; see also the beginning of Book II.

[15] In contradistinction to the founders of the Christian and Mohammedan religions.

[16] See Book II. 80.

[17] See remark 2.

[18] Proverbial saying.   Cf. Steinschneider, *Die arabische Literatur der Juden*, p. 19.

[19] See par. 49.

[20] Allusion to Ps. cii. 15 ; see also the end of the work.

[21] Original : *believers*, but the quotation of 1 Sam. v. 2 shows that we must read *Philistines*.

[22] Allusion to the founder of Islām.

[23] This remark forms the antithesis to that of the king in paragraph 6 that the Korān is written in Arabic.

[24] The Hebrew version differs here on account of a slight corruption ; see my edition of the original p. xxvii. rem. 106.

[25] The Hebrew version has here a sentence which is not in the original.

[26] Allusion to Islām.

[27] Matthew v. 39, 40.

[28] Many passages in the Talmud and Midrashim contain allegorical allusions to paradise and hell, e.g. Berakh. fol. 19 vo ; Sanhedrin, fol. 102 vo ; Bev. Rabb. ch. vi. etc.

[29] Old Testament in general.

[30] Koheleth xii. 7.

[31] Al Khidhr is in the Arab legend the name of Elijah.

[32] See Gen. v. 24 ; 2 Kings ii. 11 sqq.

[33] Numb. xxiii. 10.

34 1 Sam. xxviii.

35 In the liturgy of the daily morning prayer, according to the Spanish rite. The author reproduces it in Arabic translation.

36 See Josh. xv. 8 ; 2 Kings xxiii. 10.

PART II

1 The ב in באל שדי also refers to the following וישמי.

2 See Book IV. par. 3.

3 Cf. the words of the philosopher in the beginning of the work ; also iv. 3 and v. 14.

4 Talmud Erūbin, fol. 53 vo ; Ber. Rabba, ch. lviii.

5 See Numb. xxxiii. 13 sq. Alush was the place in which, according to Rabbinic tradition, the prohibition of gathering manna on the Sabbath was promulgated.

6 According to the Talmud Jōmā, fol. 56 vo ; Sanh. fol. 37 vo.

7 Rōsh Hash. fol. 20 vo. The author explains this sentence in the latter part of the paragraph.

8 See Book I. par. 57.

9 Which was six hours in advance.

10 Gen. i. 3.

11 For six hours later Sabbath came to an end in Palestine.

12 Viz. between China and Palestine.

13 Of the last meridian.

14 Mishnāh, Ketūbōth, xiii. 11.

15 Talmud, Ketūboth, fol. 110 vo.

16 Ibid.

17 See Sifrē on שופטים

18 Ketub. fol. 111 vo.

19 Ibid.

20 Jerushalmi Ketub. xii. 3.

21 Babli Ketub. fol. 111 vo.

22 Based on Mishnāh Abōdā Zārāh, i. 8.

23 Sanhedrin, fol. 31 vo.

24 Mishnāh Gittin, iv. 6.

25 Bābā Bathrā, fol. 158 vo.

26 Ketub. fol. 111 vo ; Pesaḥim, fol. 113 vo.

27 Ketub. fol. 112 vo.

28 Blessing after the recitation of the Haftārāh.

29 Based on Korān xvii. 1.

30 Talmud Bābā Bathrā, fol. 25 vo.

31 ' Hooks ' not mentioned in Numbers iv. 31.

32 From the well known Selīḥāh.

[33] From the Amīdāh of the penitential days.

[34] Erroneous quotation.

[35] Book I. par. 95.

[36] By striking smaller lawful animals with their claws; see p. 245,

[37] See Book I. par. 79.

[38] The Hebrew version renders: 'thousands and hundreds.' The author evidently only counts backwards to the cessation of prophecy, viz. forty years after the construction of the Second Temple. See Book III. pars. 39 and 65.

[39] Cf. Book I. par. 63.

[40] See Book I. par. 49.

[41] The author has the Arabic language in his mind.

[42] E.g. אבוא, שׁור, וַיִּשָׁתְּ

[43] Because in most cases one of them has a long vowel with virtual quiescense.

[44] E.g. נַחֲלִי or הֲלְלִי, see below.

[45] Renders Arabic metres unfit for Hebrew without modification.

[46] אָכְלָה (=Gen. xxvii. 19) and אוֹכְלָה (‿‿) In the Hebrew poems of the Spanish schools the Shevā mobile, representing ֳ, is often made quiescent, leaving the word bisyllabic. The author himself was often guilty of such liberty, e.g. in his famous Zion song, l. 2, דוֹרְשֵׁי שְׁלוּמֵךְ (dōrshē for dōrᵉshē).

[47] The ordinary liturgical Piyyut, which has not the strict form of the Arabic Kasīda, employs rhymed verses of approximately equal number of syllables.

[48] See paragraphs 76 and 78.

[49] Like Arabic, Hebrew is built upon the three fundamental vowels, U, A, I. Rather obscure is that the author considers Kāmeṣ as a great U-sound. This probably includes the Kāmeṣ hatūf (ŏ), as well as the ordinary long Kāmeṣ pronounced as a (in all).

[50] Mobile.

[51] But *short*, requiring a virtual quiescence if lengthened.

[52] The author explains almost immediately what he means by the *three forms*, viz. (1) the ordinary etymological formation; (2) changes by the rules of syntax; (3) changes by accents.

[53] Instance of the first form.

[54] This passage is wanting in the original, and supplemented from the Hebrew version.

[55] *Hē* after ṣērē only in the second form as מַעֲשֵׂה in the *status constructus*.

[56] So according to the original מַתְרוּךְ. It appears that Judah Ibn Tabbon was in doubt whether so to read, or מְחָרוּךְ ('vocalized'). The MSS. of his version vacillate between נעזב and מתנוּעע. The former is evidently better.

[57] E.g., וִיהִי־לִי Gen. xxxii, 6.

[58] E.g., וַיֵּלֶךְ Num. xii. 9.

[59] Of which the first two are short.

[60] The author read שָׁרֶךְ, although the Māsōrāh has an ordinary Shevā.

[61] E.g. אָמַר Gen. xxi. 1.

[62] E.g. אָכַל Ezek. xviii. 15.

[63] E.g. וַיֹּאמֶר Ezek. xxx. 18.

[64] ē into a

[65] Cf. rem. 55.

[66] E.g. תַעֲשֶׂה Josh. vii. 9.

[67] Since in most cases the status constr. has a shorter form.

PART III

[1] See Book II. par. 50.

[1a] Allusion to circumcision among Mohammedans.

[2] Talmud Taanith, fol. 21 vo ; Sanh. fol. 108 vo.

[3] Wanting in the original and supplemented from the Hebrew version.

[4] Passover Haggādāh.

[5] See Book IV. par. 25.

[5a] See Mishnāh, Rōsh Hash. iv. 5.

[6] Wanting in the original and supplemented from the Hebrew version.

[7] See preceding remark.

[7a] Republ. 369 C. ; 374 A. ; 464 B.

[8] Allusion to the Karaites.

[9] See p. 81.

[10] Wanting in the original.

[11] Wanting in the original.

[12] Ibn Ezra in Ṣāhōth discusses this point, quoting several other instances. He, however, prefers צדו. The author endeavours to ascribe to the Masōrāh the authority of the traditional law.

[13] Wanting in the original.

[14] See Talmud Kiddushin, fol. 30 vo ; Mass. Sōferim ix. 2.

[15] Wanting in the original.

[16] Wanting in the original.

[17] Lived about 760, and is commonly regarded as the founder of the Karaite sect.

[18] Of Nahawend (about 800), another Karaite teacher.

[19] Anan's son and successor.

[20] Literally : the problem of Exod. xii. 1. The calculation of the new moon forms one of the most trenchant differences between the Rabbanites and the Karaites, the latter fixing the calendar on the time when the new moon reappears in the sky.

[21] Refers to the incident related in the Mishnāh Rosh-Hash. ii. 8, 9, regarding a difference of opinion as to the proper date of the Day of Atonement.

[22] Proverbial saying ; see Goldziher in ZDMG, li. p. 472.

[23] The Rabbanite authorities.

[24] This distinction is only made by the Spanish rite.

[25] See pars. 65 and 76.

[26] Tōsiftā Sōtāh, ch. xiii.

[27] Mishnāh Jōmā v. 2–3 ; Shekālim. vi. 1–2, cf. Tosiftā Sōtā, *ibid.* and Sēder Ōlām ch. xxiv.

[28] See Book II. par. 64.

[28a] According to the calculation of Arab astronomers.

[29] Connexion of two places removed from each other by two thousand yards.

[30] Ritual connexion of houses within the same precincts.

[31] The author here casts a side glance at the elaborate Mohammedan legends on Solomon's intercourse with the Queen of Sheba. They are also embodied in the *Arabian Nights*, Nos. 868–878.

[32] See pars. 39 and 67.

[33] Mishnāh Hagīgāh ii. 7.

[34] Mishnāh Sōtāh ix. 9.

[35] Based on the Talmud Berakhōth, fol. 48 vo ; Kiddūshin, fol. 48 vo ; cf. Josephus, *Antiquities*, ch. xiii. 18.

[36] The Amīdāh.

[37] Cf. Talm. Sabbath, fol. 30 vo ; Jerush. Taauith, ch. iv. 2 ; Midrash Beresh. Rabb. ch. xcviii ; Sifrē towards the end.

[38] Talm. Succāh, fol. 28 vo. ; Bābā Bathrā, fol. 134 vo.

[39] According to Gittin, fol. 56 vo ; Sifrē, and Abōth de R. Nathan, ch. iv.

[40] Spurious work containing an abstract of the history of the people of Israel, calendar calculations and symbolic notes on the prayerbook.

[41] A mystic work, ascribed to R. Ishmael ; see Ph. Bloch, Geschichte d. Entwickelung d. Kabbala, p. 17.

[42] Cabbalistic writings, ascribed to the same author, see Zunz, *Gottesdienstliche Vorträge*, 2nd ed. p. 176.

[43] Talm. Berachoth, fol. 7 vo.

[44] See above annot. 21.

[45] Abōth ii. 8.

[46] See Book II. par. 64.

[47] See Mishnāh Jedaim iii. 5; Talmud, Zebāch, fol. 11 vo (Simon b. Azzāi).

[48] Talm. Ḥagigā, fol. 14 vo. This allegory typifies students of metaphysics.

[41] Ben Azzāi.

[50] Ben Zōmā.

[51] Elishā b. Abūjāh.

[52] Bemidmar Rabba, ch. xix. The late Dr. D. Cassel has pointed out (p. 289, rem. 2) that the author here mistook R. Akibah for Hillel.

[53] Berach., fol. 61 vo.

[54] See par. 12.

[55] Syro-Grecian era, beginning October 1, 312, before the Christian era.

[56] Thus enriching the Hebrew grammar and dictionary.

[57] Mishnāh Pēāh ii. 6.

[58] See Abōth ch. i.

[59] Mishnāh Edujōth viii. 7.

[60] In favour of the opponents of the Talmud.

[60a] Against the method of the Talmud.

[61] The so-called seven Noahide commandments; cf. Talmud Sanhedrin, fol. 60 vo.

[62] Talm. Berakh. fol. 3 vo.

[63] Talm. Pesah. fol. 54 vo; Nedār, fol. 39 vo.

[64] Abōth, ch. v. 8.

[65] Abodā Zārāh, fol. 19 vo.

[66] Mishnāh Edujōth i. 3.

PART IV

[1] See Part I. p. 36.

[2] See the Philosopher's speech at the beginning of the work.

[3] Against 160 as stated by the author himself, p. 178.

[4] Plato in Timaeus, ch. xxx. 13; Aristotle, *De Mundo*, ch. vi.

[5] See Part II, par. 23.

[6] The black stone in the Kāha at Mecca.

[7] The so-called *Kibla*. When Mohammed first instituted a regular worship at Medina, he commanded believers to turn their

faces towards Jerusalem. Subsequently, however, he changed this for Mecca.

[8] See p. 36 and 218.

[9] Probably the well-known saying in which Socrates declared that human knowledge was insignificant, but that he had a clearer understanding of this than most other people. See, Plato, *Apologia*, ch. vi. See also Book V. par. 14 (p. 272).

[10] Mecca.

[11] Talmud Ḥullin, ol. 4 vo.

[12] Allusion to the *Sêfer Jesirāh*, which, according to the author, contains Abraham's metaphysical speculations before God revealed Himself to him.

[13] Talmud, Sābbath, fol. 156 vo ; Nedārīm, fol. 32 vo.

[14] Cf. The philosopher's speech at the beginning of the work.

[15] See Part III. par. 35.

[16] Honorary title of the Medinian citizens who adopted Islām during Mohammed's life-time.

[17] See Part I. p. 78.

[18] The author here alludes to Arab and Persian poems in the style of Ibn Sīna, Oma Kayyām, and others.

[19] The ' Book of Creation ' (כפר יצירה) discussed in the following paragraph, is a kind of mystic cosmogony, ascribed to the Patriarch Abraham. The time of its composition can be approximately fixed as between the conclusion of the Talmud on one side and Saadyah (who wrote a commentary on the work) on the other, or between the eighth and ninth centuries. See also Bloch, l.c. p. 22 sqq.

[20] The Ptolemaean planetary system in reversed order.

[21] 69 E ; 70, A.

[22] Mishnāh Hagīgāh ii, 1.

[23] Dragon line was a name applied by early astronomers to the line which connects the two crossing points of the moon's sphere with the ecliptic.

[23a] Play upon the words עֲנָג and נֶגַע according to the position of the ע at the beginning or at the end of the word.

[24] See Talm. Hagīgāh, fol. 12 vo.

[25] According the formula $n \frac{(n-1)}{1-2}$, if $n = 22$.

[26] Formula of Permutations.

[26a] P. 18, and Part I., p. 37.

[27] Liturgy of the daily morning service.

[28] See Part IV. par. 17, and Talm. Sabbath, fol. 56 vo.

[29] Not to be found in any of Plato's writings ; cf. Steinschneider, *Zur Pseudepigr. Lit.* pp. 52 and 79.

[30] Literally : Place.

[31] See Part II. par. 64 ; III. par. 35.

[32] From the moment of the appearance of one new moon to the next. One hour = 1,080 fractions ; 793 fractions are therefore equal to 44 min. 3⅓ sec.

[33] The equinox of spring. *Tekūfāh* means course of the sun, but the term is applied to the four seasons, each lasting 91 days 7½ hours. The *tekūfāh* of Nisān begins with the entrance of the sun into the sign of Aries. From the verse Deut. xvi. 1 it is deducted that Passover is to be celebrated after the *tekūfāh* of Nisān.

[34] Talm. Rōsh Hash. fol. 21 vo.

[35] Famous Arab astronomer of the ninth century.

[36] See Part II. par. 20.

[37] See Part III. par. 65.

[38] Talm. Berach. fol. 58 vo.

[39] Termination of the conjunction and appearance of the new moon.

[40] Body physician to the Emperor Commodus, and greatest medical authority during the whole of the Middle Ages.

[41] Talmud Hullin, fol. 56 vo.

[42] *Ibid.* 45 vo (Mishnāh iii. 1).

[43] *Ibid.*

[43a] *Ibid.* 470.

[44] Mishnāh, Hullin, vii. 1.

[45] *Ibid.* viii. 5.

[46] Talm. *ibid.* fol. 93 ro.

[47] *Ibid.* fol. 51 ro.

[48] *Ibid.* fol. 47 ro.

[49] *Ibid.* fol. 46 ro.

[50] *Ibid.* fol. 47 vo. ; Sabbath, fol. 134 ro.

[51] Talm. Hul. fol. 49 ro.

[52] *Ibid.* fol. 50 vo., 51 ro.

[53] *Ibid.* fol. 65 ro.

[54] Mishnāh, Bekhōrōth iii. 1.

[55] Talm. Hul. fol. 52 sq.

[56] Mishnāh, *ibid.* iii. 1, 2.

[57] Talm. *ibid.* fol. 55 vo.

[58] Mishnāh, *ibid.* iii. 2.

[59] Mishnah, Bekhōr, chs. vi and viii.

[60] Mishnāh, Oholōt i. 9 ; Negāīm vi. 7–8.

PART V

[1] Wanting in the original.

[2] Paragraphs 7 and 8 are wanting in the Arab original.

[3] The author probably means the *Historia Animalium*.

[4] See Part I. par. 72.

[5] See p. 149.

[6] The αἰσθητήριον κοινόν of Aristotle (*Da Anima* iii. 1).

[7] Ibn Tabbon read אלעאלם and therefore translates העולם
' the world.'

[8] See p. 218.

[8a] See pages 89, 186, 210.

[9] *Kalām* (dialectic discussion) is a technical term for the
philosophic treatment of religious axioms. It originated with
the Moslem theologians of the Mutazilite school, who supplemented the simple belief in God by argumentation. On account
of their rejection of the Rabbinic tradition the Karaites were
forced to adopt the Mutazilite Kalām.

[10] See p. 145.

[11] Wanting in the original.

[12] Wanting in the original.

[13] See Part III. par 17, and IV. 25.

[14] See Talm. Berakh. fol. 7 ; Aboth iii. 15.

[15] See the Philosopher's speech at the beginning of the work.

[16] See Part II. par. 12 sqq.

[17] According to Makkoth, fol. 2 vo.

[18] See p. 21.

[19] See p. 79 and 226.

[20] See Talm. Ketubōth, fol. 67 vo ; Kiddūshin, fol. 17 vo.

[21] See the author's ' Song of Zion,' l. 12, where these words of
the Psalm are reproduced.

[22] The Hebrew version has here several sentences which are
wanting in the original, but are probably added by the translator.

SELECTED BIBLIOGRAPHY

ENGLISH

Hirschfeld, Hartwig, *Das Buch al-Chazari, im arab-ischen Urtext, sowie in der hebräischen Übersetzung,* Leipzig, 1887.

Baron, Salo W., "Yehuda Halevi," *Jewish Social Studies* III, 1941.

Baron, Salo W., *A Social and Religious History of the Jews,* Vol. VIII, Philadelphia, 1960, *passim.*

Bookstaber, Philip D., "Judah Halevi." *The Idea of Development of the Soul in Medieval Jewish Philosophy,* Philadelphia, 1950.

Cohon, Samuel S., "Jehuda Halevi." *American Jewish Year Book* XLIII, 1941–42.

Druck, David, *Yehuda Halevi, His Life and Work,* New York, 1941.

Efros, Israel, "Some Aspects of Yehudah Halevi's Mysticism." *Proceedings of the American Academy for Jewish Research* XI, 1941.

Epstein, Isidore, "Juda Halevi as Philosopher." *Jewish Quarterly Review,* New Series, XXV, 1935.

Goitein, S. D., "The Biography of Rabbi Judah Ha-Levi in the Light of the Cairo Geniza Documents." *Proceedings of the American Academy for Jewish Research* XXVIII, 1959.

Guttmann, Julius, "Judah Halevi." *Philosophies of Judaism,* New York, 1963.

Heinemann, Isaak, *Jehuda Halevi: Kuzari* (Philosophia Judaica), Oxford, 1947.

Husik, Isaac, "Judah Halevi." *A History of Medieval Jewish Philosophy*, Philadelphia, 1916.

Neumark, David, *Jehuda Hallevi's Philosophy in its Principles*, Cincinnati, 1908.

Strauss, Leo, "The Law of Reason in the Kuzari." *Proceedings of the American Academy for Jewish Research* XIII, 1943.

Wolfson, Harry A., "Maimonides and Halevi," *Jewish Quarterly Review* II, 1911–12.

Wolfson, Harry A., "Hallevi and Maimonides on Design, Chance and Necessity." *Proceedings of the American Academy of Jewish Research* XI, 1941.

Wolfson, Harry A., "The Platonic, Aristotelian and Stoic Theories of Creation in Hallevi and Maimonides." *Essays in honor of . . . J. H. Hertz*, London, 1942.

Wolfson, Harry A., "Hallevi and Maimonides on Prophecy." *Jewish Quarterly Review*, New Series, XXXII, 1942.

HEBREW

Altmann, Alexander, "Torat ha-aqlimim le-Rabbi Yehudah ha-Levi." *Melilah* I, 1944.

Beer, Y., "Ha-Matzav ha-Politi shel Yehude Sefarad be-Doro shel Yehudah ha-Levi." *Zion*, New Series, I, 1935.

Cohon, Samuel S., "Musag Eloah shel Yehuda ha-Levi." *Bitzaron* IV, 1941.

Dinaburg, Benzion, "Aliyato shel Yehudah ha-Levi

le-Eretz Yisrael." *Minhah le-David Yellin,* Jerusalem, 1935.

Heinemann, Isaak, "Temunat ha-Historia shel Yehuda ha-Levi." *Zion* IX, 1944.

Shirmann, Hayyim, "Hayye Yehudah ha-Levi." *Tarbitz* IX, 1938.

Zipronowitz, A., *Sefer Hakuzari* (critical edition), Warsaw, 1911.

INDICES

INDICES

I. NAMES AND MATTERS

II. BIBLE QUOTATIONS

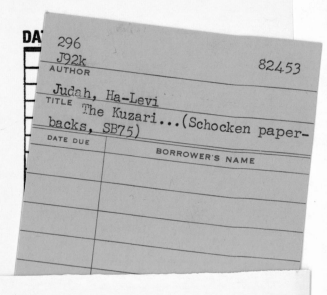